Mom,

May Your New Knees
Transport You To Some
Exciting New Destination,
And Taste Some New Delicises!

Love You,
Doug & Colleen

Take
BIG
Bites

Also by Linda Ellerbee
in Large Print:

"And So It Goes": Adventures in Television

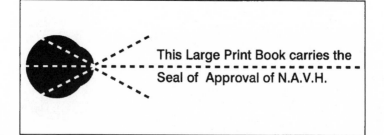

This Large Print Book carries the
Seal of Approval of N.A.V.H.

Take BIG Bites

Adventures Around the World and Across the Table

Linda Ellerbee

Thorndike Press • Waterville, Maine

Published in 2005 by arrangement with G. P. Putnam's Sons, a division of Penguin Group (USA) Inc.

Thorndike Press® Large Print Biography.

The tree indicium is a trademark of Thorndike Press.

The text of this Large Print edition is unabridged.
Other aspects of the book may vary from the original edition.

Set in 16 pt. Plantin.

Printed in the United States on permanent paper.

Library of Congress Cataloging-in-Publication Data

Ellerbee, Linda.
    Take big bites : adventures around the world and across the table / by Linda Ellerbee. — Large print ed.
      p. cm. — (Thorndike Press large print biography)
    ISBN 0-7862-7843-9 (lg. print : hc : alk. paper)
    1. Ellerbee, Linda. 2. Large type books. 3. Women food writers — United States — Biography. 4. Journalists — United States — Biography. 5. Cookery. I. Title.
II. Thorndike Press large print biography series.
TX649.E55A3 2005b

                                2005012421

For Violet, my granddaughter.
Oh, the places we'll bite, you and me.

As the Founder/CEO of NAVH, the only national health agency solely devoted to those who, although not totally blind, have an eye disease which could lead to serious visual impairment, I am pleased to recognize Thorndike Press* as one of the leading publishers in the large print field.

Founded in 1954 in San Francisco to prepare large print textbooks for partially seeing children, NAVH became the pioneer and standard setting agency in the preparation of large type.

Today, those publishers who meet our standards carry the prestigious "Seal of Approval" indicating high quality large print. We are delighted that Thorndike Press is one of the publishers whose titles meet these standards. We are also pleased to recognize the significant contribution Thorndike Press is making in this important and growing field.

Lorraine H. Marchi, L.H.D.
Founder/CEO
NAVH

* Thorndike Press encompasses the following imprints: Thorndike, Wheeler, Walker and Large Print Press.

CONTENTS

So how about spending a holiday
— or a life — in a country
not your own?

A reality check: why food,
family, and holidays will always
be messy and why it's okay.

Sometimes nibbles of elsewhere
make up a meal worth the trip.
And sometimes not.

A journey to the heart of a
devastated land in search of
hope and mutton.

An ongoing road show starring
children, weddings, red dresses,
potato chip sandwiches, and
a box of dreams.

Everybody ought to spend a month
on an island far, far away.
At least once.

James Taylor and Julia Child
accompany a woman on a 200-mile
hike to her sixtieth birthday. As a
gift, they teach her the secret of life.
And so she goes . . . on.

INTRODUCTION

Take Big Bites

I'm not crazy about Florence except for the pig museum. If, precisely speaking, it's not a museum, that's only because some fool in the Italian government doesn't recognize a national treasure when he sees one.

Consider this:

Out front there is a brown table covered by a red-checked tablecloth. Three once-living, now-stuffed pigs sit on little wooden chairs, red-checked napkins tied around their throats, real knives and forks tied to their hooves. In their glasses is real red wine. On their plates is more dead pig. Enough to make a decent docent sit up and take notice, wouldn't you think? Or perhaps you think an embalmed sidewalk salute to anthropomorphic cannibalism is in bad taste? I say it's art and I much prefer it to the Uffizi; they don't let you eat the paintings, whereas the three little pigs are gatekeepers to the world's most perfect pig meat. They are also the only way I find the shop, which is the second best thing about Florence: It's easy to lose your way. I go the distance, nodding briefly to this statue and that church, following narrow streets that meet themselves coming back, stopping to ask directions of people as lost as I am — constantly flirting with personal failure and public humiliation on foreign soil — simply because I like to eat pig and because I like adventure, by definition an undertaking of uncertain outcome.

Another way to look at it is that adventure is to take big bites of elsewhere. I believe in elsewhere. I believe in taking big bites. Therein lies a book. I hope. Be warned. I'm not a food or travel writer. I'm not a chef. There is no show on the Food Network called *Essence of Ellerbee*. There are no books anywhere called *Linda Jane's Guide* to somewhere. What I am is a recovering journalist who's traveled and eaten her way around the planet and lived to tell some tales. A few have little to do with food and only indirectly with travel, but all make up that portable library I pack without regard to weight: memory.

Adventures around the world, across the table — and from the heart. There's a connection. A memory of a different place, an unfamiliar taste, an old friend, a new love;

the root word is *passion*. I carry mine with and inevitably on me. Eat this plate of *pommes frites* or just go ahead and paste them on my hips? I like to think I make the right choice. Pasting potatoes directly on your person probably calls for Krazy Glue. I have a bad record with Krazy Glue. What the hell, I like to eat. I like to travel. I like to talk about both. A starter set: I don't like Singapore, Brunei, or Gibraltar. I'm conflicted about Turkey and turkey. I don't like nuts in sweet things or tomatoes on any sandwich but a tomato sandwich. I like to prepare and share food with friends and family as much as I like sitting all by myself at a café someplace where I don't speak the language.

There's more: What it is to be eighteen, working as a missionary in Bolivia, eating strange foods seasoned with hypocrisy; how Thai chicken tastes on a rain-scored ledge at the bottom of the Grand Canyon after you've flipped your raft in the Colorado River; how *chile con queso* changed the course of American education; where in the world — and you will not, I swear, guess the answer — you go to find the best fried-egg sandwich; how to escape one's captors in occupied Afghanistan in order to pursue mutton on the streets of Kabul;

why I decided to move to Da Nang in the first place; how a ham-and-cheese sandwich in Málaga could possibly cost $500; what Elvis had to do with the Big-Hatted Baroness and the only three-star Michelin restaurant in southern Italy; why everybody should spend one month a year alone on an island far, far away; who you meet and what you eat when you spend your birthdays alone in the wilderness; and how I came to follow the River Thames on foot, from its source to the sea, to celebrate turning sixty. Or in denial of it.

My first food adventure was colored by a tiny misunderstanding. It wasn't my fault. Nobody mentioned anything about taking the plastic cover off the TV dinner *before* you put it in the oven. It's not that I didn't grow up eating real food. It's that when I was growing up, real food was briefly extinct. Blame the Nazis. If America hadn't gone to war, a man named Birdseye wouldn't have figured out he could preserve food for our troops by flash-freezing it in cold water. After years spent shelling peas, stringing beans, cutting the corn off the cob, peeling this and slicing that and then cooking everything — in a big pot of water with a big piece of pork — until Tuesday, my mother thought Mr. Birdseye was a saint. She was not alone. Convenience food became the mantra of postwar motherhood. I understand. Preparing real food was and is more work. But it tastes better. Around our house, when not infected by the Birdseye plague, real food often meant chicken-fried steak with mashed potatoes and cream gravy, sugar peas, field peas, black-eyed peas, lima beans, green beans, all greens, ambrosia, okra, corn, tomato aspic, squash casseroles, pot roast, fried fish, chicken and dumplings, hot rolls, biscuits, cornbread, cakes, pies, fudge, divinity, and Mama's homemade vegetable soup, which was world-famous in our family. Labor-intensive stuff. But when I would ask to help, Mama would say, "Oh Linda Jane, it's easier to do it myself."

I hung around anyway. Willie Pearl Ellison, the African-American woman who worked for our family from the time I was an infant — a saintly human and my constant ally against my mother — let me help her in the kitchen when Mama was off playing bridge or having her hems shortened, or lengthened. When she made apple pies, Willie Pearl would give me pieces of dough and fruit to make a pie in my own little pie tin (when she made chocolate pies I ate the filling before I could make my pie). Willie Pearl also taught me how to do the dirty bop, which for some years was more useful than knowing how to make an apple pie.

If it was Mama who did her best to keep me from cooking, it was Daddy who gave me the idea that a foot in the road was not a bad place for a foot to be. He took me with him on business trips to other towns in Texas. Early in the morning, we would go walking and he would tell me about where we were: why New Braunfels had been settled by Germans, how the dome of the Texas Capitol came to be fourteen feet taller than the dome of the U.S. Capitol, how to read a street map and when to throw one away. He took me to a mill in Lubbock. I watched cotton bolls become thread. He took me on a fishing trip to Eagle Lake. I learned how to bait my own hook and not squeal when I caught a fish. In Galveston, he taught me to hear the sea in a shell. Everywhere we went, Daddy talked to people. When I was in high school, Daddy came home from a business trip to Missouri and told us that on his early-morning ramble he had run into a fellow he knew but had never met. My father said he had offered his hand to the familiar stranger.

"I'm Ray Smith from Houston, Texas."

The man shook my father's hand. Daddy said he had a good shake.

"I'm Harry Truman from Independence, although I was born in Lamar, Missouri."

"What a coincidence. Lamar is the name of my daughter's school. Named after the second president of the Texas Republic. Don't suppose your town was, though. How did it come by the name Lamar?"

My father and a former president of the United States stood on a street corner and talked for thirty minutes. The world was a curious place, Daddy said. I should go see for myself.

And so I did.

Some memories warm me like Willie Pearl's apple pie or the sun hitting my face when the trail opens up near the top of the mountain. Others leave me sadder but wiser, knowing that no matter how much I eat, travel, learn, or impossible though it seems, occasionally grow, I still don't get it. Life remains more question than answer. I wanted more. I always meant to understand my world, and myself, and if I couldn't, I would settle for being great. I believe I may have waited too long. There are no longer an unlimited number of Saturday nights, summers, or choices. It's too late to change my major. I'm not going to stop writing television programs and go be a shepherd. I'm not going to sail around the Cape alone. I'm not going to be an airline pilot or a rodeo clown or stop the show. And I'm never going to be a rock star — tragic, because I've always liked wearing tattered clothes and am certain I would enjoy having groupies. Oh yeah, George Burns won his first Oscar at eighty. Golda Meir was seventy-one when she became prime minister of Israel. Michelangelo was seventy-three when he painted the Sistine Chapel. Grandma Moses didn't start painting until she was eighty. And George Bernard Shaw was ninety-four when they produced his first play. Which is all well and good for Golda, Grandma, Mike, and the two Georges, but I don't write plays, perform stand-up comedy, or paint terribly well lying on my back, and being prime minister of Israel is not a job for a lapsed Protestant and committed coward.

Frankly, my dear, while complaining may not be helpful, given a choice, I would rather be young again. I had a great time and want to do it over, to fall desperately in love with the wrong man and know there's time to get beyond it. Leave home for the first time. Learn how to saddle my own horse. Learn how to ride a high one, if that is what is saddled for me. I want my children to be kids again. We'll eat Cheese-burger Salads (shred iceberg lettuce, add the cheeseburger and anything you'd put on a cheeseburger except the bun, toss with a mix of mustard and mayo, and serve it to kids — salad with training wheels). I want my twenty-five-year-old body back so I can wear a two-piece bathing suit without fear of offending the general public. (I wouldn't object to having my breasts back, either.) I want to wear my hair in pigtails and run for the sheer pleasure of running, eat my mother's fudge pie in her kitchen with her still there, drive too fast and wear no seat belt, drink too much champagne, and walk again on the wing of an airplane 3,000 feet above New York. I want to be young enough to believe in my immortality one more time.

In a book, I can do this. I can go back for second helpings. Not second chances, though. What was, is. Instead of dedicating my life to delicious gallivanting, I grew up to be a woman who worked, not because she had something worthwhile to contribute, but because she had already contributed her best shot — Vanessa and Joshua — her children, who had a habit of eating regularly.

21

Reason enough to find a steady job. This being the case, I was determined to earn a living doing something I liked better than, say, waiting tables. Honorable work, but journalism paid more and you didn't have to wear a uniform. When you would rather be traveling and eating, working at anything is a compromise, but I was lucky. Thirty-something years as a journalist allowed me to travel and eat while pretending to be working.

I'm assuming you've no idea who I am other than somebody who probably has nothing important to say you don't already know, so here are the Cliff's Notes. I grew up in Texas, dropped out of college, gave birth twice, and married thrice too often. For twenty years, I worked as a network television news correspondent. Always I worked for other people. Some said I was strange. I don't know about that; the world is a strange place. I recorded what I saw and heard. Some said the character Murphy Brown was based on me. I don't know about that either, but a network anchor whose mouth gets her in trouble — what's not to like? If I'm a maverick for not seeing the world the same way some of my colleagues do, so what? Only dead fish swim with the stream all the time.

Since the late eighties, when we both quit the network-news follies, Rolfe Tessem, my partner in life and work, and I have owned Lucky Duck Productions. For fourteen years, we've produced *Nick News* — a children's news program with serious intent — which airs on Nickelodeon. We've also produced programs, mostly documentaries (many networks, frightened that audiences will surely shy from something called a documentary, now call these "specials") for HBO, PBS, MTV, CBS, ABC, Lifetime, Court TV, MSNBC, TRIO,

TV Land, SOAPnet, WE: Women's Entertainment, A&E, and Bravo.

When we are in New York City, Rolfe and I live in an old brownstone in Greenwich Village. When we are lucky enough to be in North Egremont, in the Berkshire hills of western Massachusetts, we live at Huckleberry Hill, which began life as an old stone-and-wood hunting camp. Having traveled so long for television networks, Rolfe's idea of a satisfying trip these days is driving from Greenwich Village to North Egremont. But my foot is still in the road; my mouth still waters for new tastes and longs for the old ones. Even that particular dish I've been forced to eat more often than any other: a large helping of my own words.

Would I, the lady on the telephone wanted to know, take part in the March of Dimes Celebrity Cook-Off? A black-tie charity gala at the Plaza Hotel in New York City. Five hundred guests. Twenty-four celebrity chefs. I was flattered. Among my sillier fantasies was the one about writing for the food and travel magazines I'd been reading for years. *Linda Jane* à Table *with Knife and Forked Tongue.* Imagine being paid to eat, travel, and write about *that,* instead of the bombing down the block.

Of course I said yes to the lady.

I was to supply the March of Dimes with the recipe for a "personal specialty," calculated to feed eight people. They would do the numbers to make it feed 500. On the night of the gala, a chef from the Plaza would prepare and serve my "personal specialty" to New York society. I would stand in the booth and take compliments. Sounded like a plan. Now — what was my "personal specialty"? These society folk, I said to myself, they must be bored to death with fancy food. They dine on hummingbird tortellini three nights a week. Surely they're tired of unborn vegetables, foie gras eight ways, vertical food, farcical fusion, and the New White Meat, which we used to call pork. Normal people know when the emperor is short his shorts: the New White Meat sucks. No fat, no flavor. These days some New York restaurants wrap bacon around pork tenderloins before they cook them, as if taste were an accessory, like a Prada bag. And let's not forget foam cuisine, an especially dismal trend; foam belongs on cappuccino, beer, and the sea.

I would give the society folk something different.

When I was young, every town in Texas had a café and every café kept a big pot of chili on the back burner. If you ordered a Frito Pie, they took a nickel bag of Fritos, zipped open the top, ladled chili over the Fritos, tossed in a handful of grated cheese and chopped onion, stuck a plastic spoon in the mess, and you were on your way to greasy bliss. The recipe was foolproof. I know. One Sunday night when I was thirteen, my mother told me to go to the kitchen and make supper.

"But Mama, I don't know how to cook. Remember the TV dinner."

"Linda Jane, any fool can make a Frito Pie."

She was right. You layer (how many layers depends on how many people) canned chili *without* beans, chopped onion, grated American cheese, and Fritos (the little ones) into a casserole dish, adding extra cheese on the top, and then put it in the oven until it's heated through and the cheese bubbles. You don't have to be thirteen to make a Frito Pie, but it probably helps.

So why not make Frito Pie for the gala? The original fast food. Down-home. Witty. *Easy.* I was flying to Los Angeles when this brilliant idea struck. I called my office and dictated the recipe for Frito Pie to my clever assistant. It's often hard to hear

26

people speaking on airplane phones, but we managed. She passed the recipe on to the Plaza. A week later, I arrived at the big charity gala barely in time to climb behind my booth, where a genuine French chef — I knew he was genuine because he spoke barely enough English to tell me Americans didn't know "sheet" about food — was pulling the first of several giant Frito Pies from the oven in my booth.

"Taste thees. You weel love my Fry-toe Pee."

"Frito Pie. And it's mine, not yours."

"Whateever."

Mentally still congratulating myself for offering something newer than foamy foie gras on frappéd figs, I inspected our creation.

Houston, we have a problem.

The pie was a neon-red runny mess. I put my spoon in and took a bite. It tasted like ketchup topped with cheddar cheese.

"What the hell have you done to my Frito Pie?"

Chef Froggie went pale.

"Madame, I use only your *specialité* recipe. I have eet here. See!"

He pulled out the recipe, faxed from my assistant. Where it was supposed to read "three cans of chili," it read "three cans of chile sauce."

The airplane phone.

No wonder it tasted like ketchup and cheddar cheese. It was. The Fritos had decomposed in shame. Wish I'd thought of it first. I looked down the room past Danny Glover's crab cakes and Joan Rivers's turnovers to see the first of 500 gowned, tuxedoed, and bejeweled people, each of whom had paid $750 to sample our "celebrity cooking," headed my way. I am resourceful. During the time it took to go to the bathroom and throw up, I figured out what to say. "Please do not eat this crap," I would say. Then I would leave to kill myself in the privacy of a taxi headed downtown. But when I got back to the ballroom, I couldn't get to my booth for the people around it. A riot? Worse. An adoring crowd. What can one say? They loved my mangled Frito Pie in uptown New York City. Many, including a fellow named Trump, came back for second, even third helpings. I could have said a variety of things to those people at the big charity food bash, including my planned speech, but I believe that under the circumstances, I said the right thing. I said, "Thank you." You may say this story proves how little New Yorkers know about good eating. I say you're a cynic. I say those people were merely being, in the best sense of the word, charitable.

Adventure, food, travel, and memories from a life lived interestingly, if not especially intelligently. Growing older? My parents couldn't teach me much about that; they died too soon and, yes, it may have had to do with the chicken-fried steak. But I continue to be blessed with other teachers. After I wrote a newspaper column about turning fifty, I got a letter from a woman named Alice Warden, who lived in the state of Washington. Mrs. Warden wrote that she had something to say to me.

"Linda, on my 30th birthday, a friend said, 'Well, Alice, your life is over.' I thought of this as my birthdays went by. My life was still pretty good. My 50th came and went and I thought my friend had got it all wrong, but then my husband died when I was sixty-three and for a time my life was very dark. When I was sixty-five I met a man who told me he had only six months to live. I said don't let's worry about it. Let's go have adventures, instead. And so we did — for *fifteen years* — and what adventures they were."

I stopped reading long enough to try to imagine falling in love at sixty-five, having adventures at that age, but couldn't, so I went back to the letter. In the next paragraph Mrs. Warden wrote about a trip to California.

"We were getting into bed and he turned and said, 'Alice, do you know I love you?' I said I did. We slept. After a few hours I heard a sigh and said, 'Are you all right?' There was no answer. I called 911, but my good man had spent his last evening."

And this was supposed to cheer me up?

"It has been hard," she wrote. "I think of him when I look at the swallows' nest box he made over the window, when I walk in the garden and see the rhododendrons we planted and I work in that garden every day. I am now 86. Life is still good. Fifty years old? Oh, Linda, what a baby you are."

My trouble was, I had been allowing young to define old.

Wrong teacher.

I may be coming on to sixty, but there are still places to see, meals to eat, adventures to be had, and memories to be made.

Come along for the ride, the food, and the stories.

Go ahead.

Take big bites.

ONE

The Prism of Memory

(1995)

April 1995. Dawn. A red ball burns a hole through a rice-paper sky. Three bawdily green mountains rise from a sea the color of light. The mountains are conical like the hats of women in the sampans floating by us. I can hear the women murmur to one another, but only as background — wind chimes in the tree next door. The rest is silence. The fragility of such moments is to be cherished, and mistrusted. For one thing, it never lasts. This one ends gently.

"Good morning," people on the ship whisper to the mountains, the water, to the women in boats. "Good morning, Vietnam."

Nobody told me Vietnam was beautiful. I don't remember anybody saying so. But maybe I have forgotten. Joshua, my twenty-five-year-old son, stands next to me near the bow. Andy, whom we met on this voyage, stands next to Joshua. Andy and I are the same age. He's been here before — a Navy doctor, a young oral surgeon who identified other young Americans by their dental remains. We have talked, the one who opposed the war and the one who attended it, tripping over our histories in some mutual attempt to say it's okay now. Really it is.

Really . . .

The ship's engines are stilled.

We are in the harbor of Da Nang.

A tug pushes us closer to this improbably significant little country whose sad song soared to the top ten on the Low Moments in American History hit list. Josh was born in 1970. He has no memories of the Vietnam War, the same way I, born in 1944, have none of World War II.

On the dock, a group of Vietnamese holds up a hand-painted welcome banner. Others are setting up stalls to sell us stuff. Three soldiers bustle about, preparing to hawk something from the back of a Vietnamese army truck. Vietnam is new to American tourists. The embargo was lifted only last year. Heading for the gangway, my son and I are accosted by the terminally sincere Shore Excursion Director, who wears hair too big even for Dallas and an I-was-this-close-to-being-an-anchorwoman-in-Mobile smile. Her lip gloss matches her shoes.

"You *must* go on the bus with everybody else," she says. "There's no other transportation. The port isn't near the city. This time there can be no question. Why don't you like our bus tours?"

Her face says I will be sorry if I don't do what she says. You know the look. Bad schoolteachers have perfected it. I thank her for her concern and say we will take our chances. She walks away disappointed in me. Again. My son wants to know how we plan to get around. What if the cruise director is right? Josh is not as practiced as I am in the art of zagging where zigging is what is called for. But he's a quick study. I point to the far side of the dock, beyond and to the right of the instant mini-mall.

"What do you see?"

"Black cars," Josh says, "and guys standing around talking to one another."

"We'll go over to one of those men and say that while we're here we want to hire him and his car. He will name a price. We will say yes or offer another price and then he will offer another price and this will go on until everybody believes they've won."

"How do you know this?"

I know this because there are always guys with cars. Forget politics; *this* is the way the world works. But I need to not show off right now. More than the moment is fragile. I saw this trip as a mother-son adventure, and in my campaign for his company, I had painted many a verbal travel poster. I promised him palm trees, vine-covered ruins, and black sand beaches. I promised him juicy fruits that had no names in English, and the taste of fish that swam in different seas. I promised him different seas.

"China. Hong Kong. Brunei. Vietnam. *Malaysia,* Josh. Doesn't just saying the word feel good? Malaaayyssshiiaaahhhh."

I also promised him engaging companionship. Once on board the ship, Josh discovered he was one of three people under the age of forty. The other two were on their honeymoon. I had warned him. Okay, maybe I left out a detail or two. I definitely had mentioned that his looks might put some people off, but I hoped they would see past his long hair the same way I hoped he would see past their gray hair.

"Is your son a hippie?"

She can't mean that. A hippie? *In 1995?* What this woman means to ask is if my son is the one with the long hair.

"No, ma'am, my son is not a hippie," I say. "His mother was."

She is seventy-five. I am fifty. My son is twenty-five. There is as much age difference between this woman and me as there is between my son and me. Learning to speak Urdu might be easier for us all.

Singapore, where we boarded, was hideous, one skyscraper after another, a city so paved over with progress they had built a Disney version of its past on an island in the harbor. They even created the island, as God might have done if he had such cheap labor, which had become a tourist attraction especially attractive to the young people of Singapore, who'd grown up in the shadow of the city's brave new skyline. A tram separated the city from what I thought of as Singaporeworld. There were trees and monkeys and flowers. Some were real. Surrounding a movable walkway was an aquarium bigger than Walden Pond. You glided, protected by nothing but glass and blind faith in the structural engineering skills of the lowest bidder, from large sharks that looked at you from both sides now. In Singapore, Josh and I had watched the news on television in our hotel. There were black holes in the BBC newscast. The government of Singapore had removed stories it believed might upset people. Oh good God yes. Reality? Edit it. Our first day aboard the cruise ship, when we plunged into obligatory small talk with other passengers, all we heard was how everybody loved Singapore.

"So clean."

There was a $500 fine for littering. Josh and I had littered on principle.

"So orderly."

There was a $500 fine for chewing gum. Although neither of us was fond of gum, we had gone out of our way to find some and chew it in public.

"Such nice restrooms."

There was a $50 fine for not flushing. Josh and I had not flushed.

"And so well run."

Josh and I looked at each other, coconspirators and longtime disciples of Mr. Rogers, and silently mouthed the words together: Can you say "police state"?

But that was another morning, in another country, not this one.

We get off the ship, easily hire a car and driver, and head for Da Nang, passing the ship's buses on the highway. We are good. We do not wave. We look at Vietnam instead. Everything I see is through the prism of memory. If I see children play, I see them through a TV screen in which a village burns in the background. If I see red flowers, I see blood. If I hear people laugh, I hear Lyndon Johnson saying he will not run again. When we drive by the old air base, I see news film of people throwing babies into the last American plane to get out of Da Nang and, as the plane takes off, those who tried to ride in the wheel base falling, one by one, into the South China Sea.

I turn to look at that sea, inhaling and exhaling an elsewhere that is more an elsewhen. The sea does for me what seas do; after a while, when I look back, I see a jogger; a karaoke bar; a tank; houses made of straw, tin, stone, paper, and wood; two men in a bamboo garage working on an American Army jeep; a woman with a cleaver chasing a chicken into a noodle shop. I see men, women, and children wash, chop, talk, eat, drink, walk, bike, fish, sell, mend, and build. Everybody is *doing* something and almost everybody smiles at us. But then almost half the population is under twenty-five. We get out of the car at the central market area. Small outdoor restaurants have sprung up as if from the roots of the large tree each cook shack seems to have claimed for its center pole. *Have shade, will feed people.* Generally there are three or four tables and a hot plate. It is just after sunrise. All the tables at all the tree restaurants are filled with Vietnamese and everyone is eating the same thing. I spot an empty table under a spread of green and persuade Josh to follow me. We are, I say, on an investigation.

A young woman, also smiling, approaches us. I point to the dishes on the other tables.

"We'll have some of that."

Josh is worried. He has not forgotten Canton, where we went to the open-air food market. There were vegetables, fruits, rice, and sweets. Almost everything else that was for sale, except for the dried lizards on a stick (Lizard Lollipops, an idea looking for a franchise), was live. We got by the eels, fish, parrots, turtles, piglets, and baby lambs, even the bunny rabbits, but then we came to the part of the market filled with cages of live puppies and kittens. A woman was hefting three puppies onto a scale. We must have looked horrified.

"Pets," she said. "You understand? These — pets."

And when was the last time you bought a pet by the pound?

In Da Nang, at our tree café, we're served big bowls of rice noodles topped with thin slices of raw beef, beef tendon, and chopped peanuts. A young woman places on our table small bowls and plates containing fresh basil, sliced limes and scallions, chopped garlic, chile paste, and tiny red peppers you know plan on making a major statement to your insides. There's a bottle of nuoc mam, the national condiment — a clouded liquid made from fermented fish — and a bottle of hoisin sauce, a sweet-tasting concoction familiar to regular customers at Chinese restaurants everywhere. Josh and I stare at our food, not sure what to do with it, or in what order. The young lady is back, carrying a large steaming pot and a ladle. She scoops, and our noodles are covered with clear brown liquid.

"Ah hah," I say. "Soup."

"Soup for breakfast?"

Josh is wary.

"It's another country," I say, gently.

"It's seven a.m.," Josh says, less gently.

I look around. Nobody seems to think we ought not to be there. It is a lovely morning in Da Nang.

"Try your soup, son."

The broth is simple and complex; there's a hint of anise, maybe cinnamon too, but the base is good beef stock. I begin adding condiments, experimenting. The young lady returns. She is still smiling as she puts down two warm baguettes and individual espresso drip pots, plus cups and saucers. Now Josh is smiling too.

"This is okay."

"Blame the French."

The French once thought they controlled this land. They, too, were wrong. But the Vietnamese are not fools. When they threw out the French, they kept the bread and the coffee. What, I wonder, have they kept from the American follies here in their country? Meanwhile, something is going on inside me. It takes a few moments to discover precisely what it is, and then I understand. This odd feeling is euphoria. My soup, laced with hot peppers and everything else on the table but the bread and coffee, tastes unlike anything but its own self. It's causing me to break out in a sweat. I like that. Back in Eagle Pass, Texas, down on the Mexican border, I'd go to a certain Mexican café for lunch just to eat a *carne guisado* so hot tears would roll down my face with each reality-altering bite. Heaven. I know it makes no sense; why would anyone willingly eat something that causes pain? Perhaps because, like hitting yourself in the head with a hammer, it feels so good when you stop, or maybe it's because of a piece of folk wisdom with which I am entirely familiar, that goes like this: eating hot food when it's hot outside, or drinking a hot beverage, cools you off. You eat, you sweat, you chill. When I was growing up in Texas, people swore by this theory. They didn't eat chiles for breakfast (well, we sorry-assed, white-bread Anglos didn't), but they drank strong, black, hotter-than-the-third-ring-of-hell coffee all day. They said you had to, to keep cool. Then they air-conditioned Texas and everybody switched to iced tea.

I ask the young woman who brings us re-fills on the coffee what this wonderful soup is called, feeling like a person from San Antonio walking into a New York deli and asking what a bagel is. She opens her mouth and puffs at me. I can't tell if it's a word or an expression of Vietnamese dis-gust at American ignorance.

"Pardon me?" I say.

She puffs at me again. Actually it's not so much a puff as a fuff. Maybe a *fuh*.

"Fuh," she says once more, as if to an especially slow child.

I try it.

"Fuh?"

"Fuh."

41

Later I learn what I am eating is called *phô*, pronounced "fuh." It is the national breakfast dish of Vietnam. Later I seek out and find *phô* in all American cities in which Vietnamese have settled, including an outstanding *phô* parlor in Austin where cowboy/trucker/good ole boys in gimme caps and Stetsons line up at opening time. Later I even learn to make *phô*, but at this moment all I know is that *phô* beats the devil out of a bowl of Wheaties; *this* is the breakfast of champions. We finish, pay up, and leave. I tell Josh I am thinking of moving to Da Nang. I need to be near the *phô*.

China Beach is a pretty piece of sand and water once enjoyed by U.S. Marines stationed at the base in Da Nang and now enjoyed by Vietnamese families on holiday. There is a small market at China Beach. My eyes light up.

"Josh, it's time to see what they have for sale in the market."

My son gives me a dark look.

"We are not going to eat more soup. We are *not*."

"Inedible stuff, I mean." Of course I do.

The woman is unable to tell me much about the cigarette lighter she wants to sell me, either because her English is not up to it, or because she does not know, or does not wish to tell me. The lighter is an old Zippo. Holding it in my hand, feeling its familiar heft, is like holding a piece of America that no longer exists, something from a time when cars were Cars and chrome was good, a time when people smoked, and ate bacon for breakfast, a time when we went to war in and over a little green country halfway around the world. Engraved on the Zippo are a name, a serial number, and the words "U.S. Marines. Vietnam. '68." Troublesome decision. If I buy the Zippo, am I buying something taken from the body of an American soldier? Or something manufactured yesterday in Da Nang? Is a war souvenir, genuine or not, something I even want? But if it's real, maybe I can return it to its owner. Well, this is what I tell myself. I buy the Zippo.

Driving over the pass on the way to the imperial city of Hue, we stop in villages and at shrines. Although I can't see anything that looks like marble, Josh and I decide to climb what is called the Marble Mountain. Two young girls — twelve years old? Eighteen years old? I cannot tell — insist on holding my hands as I climb the path, which is not *that* steep. I must look old to them. Could it be the *phở?* We climb some more. Now I *am* winded, and it shows.

"No pain, no gain," says one girl.

"Totally awesome," says the other.

What I say is best left on the mountain.

We enter a rock passage. They show us Buddhist shrines set in big, high-ceilinged caves inside the Marble Mountain. They point out how the light hits the Buddhas through large holes in the mountain. I say that it must have been quite an engineering feat, getting those holes over the caves in such a way that the light would fall so precisely and prettily on the Lord Buddha. One of the girls smiles (Why is everybody in this country smiling at me all the time? Have they no memory?) and says I have it backward. The holes in the mountain were made by American bombs dropped from airplanes. Every place a bomb created a cave, the Vietnamese built a shrine.

"Isn't it beautiful?" she asks.

I smile back. "Yes, it's beautiful."

And crazy.

In Da Nang, streetlights are hung with banners. Tomorrow is the twentieth anniversary of Liberation Day. Liberation from us, they mean. We stop at a corner and get out of the car to watch a parade pass.

Down the street comes a group of what appear to be ex-soldiers. They are in uniform. They are marching. They are not young — and they are not smiling. We have found Vietnamese with memories.

Now they want us back, or at least they want our money, our trade. If Vietnam doesn't look or feel like a Communist nation, it doesn't look like the rest of Asia either. In Da Nang, time seems to have stopped sometime around 1948; the place is not yet crowded with the battery shops, the T-shirt vendors, the brand-name billboards that clog Malaysia, Indonesia, even China, and the pollution that seems to follow modernization like coffee follows *phô*. Do they seek their own way here, not ours? Or is it that the embargo has been lifted so recently? If I return next year, will a swoosh be carved into each *phô* parlor tree? Is this what we fought for? Is this what they fought against? The ghosts of Lyndon Johnson and Ho Chi Minh are dissolving in my head. There are other villains loose in the world now. Instead of names, they have logos and government contracts. They hire children to work in their factories. And with them come the poisons of the modern world, poisons that when they get into you, make Agent Orange look like a mild case of chicken pox.

The man driving the water taxi in Brunei had spoken no English, but he talked as hard as he could as he showed us around the Kampong Ayer, the world's largest water village, home to 30,000 people, roughly half the population of Bandar Seri Begawan, capital of Brunei and home to the sultan of Brunei, the (then) richest man in the world. Eventually, the water-taxi driver had decided his gestures were not enough to say all he wanted to say. He took us to the water village home of his cousins, Zia and Roz, two women in their twenties who taught English and, there-fore, spoke it.

Zia and Roz invited us inside their house, which, like the others, sat on stilts six or seven feet above the Brunei River. These new houses had been built by the sultan after a terrible fire destroyed hun-dreds of the older, wooden ones. The women wanted to show us how modern everything was: the kitchen with its refrig-erator, the living room with its television. They offered us cans of pineapple juice and asked had we seen the sultan's palace, with 1,788 rooms, including the banquet hall that seats 4,000. No? Had we seen the new mosque with its solid gold chandeliers?

We had seen the mosque. Josh saw more than I. It was hard to see anything looking through the eye gap in the black chadoor that covered me from head to foot, which, being a woman, I was forced to wear so as not to offend God. The sisters were proud of their country. Did we know that Brunei was very rich; that because of the oil, Brunei had the second-highest per capita income in the world? Did we know that Brunei offered its 260,000 citizens a welfare service that encompassed pensions, medical care, education, and sports facilities, none of which was financed by taxes — because there weren't any? Did we know that for the citizens of Brunei, interest-free loans were available for essential purchases, such as homes and cars?

Roz and Zia told us how much they earned. They wanted to know what teachers earned in America, and if they were respected. I told them teachers did not earn enough (many did not, in fact, earn what a teacher in Brunei earned) and were rarely respected enough. Both women were shocked. Perhaps teachers in America made do by catching their own food? They showed us how they fished for shrimp off their front porch. My son and I could not help but notice the amount of garbage in

47

the river. We spent nearly two hours with Roz and Zia, intelligent women who were well read, outspoken, and, they told us, progressive thinkers in a progressive country. When we got ready to leave, we asked what we should do with the empty pineapple juice cans, and two intelligent, well-read, outspoken, progressive-thinking women in a progressive country looked at us as though we were crazy.

"Throw them in the river, what else?"

They made no distinction between "the river in which we throw our garbage" and "the river from which we get our food."

Will Vietnam become Brunei? Or did defeating the most powerful nation on earth give them a new dream? I'm not going to be in Vietnam long enough to find answers to all my questions. I see what I see. I talk to Vietnamese people. So does Josh. He has no fear of foreigners; instead, he uses English, French, his hands, and his own winsome smile to make people comfortable, communicating far better than I. We stop to have coffee on the road back from Hue, and by the time we leave, Josh knows the names, relationships, and hopes of all members of the family that owns the coffee stall. They seem sad to see him go. I know the feeling.

By the end of our visit, the prism behind my eyes has shifted. I see different colors. I see another Vietnam, a beautiful and busy place, filled with people hurrying to catch up with a future they may one day regret chasing. I think of the stink of Canton, the paving-over of Singapore, the backward-forward water village of Brunei. But who am I to decide? It is their country, not ours. It never was ours. When I get back to New York, I give the Zippo to Lori Seidner, a young woman in my office who loves a challenge.

"This is probably a wild-goose chase, but . . ."

I promptly forget about the Zippo. Lori does not. She calls various Vietnam veterans' organizations, most of which suggest placing an advertisement in their magazines. Lori turns directly to the few, the proud. The Marines explain it is a server number, not a serial number, which is what they used before they began using Social Security numbers. They confirm the name and come through with the guy's last known address, which is in Carbondale, Pennsylvania. Trouble is, the address is from 1976. What are the odds he still lives in Carbondale in 1995? But a check with information in Carbondale gives up a telephone number, and a new address, same town, different street. I pick up the telephone and call the number.

A man answers.

"This is an odd question, but are you by any chance the Michael J. Matichak who fought in Vietnam?"

Turns out he is. Michael J. Matichak of Carbondale, Pennsylvania, went to Vietnam when he was eighteen. He enlisted in the Marine Corps because, he said, his buddy did. Mr. Matichak pulled three tours of duty in Vietnam and was stationed at the air base in Da Nang in 1968.

"Mr. Matichak, I think I have your lighter."

"My what?"

"Your lighter. Your Zippo. From Vietnam."

"You're kidding."

I tell him where I bought the Zippo. Had he ever been to China Beach?

"Yeah, it was supposed to be a place to relax, but it was all crisscrossed with barbed wire, and it's hard to get a suntan holding a rifle, anyway."

Michael J. Matichak works as a psychiatric aide at the state mental hospital. He has six children. He says he still smokes. I say I will send him his lighter. Before we hang up, I ask him if he has any thoughts on his time in Vietnam?

"I really don't think about it. I'm glad I went. I'm glad it's over. I'm glad to get my Zippo back."

The evening we sailed out of Da Nang harbor, I had looked for Andy, the oral surgeon, wanting to tell him — what? That I, like so many others, had never been against the American soldier, only the war — *and didn't that sound like the cop-out of all time?* I kept on looking. I thought it was important. But it wasn't. It's not. Andy has his own prism. Michael J. Matichak has his. The Vietnamese veterans we saw on parade in Da Nang have theirs. Josh has his. I have mine. We all see the world through our little private prisms, reality refracted by our different truths.

An American woman came to stand by me at the rail as the sun, sinking, turned red again and the ship began to pull away from the dock. I resented the interruption. I was enjoying the moment and, okay, figuring out how I was going to persuade my family that lime-flavored beef noodle soup with chiles was a first-class way to start the morning.

"Such a poor place," she said.

She was right. Despite its natural beauty

and the enterprise of its people, Vietnam was still a poor place. But just you wait, I thought.

"And so few Americans," she said.

I turned and looked at her.

"Excuse me?"

"I mean, you'd think we would have at least kept a base here, wouldn't you?" she said.

"Uh, ma'am, we lost the war."

"Well, then," she said, "a small base."

I smiled at the lady. It's what any sensible, forward-thinking, *phô*-eating Vietnamese person, confronted with a newer, possibly even more stupid world, would do. I'm sure of it.

Phô

SOUP

4 quarts homemade beef stock, preferably made with shinbones or oxtails

6 quarter-sized slices fresh ginger

4 star anise pods

3 tablespoons nuoc mam (Vietnamese fish sauce)

Freshly ground black pepper

6 ounces flat rice stick noodles

8 ounces small, paper-thin slices of very lean beef sirloin (freeze it a little first to make slicing easier)

2 cups bean sprouts, rinsed and drained

$1/4$ cup julienned fresh basil leaves

4 green onions, crisp green parts only, thinly sliced

$1/4$ cup finely chopped fresh cilantro leaves

ACCOMPANIMENTS

1 lime, cut into 6 wedges

1 fresh red chile, stemmed, seeded, and very thinly sliced
2 tablespoons hoisin (plum) sauce (optional)
1 cup peanuts, chopped (cashews work too)
1 bottle *Sriracha* (chile-garlic sauce found in Asian markets and some supermarkets)

1. Simmer the beef stock with the ginger and star anise for 20 minutes. Let it stand for 30 minutes, then fish out and discard the aromatics and add the nuoc mam and a pinch of pepper. Bring to a slow simmer and cover.
2. Soak the rice stick noodles in hot water for 15 minutes, until softened. Cook in boiling water until tender, about 1 minute. Drain well and divide between six large, deep bowls.
3. Add the sliced beef and bean sprouts to the beef broth and bring to a boil. Cook for 1 minute, and then ladle the broth, beef, and sprouts over the noodles in each bowl. Scatter with the basil, green onion, and cilantro.
4. Serve the *phô* immediately, with the lime wedges, chile, hoisin sauce, peanuts, and *Sriracha* sauce in tiny saucers on the side.
5. Tie a bandanna around your head to catch the sweat.

TWO

A Table for One

(1950–2004)

James J. Walker was mayor of New York in the twenties. He lived on my block. The park across the street is called James J. Walker Park. A bon vivant who loved his town, Beau James is remembered for saying, "Who'd want to be president when you could be mayor of New York?" He's also remembered for participating in or at least condoning a few distinctly shady deals, which led him to say something else, shortly before he left the country: "There are three things a man must do alone: Be born, die, and testify."

I would add a fourth. Travel.

While I believe two people can take a trip, and I've enjoyed some doozies, I think you must be alone to really travel. If you're with someone else, it's possible to become so involved with each other you could be in Outer Mongolia and never once have a conversation with an Outer Mongolian.

Alone, you're forced to engage with a people and a culture, both of which, presumably, are different from yours. Or you can choose to speak to no one; you can stand a lot when you can stand your own company. Traveling alone, I never have to say, "What would *you* like to do today?" No one ever says, "Surely you don't think that stupid green vase is worth thirty *zupatas?*" I get up when I want, go where I want, buy what I want, sleep when I want, and eat what I want. I choose. I like choosing. I've traveled on my own since I was a little girl, and it doesn't matter that those first journeys into the big world were short — my mother put me on the train in Houston and two hours later my grandmother fetched me off it in Trinity, the porter having been bribed to look after me during the ride. Of course like all good little girls, I was taught never to talk to strangers. I liked talking to strangers. They told stories I hadn't already heard.

This is a story of traveling alone, of three countries, four cities, one village perched on a mountaintop, an Italian chef who wouldn't take yes for an answer, a Turkish jeweler who helped me break into a bank, a pompous London maître d', a German baroness, and a thoroughly annoying fellow.

It's a love story.

Begin with the thoroughly annoying fellow.

My first day in Istanbul I spent the morning walking. Of Istanbul, I knew nothing and was content; it left so much to learn. Vanessa, my daughter, had once lived here. People would ask me why. I thought the answer was obvious. When she had set off to see the Old World, I had given her a Eurail Pass; Istanbul was the last stop on the line.

Now my daughter lived in Seattle and I was in Istanbul. I'd asked Vanessa where to get the best meal in town.

"Go to the docks by the Galata Bridge," Vanessa said. "Men build fires in oil drums. There's a grate over each fire. A man will take a baguette-sized fish and throw it on the grate until it's blackened outside and still juicy inside. Then he will slice open a real baguette and lay the fish on one side of it. He'll add slices of raw onion and squeeze lemon juice over the top. Hot sauce too, if you like. He'll close the baguette and hand it to you. Pay the man and *don't go anywhere*. Stand at the dock and eat a fish that was swimming between two continents earlier that morning."

This, Vanessa said, was the best meal in

Istanbul. I did what she said and thought it was one of the best meals anywhere: fresh, simple, and consumed under extraordinary circumstances. The day went downhill from there. At the spice market, I wandered about, getting drunk on color and smell, and then noticed I was being followed. He was unsavory — make that dirty — talking trash and acting as if he were doing me a favor.

"Lady, you lonesome? You want company? I be your man tonight."

He stuck out his tongue and waggled it at me, in case I didn't get his meaning. Always a charming gesture, I think.

"You like me, lady. You come with me. I got something *big* to show you."

I wasn't frightened. I've never been frightened traveling alone, and even if I were, I still wouldn't stay home. I refuse to accept that the words *solitary* and *confinement* go together. Just the opposite. I find a strong connection between solitude and freedom. Perhaps it's self-confidence, or perhaps I'm a fool, but if I'm to be bound by a cage, let it be the natural limits of the planet, not my own cowardice. Besides, as a woman, I've had years of edifying experience walking by construction sites. You know what I mean. They're putting up a new building. They're repairing a highway. They're just standing around waiting for someone to tell them to get back to doing something. You approach, tensing in anticipation of the formal greeting of the hard-hatted male.

Heysweetmamahowwouldyouliketositonthis!

Like most women, I'd never truly understood why they did it, or what I ought to do about it. Shout something equally ugly back? Walk over and in simple declarative sentences, the kind any four-year-old might be expected to understand, explain that women are neither sexual objects nor deaf? In the end, I would do what most women do: I would pretend they weren't there. And then one day I strolled by the guys and nothing happened, and I heard a voice inside my head point out that for a while now nothing had happened when I passed a construction site. What? I had become invisible? I wasn't twenty-five anymore, but I didn't look like someone who ought to wear a sack over her head. Although no woman likes being leered at — when I was fifteen, I chose to lifeguard wearing a sweatshirt over my swimsuit — being ignored was unsettling. I began to test my invisibility in other situations: asking for help in stores, attempting to get the attention of waitpersons, jockeying for space on the subway, negotiating a large party. I discovered those most likely not to see me were usually young and/or male. How ungrateful. All those years curling this, straightening that, holding my tummy in, lining my eyes, lacquering my nails, glossing my lips, and keeping my mouth *shut* (or trying) and now suddenly I'm not here? I complained to Marshall, a friend my age who'd recently been divorced. Marshall had just begun to date again. He said that Bob, his trainer, had advised him never to see a woman over thirty-five. It didn't immediately occur to me Bob might mean that literally.

The more I became invisible, the more I began to feel about it as Edna Ferber did about being an old maid; she said it was much like death by drowning, a really delightful sensation after you have stopped struggling (she didn't say how she knew what it was like to die by drowning). I discovered being invisible was useful to a woman addicted to traveling alone. Curiosity and restlessness were encouraged in a boy, but when I was growing up, it was taken for granted that a young woman traveling alone was in desperate need of a companion. Even today, a thirty-year-old woman who goes on vacation by herself is seen to be searching for someone. A twenty-five-year-old woman who sits alone in a hotel lobby is (still) suspect. But if, at first glance, I no longer counted to some people, I was free to be me at all times. My invisibility made me invincible. So what if you don't see me? I see you.

Okay, I have to admit there are times I miss the wolf whistles and the attention any woman gets for the accident of being young and not entirely ugly. This, however, was not one of those times, and this annoying fellow was not what I had in mind in the way of getting to know the citizens of Istanbul. I ignored him. Not easy to do. He was loud and persistent in his offer to make me a happy woman. By the time I found my way to the Blue Mosque, I'd had enough. I turned to him.

"Please leave me alone," I said in a polite but firm voice. *"Please go away."*

He got his knickers in a knot and began to yell at me, which caught the attention of other foreigners in the vicinity, who stared at both of us. I was embarrassed — from his tirade, you would have thought I'd tried to chip off a piece of the mosque and put it in my pocket.

"*You* do not tell *me* to go away!" he screamed. "This is Turkey! This is *my* country! *You are not Turkish!*"

Well, Clyde, if you can't bite, don't show your teeth. I do not like scenes, but was raised not to shrink from one when a scene is what is called for. I smiled at the many people now watching us. I smiled at the thoroughly annoying fellow. And then I spoke to him in a voice I can summon when needed. It's not a screech, not a bellow, not even horribly loud. It does carry to the upper balcony of anywhere.

"Please forgive my bad manners. You are, of course, right. I cannot tell you to go away. I am not Turkish. *I* am a New Yorker. So why don't you just go fuck yourself?"

He went away.

And they say language is a barrier among strangers.

But still, aren't I, as a female alone — no matter what my age — intentionally making myself a target, especially in countries where a stump-broke goat might still be worth more than a woman? Maybe, if all men were like the fellow in Istanbul that afternoon, but they're not. Not at construction sites at home. And not in Turkey. I met Zeki in the port town of Kusadasi. This time I skipped the nearby ruins at Ephesus, although they are some of my favorite ruins, mainly because no one has ever thought to rope any part of them off. Ephesus is said to have been founded by Androcles of thorn-in-the-lion's-paw fame. It is fact that at one time Brutus was there. Cicero, Mithradates, Mary Magdalene — they were all there. Ephesus was a port, and a center of trade and learning, up to and through the Byzantine era. I had twice walked the long stone path — I thought of it as a really old Main Street — that sloped gently down to where the city used to meet the sea. Over time the sea had receded. Now ruins and road ended a long way before water began. The place was no less appealing for it. I had sat in its amphitheaters — there were two — and imagined watching a performance of *Antigone* with the original cast. I'd seen the beauty of new flowers growing out of old marble. I'd gazed in wonder at the carving of Winged Nike, goddess of victory and running shoes. This day I thought I'd see what the town of Kusadasi had to offer, other than people who wanted to sell me rugs.

Although Kusadasi was now something of a resort town, there was still an old quarter. Old quarters are the best quarters. Because I would need money for coffee and food, if nothing else, and was out of

Turkish money, I stopped at a bank with an ATM attached and fed the machine my Visa card. The machine ate my Visa card. Naturally it was Saturday. The bank was closed. I wasn't going to be in Kusadasi on Monday. A lesser woman would have burst into tears. A smarter woman would have not run out of Turkish money. I decided to eat something. A fisherman was standing on a rock near shore. He caught a little fish. It seemed to make him happy. He caught another little fish. Then another. He turned and gave me a great big fisherman grin, as if to say, "One by one, little fish add up to a meal." I wondered if he would take dollars for those little fish. The waiter at the Ali Baba restaurant, near the fisherman, next to the water and a foot above it, said he would take any legal tender I cared to offer. A cheese omelet was cheap and comparatively healthy. The plate of fried potatoes was compensation for losing my Visa card. When I finished my meal, the waiter brought me fresh melon and cherries.

"A gift," he said, "for a beautiful woman alone."

Sweet. If he could tell lies like that, so could I. I told him I loved cherries. I hate cherries. I wrapped them in a paper napkin

and shoved them into my backpack so as not to hurt his feelings.

The waiter's lie, the fisherman's smile, the potatoes, and the sweet melon improved my attitude. But not by much. My Visa card was how I got foreign currency. Without it, the rest of my trip was going to be one long diet. Might as well e-mail home and cancel the card. The Internet café was above a jewelry store. A man who said his name was Zeki said he was the owner of both. I asked if I could pay for some Hotmail time with dollars, of which I had not many left. I explained why.

"Not to worry," Zeki said. "I will call the bank manager at home."

After the phone call, Zeki said the two of us would now return to the bank, where the manager would meet us in five minutes.

Yeah. And I love cherries.

Zeki shrugged. "That's a Turkish five minutes, you understand. . . ."

We were both amazed when it really was five minutes. The manager unlocked the bank, opened up the back of the ATM, and retrieved my card. He wouldn't open up the vault and give me Turkish money; he said he wasn't cleared for vault-opening on a Saturday. He directed me to another ATM. This one gave me money *and* returned my card. Zeki and I went back to his jewelry store. We drank tea. He asked what I did. I told him. He said I was the first American television journalist he'd ever met. I told him he was the first jeweler/computer geek I'd ever met. He asked if he could take my picture. I said he could if I could take his. When we said goodbye Zeki kissed me on both cheeks, and it was only as I left that I noticed the name of his jewelry store. Kismet. Well, why not? Fate, in the form of a strange man, two strange men, had been good to me that day.

There is a codicil to this story.

A few years later a friend told me she had seen the oddest thing on a visit to

Turkey. She said my photograph was hanging on the wall of an Internet café over a jewelry store in the town of Kusadasi.

"How is that possible?" she said.

I told her it was kismet.

It would be a lie if I claimed that being a woman alone in a foreign country — and possibly in your own — is always easy. There is never a shortage of dickheads. When I go to London, I stay, if I can, at the Connaught, pretending I'm landed gentry come up to town for a few days' shopping. It costs way too much, so it helps that I'm never there more than a day or two. The first time I stayed at the Connaught, I arrived at night. Jet-lagged and hungry, I ordered dinner from room service: pâté, a veal chop, and a small salad.

The waiter brought the pâté.

"Excuse me, where's the rest of my meal?"

He looked at me with a sad kindness — or a kind sadness — as if I'd fallen off a turnip truck the day before.

"Madam. There is a button on the table next to your bed. If you will push it when you are ready for the rest of your meal, I shall bring it. Otherwise the veal will get cold while you enjoy your pâté."

I looked around for my turnip truck.

Until then, I believed that if you happened to be in London and hungry, the kindest thing you could do for your stomach was to leave your hotel as quickly as possible. For years the best food in London was in Indian and Chinese restaurants. There were places offering traditional English food, and because I like eating what comes naturally to wherever I am, I wanted to like them and would have, I'm sure, if what they served hadn't seemed specially created for people who had never gotten beyond the kind of sustenance you spoon into small children before they have grown taste buds. Mushy peas? How could a people who ate something called mushy peas have conquered half the known world? Spotted dick? I don't want to know. The only English food you could count on was breakfast: the odd bacon, the white sausage, blood pudding, golden-yolked eggs, sautéed mushrooms, and grilled tomatoes. Heart-stopping, but wonderful. Toast? The English knew how to toast bread, but they served it in a rack designed to ensure the toast would get as cold as possible as fast as possible. I imagined English engineers perfecting the design of those toast racks.

"Let's see, we lost an empire, now how can we screw up toast?"

In the late seventies and early eighties, food in England began to change. Restaurants purporting to serve a New English Cuisine sprang up like dandelion greens doused with kiwi oil. Most of this early new food was a combination of lame and precious. Banger and mash topped with aioli is still sausage and mashed potatoes topped with garlic mayo, and a bad idea. If I was going to eat English food, I preferred Langan's Brasserie, which served English nursery food with a French accent. Langan's offered a first course consisting of Lancashire cheese stirred into a béchamel sauce, ladled over pieces of sautéed bacon and field mushrooms, and then broiled. I've been known to eat two portions, get a goofy look on my face, and look around for my nanny.

But then I discovered the Connaught. In the Grill Room, giant trolleys with silver platters of joints of beef and lamb were rolled around by little old men with big knives. The food, the room, the service — everything combined to fulfill my Anglophile fantasies. Chef Michel Bourdin offered well-prepared traditional British dishes, and more. I learned from *Saveur* magazine

69

about the *Oeuf en Surprise,* a specialty of the house not on the menu. Lobster soufflé with a poached egg inside? How did they do that? Why didn't the egg harden when the soufflé was baked? I didn't care. I knew only that if you wanted it for dinner you had to tell them that morning. One year I spent four days at the Connaught. A fifth day would have put me in debtors' prison. Every morning I told them I wanted an *Oeuf en Surprise* that night. By now the waiters and I were on friendly terms. They knew I ate early. They knew I preferred Table 8, where I could sit with my back to the wall. I hate to eat in the middle of a room. Call it a fetish. There are worse ones.

In the evening I would wait in the bar until my soufflé was ready, watching the real landed gentry sip whiskies without ice. I drank water with ice. The bar used a beautifully shaped crystal water pitcher. No matter which way you turned it, the crystal caught the light. Water poured from this pitcher tasted better.

Apparently, the regular maître d' of the Grill Room had been on holiday until this, my last night at the Connaught. I introduced myself to him and asked if my table was ready. He looked down his list. He looked down at me.

"Sorry, madam, I have no reservation for you."

"But you must have. I'm a guest in the hotel. I make the reservation with the front desk every morning at the same time I order the *Oeuf en Surprise*. I always" — for a whole three nights — "eat at Table 8. Please check again."

He repeated that there was no place for me. Well, call me a feminist bitch, and you wouldn't be the first, but the next morning I called the hotel manager. Was this how the Connaught treated a woman alone? Was I less welcome than a man alone? The manager said he was sorry. He even sounded as though he meant it. He asked how he could make things right. I thought about it. The maître d', who had been there longer than I ever would be, was not going to apologize and management wasn't going to make him. But I wanted something to assuage what I considered indignities to person. All right. I really was a bitch.

"You know those lovely crystal water pitchers you use in the bar . . ."

Whenever I fill mine with water, or fresh flowers from our garden, I think about what a friend once said of sex: "It's not what you have or even what you do with it. It's the cute way you get on and off." It's not that world-class hotels never make mistakes. They do. It's the cute way they make up for them. As long as I can afford it, I will never stay at any other London hotel. But I continue to stand up for myself. If you are afraid of being lonely, don't try to be right.

Let's see, so far, in describing my love affair with traveling alone, we've covered the pompous maître d', the Turkish jeweler, the thoroughly annoying fellow, three cities, and two countries. That leaves The Baroness, the chef who wouldn't take yes for an answer, the village perched on a mountaintop, one city, and one country: Italy.

Italy is a particularly satisfying country for a solitary sojourn. People often behave as if they're glad you're there. I've walked into restaurants where there was no one not with someone else, only to have the proprietor rush to greet me as if I were a friend who had been there the night before and would be there again the next night. He clears a table on the terrace. Is the table to my liking? Can he bring me some wine before we get down to the serious business of talking about what I shall eat? How long have I been in Italy? Do I like his country? Have I been to his *ristorante* before? No? Well, then, I've missed the best food in all of Italy. I want to believe it happens because I come to a country, a restaurant, a person, visibly ready to enjoy the experience. In truth, I think it has more to do with Italians. They seem to have been born with the welcome mat out.

The first time I went to Rome *alone* I called ahead to Alfredo, a charming man who, during the years when NBC News had a Rome bureau, was driver, translator, fixer, and friend to the employees of that bureau. I had met Alfredo the year the *Today* show broadcast from Rome, but I hadn't seen much of him that week. He was busy driving Jane and Bryant. This time, Alfredo met me at the airport. On the way to town we talked about the good old days at NBC News, when networks spent money like a sailor on shore leave. I asked Alfredo if he had learned to speak English so well while working for NBC News. He thought this was a funny question.

"From NBC, I learned how to curse in English when things do not go right," he said. "I learned to speak real English by listening to the songs of Frank Sinatra. I still listen to those songs. Sinatra cures my ears."

And Rome cures my heart.

The next day I got up early — my secret for seeing anything anywhere before everyone else. For instance, if you get to the Forum before 9 a.m., there is no one to charge admission and no fence to keep you out. Think of the Roman Forum as an ancient cross between Times Square, Wall Street, a chat room, an Army recruiting center, and an open-air shopping mall. When the empire fell, so did the Forum, given a little help from outsiders with truly fantastic names such as Alaric the Visigoth and Genseric the Vandal. What they couldn't carry off they tried to destroy, and kept on doing so until the cows came home. Literally. By the Middle Ages what had been the Roman Forum was known as Campo Vaccino: the cow field. So why go there? I go to old places to look for the shape of old dreams. In that, the Roman Forum is much more than a bunch of crumbling façades circling a weeded square. It is a shrine to a great dream gone wrong, to a republic that turned imperial, tried to rule the entire world, and failed. When you put your feet on the Via Sacra, the Sacred Way, the road along which returning heroes marched triumphantly, parading prisoners and prizes from distant military victories, you know you are where stones really do tell stories, and you wonder if there will come a day when people walk up a broken road lined with the remains of buildings now covered with vines, and tell one another, "Once upon a time, they called this Constitution Avenue."

As it was near Easter, I was on a mission. I meant to eat *abbacchio,* the baby lamb served at that time of the year. A guidebook recommended a restaurant said to do a good job with *abbacchio.* I decided to take a taxi. The driver, an older man with a lion's mane of white hair and a true Roman nose, could not find the restaurant from my map or his. After fifteen minutes of not finding it, he got angry and shut off the meter. He said the fault lay with the maps or the restaurant — or him — but not with me, and if I still wanted to go there, he would not be defeated in his effort to take me there. After stopping to engage several people in heated conversation, we finally found the restaurant, which we'd more or less been circling for the better part of an hour, at no cost to me. I came close to inviting the taxi driver to dinner. He was so completely unlike most New York cabbies, who listened to music that didn't sound like music, spoke on their two-way radios in languages that didn't sound like language, and then turned to ask you how to get to Times Square.

One night, I decided to eat at the restaurant on the roof of the Hotel Hassler, more for the view than the food. It was early in the evening. If you're traveling alone, eating early is a good idea. A restaurant is more willing to accommodate one person taking up a table for two, or even four, if you're going to be gone before most people arrive. I had a reservation and there was no one else in the restaurant yet, but the maître d' appeared reluctant to give over the corner table, the one with the best view of Rome. *Excuse me, but do you have a brother at the Connaught in London?* I was about to pull a small hissy fit when I remembered where I was. In a soft voice, I explained that it was my last night in his city and it would be such a shame, would it not, to be forced to forgo *this particular memory* of Rome — and the generosity of a man who would understand the wish of a lady traveling alone in this most wonderful of countries. . . .

I enjoyed that corner table.

As much as I love being alone in Rome, I love the Amalfi Coast more. When I used to think of the Mediterranean, I would think of young. Young girls. Young bodies.

Young love. Maybe it was memories of photographs from the Cannes Film Festival. Gina Lollobrigida in a bikini. Sophia Loren falling out of one. Brigitte Bardot not bothering to wear the top of hers. Or maybe it was Françoise Sagan. *Bonjour Tristesse?* So sad. So sweet. So *young.* Or maybe it's because the first time I went to the Mediterranean, *I* was young. Now when I think of the Mediterranean, I think of a small restaurant called Don Alfonso 1890 in the village of Sant'Agata sui Due Golfo, on the top of a mountain with the Gulf of Salerno on one side and the Bay of Naples on the other. I went there to eat lunch, being more or less in the neighborhood already, having spent the morning cowering in the back seat while Carmelo, a taxi driver I'd hired for half a day, played chicken with buses on the Amalfi Coast Road. Carmelo was proud of the famous Americans he'd had in his car, a Mercedes old enough to have been on a first-name basis with Adolf. He said he'd driven Gore Vidal, who lived nearby. He showed me a card Vidal had signed for him. He showed me a card Mario Cuomo had signed for him. He showed me a card signed, "Whodi Alan." Carmelo said this one was his favorite. Mine too.

I was apprehensive about lunch. Only three Italian restaurants rate three stars in the Michelin guide. Don Alfonso 1890 was one of them. I'm not a three-star girl. I'm more a can-you-tell-me-where-the-locals-eat gal, but I was hungry and both my kids were done with college, so I forged ahead. Don Alfonso Iaccarino turned out to be the name of the owner/chef as well as the name of the restaurant. His wife's name was Livia. They looked to be near my age and made me feel as if they'd opened their restaurant eighteen years ago on the off chance that one day I might stop by for a bite. *Alone.* When I told Don Alfonso how much I was looking forward to eating his food, he took the menu from me. He said to forget the menu.

Wonderful surprises began to arrive. Costanzo, the maître d', brought them, smiling every time he did so; obviously he had no relatives in London. The first dish was a plate of nickel-sized full moons of sautéed zucchini from Don Alfonso and Livia's farm. The zucchini rounds were dotted with bits of roasted baby goat. Four homemade breads — ciabatta, fennel, tomato, and spinach — were placed next to a dish of olive oil from Don Alfonso and Livia's olive trees. Don Alfonso came out

Don Alfonso and Livia

from the kitchen to watch as I tasted his olive oil.

"Is good?"

"I could drink it."

He looked relieved when I didn't.

I ate fresh asparagus tossed with capers and bite-sized pieces of flying fish. Fried chunks of lobster coated with caramelized onions and saffron threads. Homemade candle pasta with bacon, baby peas, and garlic. A white fish — what, I don't know — topped with newborn fava beans and littered with fried baby leeks. In between their trips to the kitchen, Don Alfonso, Livia, and I talked. Of work. Of gardens and cities. Of wine and roses. Of Elvis and olive oil. Mostly we talked of our families.

Don Alfonso's grandfather had opened a hotel in Sant'Agata in 1890. He earned the "Don" honorific because he was a benefactor to the town, bringing in its first electric power lines, bus, automobile, private aqueduct, and movie house. The present Don Alfonso was supposed to be a hotelier too, but he and Livia, who'd married in 1969, were more interested in cooking. They transformed an abandoned annex into a restaurant and filled it with cast-off furniture from the hotel. He said farmers were abandoning the land for the tourist trade; local products were being replaced by foods that came from somewhere else and were mediocre. He said he and Livia intended to save the old flavors and the simple dishes, but they wanted them to resonate.

"We want them to be heard ten kilometers away."

Costanzo joined us.

"I was twenty-five when they started the restaurant. Don Alfonso said he needed a waiter," Costanzo said. "My qualifications?

80

Alfonso and I played soccer together when we were young."

Near the end of my meal, I became aware of another solitary woman in the dining room. She wore a wide-brimmed black hat with a shocking-pink ribbon around the crown and spoke Italian to Don Alfonso and Livia, but I could tell it wasn't her first language. Now she turned and spoke English to me, but I could tell this wasn't her first language either. She invited me to join her at her table. I thought of her as The Baroness, not because she was one but because to a simple American who'd never met a baroness, she looked the way I imagined one ought to look. As it happened she was the *grande dame* of German food critics, whose name I withhold for her own sake and because I can't spell it. Over Sunday lunch, The Baroness instructed me.

About food: "Remember that no war was ever started over the dinner table. Not if the food was any good."

About age: "As a woman gets older, her hats should get larger and more grand. One must give the gentlemen something fine to look at before they get to your face."

About life: "Americans talk about life as

though it were good or bad. What nonsense. Life *is*. That is all there is to say about that."

About traveling alone: "Oh, just be yourself, my dear. After all, who else is better qualified? Now what shall we have for dessert?"

We had lemon crème caramel sprinkled with candied lemon peel and served in hollowed-out lemons. Like swallowing sunshine. After the meal, Livia gave me a tour of the garden and the Roman cistern below the restaurant, home to several thousand bottles of wine, most of them older than I was. The Baroness, asked to join the tour, said climbing stairs was bad for digestion. When we returned, she was gone. Curious, I asked if she'd paid her bill first. Livia said she wasn't meant to; her job, you know. Don Alfonso and Livia said my meal was free too. I explained I wasn't a food critic. I was a customer. They explained I had enjoyed my lunch so much, they couldn't possibly let me pay for it.

"Yes. Exactly. That is why you must let me pay. Because I enjoyed my lunch so much. Take yes for an answer," I said.

"No."

The following spring I returned. I wrote to Don Alfonso and Livia to tell them I was coming. They were waiting at the door, along with Costanzo.

"*Leenda!* You are back! Welcome."

Like we were kin or something.

There were kisses and hugs from Livia and Don Alfonso and more of the same from Costanzo. Were they running for office, these people? No, merely decent human beings, and Italian.

They were the strangers you travel to meet in the first place.

We talked as if our conversation had been interrupted only moments ago instead of a year ago. How are the children? Theirs? Mine? Livia tells me their son was twenty-nine last week. I tell her mine was twenty-nine last month.

"And the farm?" they ask.

Theirs?

No, mine.

My *farm?* I explain they have misunderstood. Rolfe has an old house in the country. But we don't grow food — not counting herbs and four kinds of chiles.

"Ah . . . but is a start?"

This from people who grew a dizzying array of what the earth offers those who love it enough to coax forth the goodies.

The Baroness was not there, but Alfonso and Livia had seen her recently.

"A bigger hat, *Leenda*."

How could this be possible? The one she was wearing when I met her was the size of a Fiat.

"A bright-green hat," Livia said. "With a big red rose on it. She is a monument, is she not?"

Talk turned to food.

"You must be hungry. It is a very long drive from Positano."

The drive from Positano was all of twenty minutes, but Don Alfonso rushed to the kitchen in case I might faint from lack of something to eat. What can I say? The food was even better and there was more of it. As I mentioned, I don't eat at a lot of three-star restaurants; actually, this was only my third, so I'm not qualified to do justice to what I ate. Let me say that the first course was a little thingy of fried potato topped with a doodle of mashed potato and a dabble of olives and dried tuna roe. Does this description sufficiently explain why I'm not a food critic? Suffice it to say my meal was varied, plentiful, and fabulous. There was, however, one totally unforgettable dish. Such a simple thing — small gnocchi with tomato sauce, basil, and smoked mozzarella — but so perfectly made that when one little *gnocchetti* fell off my fork onto the floor, I would have dived for it if Costanzo hadn't been watching. On the other hand, he probably would have helped me retrieve it. I couldn't help myself. I asked if it might be possible to have one more plate of the little darlings.

"*Leenda*," Costanzo said, with such a sigh you'd think he and not I had been waiting all year for this meal, "is so good you are here again."

Gandhi said there are limits to self-indulgence, none to self-restraint. I feel certain that had he been with me that day he might have been persuaded to reverse the thought. Sometimes in life, if you're lucky, you are allowed to understand you are where you most want to be at *that* moment. At the conclusion of the meal, I behaved badly. I made my hosts unhappy. I didn't mean to. All I did was ask for the check.

"But *Leenda*," Livia said, softly, "you are our guest."

I persisted.

"Please. I'm not The Baroness. I don't write about food." (Well, I hadn't so far.) "I can't give you any more stars. I *will* pay."

They looked unhappy. Someone didn't understand something but *who* was still unclear — that is, until Don Alfonso made it clear.

"*Leenda,* don't you know cooking is too hard a thing to do for money only?"

Stopped me cold.

"Thank you," I said. "I shall treasure the memory of this meal and your generosity to a stranger."

"But *Leenda,* you are not a stranger. You are a *regular!*"

In September 2001, when planes like flaming swords sliced through the twin towers of the World Trade Center, some fourteen blocks from where I live, one of the first letters I received was from Alfonso and Livia Iaccarino. They wanted to know if my family and I were safe.

That's the thing about traveling alone. You *do* talk to strangers. And once you talk to them, they're no longer strangers.

Don Alfonso's Gnocchetti

SERVES FOUR AS A FIRST COURSE

GNOCCHETTI
1 pound waxy potatoes (Yukon Golds are
    good; no Idahos or reds)
3/4 cup flour
1 egg yolk
Salt

SAUCE
1/3 cup extra-virgin olive oil
1 small garlic clove, minced
1 cup Italian-style tomato sauce, bottled,
    canned, or homemade
1 cup diced fresh tomato (peeled and
    seeded)
18 basil leaves, julienned
Salt to taste
7 ounces smoked mozzarella cheese, diced,
    at room temperature

1.   Boil the potatoes in their jackets. Peel

and mash while still hot. Spread on a baking sheet and let rest until the potatoes are tepid and dry.

2. With a fork, mix flour, egg yolk, and a little salt into the potatoes. Divide the dough into smaller portions and, on a floured work surface, roll each portion into a long, ropelike form about ¼ inch in diameter. Cut each rope into ¼-inch-long pieces. You want pieces smaller than the first joint of your little finger.

3. Heat 2 tablespoons of the olive oil in a sauté pan and add the garlic. Remove the garlic as soon as it begins to brown and add the tomato sauce, the diced fresh tomatoes, one-third of the julienned basil leaves, and a pinch of salt. Cook for approximately 3 minutes. Take off the fire and let stand until the pasta is almost cooked, and then add the remaining oil and warm through.

4. Cook the *gnocchetti* in a large pot of gently simmering water. As soon as they rise to the surface, remove with a slotted spoon, drain, and add to the pan of warm tomato sauce and olive oil.

5. Add the smoked mozzarella (which

must be at room temperature by now) and 4 of the julienned basil leaves. Toss for a few seconds until the cheese is barely melted. Top with the rest of the julienned basil leaves. Serve immediately.

THREE

Whatever You Do ... Don't

(1963)

The first time I traveled to a foreign country, the sixties were barely born. I went on behalf of an American Protestant church to save the souls of Our Smaller Darker Brothers and Sisters in what was described to me as the Tibet of the Americas. You would probably call it Bolivia. The church said we had powerful enemies in the Tibet of the Americas: the heathens, the Catholics, and the Communists. All I had to do, they said, was to bear witness. I thought this meant seeing and then telling the truth of what you saw. Nobody said anything about ditch digging until much later, when someone put a shovel in my hands. It was a revelatory summer in so many ways, but according to the church I was a failure, and all I did was what they asked me to do. I bore witness.

At the time, I was a student at Vanderbilt University planning to major in Latin

American Studies and would much rather have joined the newly formed Peace Corps. When John Kennedy said the torch had been passed to a new generation, I knew he meant me specifically. Mama said he certainly did not, that I should forget about the Peace Corps and concentrate on finding a husband, or at least study something useful like elementary education — so I would have a way to pass the time until my prince came to rescue me from a tribe of someone else's snotty-nosed first-graders in order to set about begetting my own. Mama worried where she'd gone wrong, and then decided she hadn't, I had. One afternoon, over Thanksgiving break, I heard her tell her bridge club what a good Christian girl I had been (in my mother's language this meant "obedient") until I got mixed up with those Greeks. Since we didn't know any Greeks, I asked whom she meant.

"Plato, Aristotle . . . you know. Those Greeks."

My mother regularly forwarded me the bulletin from our church in Houston. Sometimes I read it, which is how I found out the national church organization planned to send five college students to work for three months at its missions in

Bolivia. A free trip to Latin America? I was ready. Problem was, I'd stopped going to church when I was thirteen. Someone might see this as grounds for not picking me. And then I read the magic words: the five students would be chosen on the basis of a written essay. As good fortune would have it, I had not stopped going to English class; I penned an essay, the point of which was that they got a chance to save me too. When I was selected, Mama was confused. I was going thousands of miles away to a country where they didn't even speak English (most didn't even speak Spanish, but neither of us knew this); there was no telling what trouble I might get into. On the other hand, I would be in the company of Christians. The experience, Mama decided, might bring me to my senses.

At the end of May, I took a plane to La Paz, where the five of us, all from different universities, were to meet at the church's Bolivian headquarters before being assigned to various missions around the country. Inside the La Paz airport, I learned my clothes had gone elsewhere, perhaps to the Tibet of the Himalayas; Braniff said it would inquire. I was delighted by this turn of events. The church had sent a list of clothes to bring: work clothes and four plainly made dresses of subdued color, suitable for wearing to church. Mama — who preferred to think of my trip in terms of Jackie Kennedy being driven around Bolivia, carrying a sheaf of lilies and waving benignly at the heathens, the Catholics, and the Communists — had decided plainly made dresses did not preclude lace collars or tulle petticoats and was sure subdued colors included hot pink, turquoise, and lemon yellow. She also had packed girdles, a nylon bathrobe with bluebirds appliquéd onto it, white gloves, and my almost-real pearls. As a final touch, she'd stuck in a framed photograph of herself and my father in case in three months I might forget what they looked like. I walked out of the La Paz airport with nothing but what I had on my body: underwear, a flannel shirt, jeans, a pea jacket, cowboy boots, my New York Yankees baseball cap, and a knapsack containing passport, cash, ten paperback books, and a pack of Kents.

There was no La Paz in sight. Unless you counted dirt, there was nothing in sight. I got on what somebody told me was the right bus, which proceeded to rev up and aim for the edge of the world. You could see where the land stopped and nothing else began. I was going to fall into an abyss on my first day; I would be dead, but Mama would be vindicated. At the last minute, the road turned sharply and we began to wind down into a valley, or a large hole, depending on your point of view. The Bolivian capital city of La Paz was at the bottom. Even so, the altitude of the city was 11,000 feet above sea level. Houston was 50 feet above sea level. We passed walls with graffiti scrawled across them. None of it said, *"Viva Jesús!"* Some of it said, *"Viva Fidel!"* The government *du jour* of Bolivia, at that time the poorest country in the Americas — and the only country in the world never to have won a war — practiced what it called "state capitalism," a bizarre Marxist free-marketplace system that worked about as well as you would expect. Meanwhile, real Marxists were afoot, and if nothing else, it was clear from the bus ride into town that they had paint.

Mission headquarters was a concrete compound with many locks on its gates. The window in my room had bars on it. Suffer the little children to come unto me and remind them to bring their keys. At dinner that first night, the four other student-missionaries and I were served watered-

94

down Campbell's vegetable soup and canned apple juice. The missionaries said the apple juice was a special treat, and it was, if you think it's special to drink juice from a can whose sell-by date had expired the same year I got my first period; worse, this awful meal was served to us by Indians we'd come to save. In the next few days I noticed that Indian servants performed all chores at the compound, and this was no mean feat. It was the only time in my life someone ironed my underwear. I went to the chief missionary. What was the deal with servants serving missionaries? He said I didn't understand; God needed many hands for his work.

We had four days in La Paz before heading to our assigned missions, but were warned we would get altitude sickness if we tried to do much more than read our Bibles. I'd read mine once, which seemed sufficient unless there was going to be a test, so I set off to explore La Paz, and it was during those four days that I first discovered the pleasure of getting lost in a strange city. I began with the Presidential Palace. Doesn't take me long to look at a palace, so I moved on, followed a broad avenue, turned into a small street, then a smaller one and so on, until, completely lost, I stumbled onto the Mercado de Brujas, the witches' market, where you could buy medicinal herbs and other Indian remedies of which I was certain neither my church nor my mother would approve. I tried to buy some beads a saleswitch assured me were magic, but we were defeated by language. Bolivia had three official languages: Spanish, Quechua, and Aymara. I spoke only one of those, and poorly. Too bad it wasn't the one she spoke. I walked everywhere, talked to everyone, or tried to, looked at everything, and ate anything. Mornings meant *salteñas*, flaky fried pastries wrapped like turnovers and filled with diced meat, onions, raisins, olives, potatoes, eggs, and chiles. I bought my *salteñas* from street vendors and ate them standing, happily dripping *salteña* juice on me and the street.

"Whatever you do," Mama had said before I left, "don't eat anything sold on the street."

In small outdoor cafés I ate *lomo montado*, two eggs on a tenderloin steak set on a bed of potatoes fried in lard. The dish was a Bolivian history lesson. Cattle were not indigenous, but when the Spanish came, saw, conquered, and stayed for three centuries, they'd asked, "Where's the beef?" and, not liking the answer, imported their own. They'd also brought pigs to the New World; think of the lard as carry-on luggage. In exchange, Spaniards sent back to the Old World a funny-looking tuber they found growing in the Andes. They called it a *batata* because it reminded them of yams they had seen in the West Indies (the English later corrupted *batata* into "potato"). Bolivian Indians, those who had chickens, already had eggs. Put it together and you got *lomo montado*. History on a plate.

Along with this heart-healthy meal, I consumed large amounts of fresh lettuce and tomatoes.

"Whatever you do," Mama had said, "don't eat fresh lettuce and tomatoes in a foreign country."

At one café I was asked if I wanted *una copa de vino* with my food. Until then, I had drunk nothing but water with meals in Bolivia.

"Whatever you do," Mama had said, "don't drink the water."

Being offered wine was thrilling. I could not legally drink alcohol at home, "legally" being the key word there. What should I order? I knew nothing about wine except that there probably was more to know beyond Thunderbird.

"*¿Uh . . . que clases de vinos tienen ustedes?*" What wines do you have?

"*El rojo.*" Red.

"I'll have *el rojo.*"

"Whatever you do," Mama had said, "don't drink alcohol in a country where women wear black lace veils. They're probably hiding blue-veined noses. Actually, don't drink alcohol at all. You're too young."

Mama had neglected to warn me about ice cream. I suspect she thought it was available only in the States. Until many years later, when I discovered Vivoli's gelato shop in Florence, this was the best ice cream I'd tasted. I ate some every hour to keep up my strength. The missionaries were becoming a trial; they seemed to think I should be lying in bed reading scripture while someone ironed my socks, not roaming the city alone, mouth rimmed with chocolate ice cream. Look at the other student-missionaries, they said. *They* were laid low with *soroche* (altitude sickness), righteously suffering from dizziness, headaches, and nausea. What was wrong with me? *And where did I go at night?*

There was no rule against leaving the compound after dark, but none of the other student-missionaries did. (How could they?

They could barely make it to the bathroom down the hall.) One place I went was to the movies. Watching American films with Spanish subtitles seemed a fine way to practice my Spanish. As some of the Bolivian guys at the movies were cute, I practiced my Spanish on them too. Although "no" meant "no" in both languages, many young men (the world over, I would learn) seemed never to have heard the word. I like to think I contributed to their basic education in this matter. There *was* a brown-eyed handsome man named Ernesto, but he didn't count. I'd never kissed a foreigner. It would be a shame to return to the States without having borne witness to such an available and rewarding cultural experience.

On the fifth day, they shipped me off to the Andes. My assigned mission was in a tiny village on the Altiplano, a bleak high plateau where temperatures fluctuated wildly and daily. At noon it was summer, at midnight, winter, and the wind never stopped. On the shores of Lake Titicaca — at 13,000 feet, the world's highest navigable body of water (and with a name hard to say without snickering) — the village was home to two hundred Aymara Indians, one Catholic church, and a Protestant missionary family from the Midwest, with whom I lived. There wasn't much to burn on the Altiplano, but come late afternoon, the missionaries built a small fire in the dirt surrounding their house. You put stones in the fire until they were hot, then wrapped the stones in rags and stuffed them in the bottom of your sleeping bag. Bedtime was an hour after dark. You always knew when it was 3 a.m. That's when the stones got cold. Mornings we drank the green tealike beverage called *maté*. Indians back to the Incas and before had believed *maté* improved health and contributed to long life; today it's advertised in the United States as an After-Workout Energizer. You had to drink fast. In the Andes, a boiling cup of *maté* cooled in less than a minute. Then it tasted like shit.

The missionaries were nice people, I thought, although I also thought there was too much preaching and too little doing, especially after Peace Corps volunteers came to the village and in one day showed the Aymara how to boil water quickly and in large amounts by digging shallow parabolas in the earth, lining them with aluminum foil, and letting the intense Andean sun do the rest. When they left, I wanted to go with them, but I was stuck giving

Protestant lessons to the Aymara, who listened politely, mentally scratching their heads. Most Indians already had been converted from their native religion to Roman Catholicism. Now we were telling them to give up Catholicism for another kind of Christianity. They were confused and I was no help. One of my assignments was to teach the Aymara to sing "Onward, Christian Soldiers" in Spanish, a language neither they nor I spoke or understood very well. When I tried to explain the words, they thought I wanted them to take up arms, leave their crops to rot in the fields, and march off to shoot people. My best friend in the village was a girl close to my own age who spoke some Spanish. Her (literally) Christian name was María. I could not pronounce her Aymara name. María spent most of her day working in the fields or minding her nine younger siblings, who, with María and their parents, lived in one room. I asked if she got cold at night. She said twelve people on one pallet made a fine blanket as long as you managed not to end up on the outer edge. We spent as much time together as possible, poking our noses where we shouldn't and trying to get out of work. María's most treasured possession was a transistor radio left behind by a departing missionary. She turned it on every few hours in anticipation of a miracle she was sure would come one day. I said the miracle needed batteries. She said that for a person who knew how to read and write, I was incredibly dumb about miracles.

My other clothes never arrived, but by then I had gone native, trading my pea jacket for a brown alpaca poncho and my baseball cap for a brightly colored wool cap like the ones Bolivian men wore — Bolivian Indian women wore the kind of bowler hat North American men had sported around the turn of the century and I had no intention of going there. I tried to fit in. I ate stewed guinea pig in the market. If anyone asks you, guinea pig does not taste like chicken. Snake tastes like chicken. Guinea pig tastes like goat. I ate purple potatoes and boiled grains we would later call quinoa and think we discovered. In general, the Altiplano diet was heavy on carbs and lacking in protein. The U.S. government had tried to help, if not entirely for humanitarian reasons. Hoping to prevent a Communist revolution they were sure was at hand, the State Department had pumped great amounts of money into Bolivia during the fifties. One swell idea had been sheep, and it was only after doubling the sheep population on the Altiplano that the State Department had discovered that sheep overgrazed the already sparse grass, and that Indians preferred chicken and beef to mutton anyway. María said she ate mutton once. She said it tasted like old llama. A rich Christian from the United States also had tried to help. Thinking to provide a continuous source of protein, he had spent a small fortune stocking Lake Titicaca with edible fish — trout, I think it was. His good intentions were thwarted by gods other than the one in whose name he acted. Because there was nothing in Lake Titicaca to prey on them, the new fish had grown to such size most Indians decided they must be spirits, and for a long time would not eat them. María said she ate a slice of such a fish once. She said it tasted like sin. She said she liked the taste.

I would get up before dawn and walk to the edge of a high cold lake in the middle of a high cold nowhere to see the sun rise, turning the water from black to aquamarine, turning the land from cold to hot. As I watched men ply graceful handmade reed boats silently across the lake, as they had done for a thousand years, it seemed to me that God, by whatever name you called

him, her, or it, must be in everything: in the lake, in the sky, the sun, the land, the potatoes, the fish. In the people. Maybe even in me. Maybe even in religion. Or not. There was no electricity in the village, no sewer system, no water purification, no doctor, and no school. The Indians grew their own food, wove their own cloth from llama and alpaca wool, made their own clothes, and bartered for what they could not raise or make. When I was there, the life expectancy of an Aymara woman was forty-five years. My friend María had already used up nearly half her life. As much as I thought what the Protestants were trying to do might be futile, I thought what the Catholics had already done might be worse. The Catholic church in our village, a simple adobe structure, was unlocked only one day a year, when the priest came to perform proper Christian ceremonies over anyone who had died, been born, converted, or married since he was here last. I was around the day the priest came. When he opened the church, I saw a room filled with gold and silver. The sale of a chalice would have fed the village children for two years. I bore witness; I told the Indians the Catholic Church was rich, they were poor, and the Protestants weren't likely to change this. Perhaps acting on the theory that I would cause less trouble rolling bandages than teaching the Aymara Christian war songs or asking if they'd heard of Che Guevara, the Protestants reassigned me to a mission clinic in the more fertile highland valleys of Bolivia. I said goodbye to María and promised to send her batteries when I found some, but now I was off to save the Quechua.

The Aymara and Quechua were two separate peoples. Traditionally they had not intermarried and they spoke different, equally hard-to-understand languages. The clinic to which I was sent (banished?) had few beds and not enough medicine. What it did have was a North American doctor who'd donated a year of his time to come to Bolivia to work for free. I thought he was sexy — Montgomery Clift, only saner — and admired his dedication, especially after the Indians decided to kill us.

Persuading any of the Quechua to come to the clinic was tough. Call it a cultural collision. Native healers, whom modern health practitioners regarded as witch doctors, were pitted against modern health practitioners whom Indians regarded as witch doctors. Only a great deal of cajoling had gotten the fellow with the rather nasty and not self-inflicted knife wound to come in for treatment. The doctor patched him up and talked him into spending the night in the clinic. The rooms had no light or heat except for gas lanterns. During the night, the man blew out the flame in his lantern, in his windowless cubicle, with the door shut. When we found his body, his stomach, site of the knife wound, had bloated until it burst open around his belt. The man's family decided the Christian doctor had killed their kinsman and went home to get their guns. I'd never been shot at before. A sobering experience. By nighttime the Indians had run out of bullets and decided to settle for money. You could put cash to more use than you could a handful of dead Christians.

Although I was pretty sure the death of the man was not my fault, the missionaries put me on a bus and sent me down to the lush Bolivian jungle, called the Yungas, to work in a leper colony. The bus was packed with more people and chickens than it had been built to hold. I found a place to curl up in what passed for the aisle. My fellow passengers did what you might do on a bus driven by a maniac determined to bring you closer to God by flinging his vehicle off a high mountain curve — they got drunk. After too many swigs of *chicha,* a fiery home brew made from fermented corn, a large fellow standing above me opened his fly and peed on what he probably thought was a lump of old clothes piled at his feet. Drinking *chicha,* it turned out, was not as awful as wearing it.

The Yungas was a wild place. My old buddies the Aymara lived there, along with nine other linguistic groups and thirty subgroups. There were Negroes too. The Spaniards, never bothered by enslaving a people when slaves were what was called for, had imported Africans to work in the silver mines, but the altitude had killed them off so rapidly that those who survived fled south, learned to speak Aymara, and became one of the Yungas subcultures. The Spaniards didn't mind; in the Yungas they used Africans to cultivate coca. Chewing coca leaves had once been a privilege of the Incas, but eventually highland Indians had found it too useful to be left to a disappearing culture. Chew enough coca leaves and you wouldn't notice how cold mining could be, or how hungry you might be. The Spaniards found it useful too; miners without appetites were cheaper to feed. I saw Indians chewing coca leaves on the Altiplano and in the highland valleys and the Yungas. But I never tried coca or its derivative, cocaine, not until the eighties, when, along with so many others, I pretended to be a Bolivian miner.

My time in the Yungas was short and no one shot at me. The "whites" treated me as an honored guest. "White" meant people of Spanish descent who might have some Indian blood but definitely did not think of themselves as Indians or even mestizos. As in the rest of Bolivia, food was important in the Yungas, and there was more of it.

Food grew on trees, roamed the jungle, or was tied to a rope in the backyard. At the "white" houses, dinner consisted of three courses, a beef soup with fresh vegetables and local herbs, followed by more meat — slices of grilled beef or goat — and more vegetables or fruit, sometimes papaya but usually plantain, a kind of stunted banana that is inedible until it is cooked. I ate it fried, baked, and mashed. I ate it as a side dish. I ate it as dessert. No matter what they did to a plantain, I hated it, but then I don't like bananas.

If the Altiplano smelled like the wind, the Yungas smelled like overripe fruit, but not as overripe as the lepers. As in almost all "civilizations," lepers in Bolivia were ostracized. The ones I met at the mission station were in general nice folks who remained uncertain exactly whose gods had laid on them such horrifying punishment. One day, a leper named Jorge told me I was a beautiful young woman. I asked him how he knew. He said he could feel it. He also said he was a beautiful young man. Jorge was sixty-seven. He had no toes, fingers, or sight. He deserved better. They all did. By then there were treatments, which, if used in the early stages, could have prevented the deformity and disability.

I complained to John, not a doctor but a missionary whose personal mission was simple: fight leprosy any way he could.

"Why," I said, "didn't we demand the church, or the U.S. government, send the medicines?"

John looked at me as if I were the fool I was. Did I think they hadn't asked, no, begged for medicine? Did I think all missionaries did was go around trying to convert people?

Well, yes, I guess I did.

I'd seen missionaries care more about saving souls than lives. I'd seen missionaries more concerned with the impression they made on the church bureaucracy than the good they might do. I'd seen Indians ironing missionaries' jockey shorts. But hadn't I also seen missionaries who gave with a hand as well as a heart, who got dirty with hard work, got shot at, gave away what they had, lived in poverty — missionaries who did anything they could to brighten the corner where they were?

I got off my high horse and asked what I could do to help.

John said why didn't we see if a shovel fit my hands? I dug trenches that could be used as latrines. I dug ditches. I dug graves. The day I helped dig Jorge's grave,

I wrote a passionate letter home about the injustice of it all. I wrote home about everything I saw. Wasn't I bearing witness? Wasn't that what I'd been sent to do? The letters were scribbled in small, cramped script on thin paper that folded in upon itself to become its own envelope. We'd been told the Bolivian government might open our mail. Exactly why was unclear, but they said the government was unstable and anything might happen. It did. Only a year later, the United States helped establish a right-wing military dictatorship that lasted until the 1980s. Now the monthly pay of an army lieutenant would be quadruple the annual pay for a teacher. And wouldn't that be progress.

In September, I left Bolivia. I didn't save any souls. I didn't change anybody's life but mine. I never knew if María received the batteries I sent and if so, if she found the outside world as fulfilling as her imagination. Waiting for my plane at the La Paz airport, I hit the bar, certain it would be the last drinking establishment to serve me for another three years without wanting to see an ID first. I said to the bartender that I wanted a real Bolivian drink. The bartender suggested *chicha*. I said no thanks; I'd absorbed a lifetime's worth of *chicha* on a bus ride to the Yungas. Was there another, equally traditional drink? He thought about it and then with some ceremony mixed a concoction that tasted like eggnog on speed.

"You like it?" He looked hopeful.

"Strong," I gasped. My vision was starting to blur. "What's it called?" I said, hoarsely.

"*La Biblia,*" he said. The Bible.

On returning home I discovered Mama had sent copies of all my letters to the church's national office. She was sure they would like to see what a good writer I was. The following year the church revised the rules for its student missionary program: no eighteen-year-olds from Texas who smoked, drank, ate guinea pig, or thought Indian healers might be on to something and that Che Guevara might be nearly as interesting as Billy Graham need apply. Bearing witness, I'd learned — seeing what you see, hearing what you hear, and then telling others about it as truthfully as you can — will not make you popular. But it just might, one day, make you a journalist.

La Biblia (The Bible)

MAKES FOUR BIBLES

$^1/_4$ cup sugar
4 whole eggs
1 cup of *singani* (see Note)
Ground cinnamon or nutmeg

1. Beat the sugar and eggs together until the mixture is thick. Use a blender if you wish.
2. Add the *singani* and keep beating. Or whirring.
3. Serve the Bibles in wineglasses. Sprinkle each with cinnamon or nutmeg.
4. Operate no heavy machinery.

NOTE: *Singani* is a grape-based liquor that is made in Bolivia. You can substitute pisco, a Peruvian brandy that is much easier to find.

Salteñas

Salteñas are Bolivia's national dish. I bought them from Indian street vendors, who learned from the Spaniards, who stole the basic recipe from the Moors. Add Las Biblias and throw a party.

The dough and the filling have to be made the day before.

PASTRY
6 cups flour
6 tablespoons lard
2 egg yolks
$1^1/_2$ cups lukewarm water
$^1/_2$ cup milk
1 tablespoon sugar
1 teaspoon salt

Mix all the ingredients together and knead well. Wrap the dough in a damp cloth and keep refrigerated overnight.

FILLING
1 cup chopped onion
3 tablespoons lard or other shortening
1 pound ground beef
1$^1/_2$ tablespoons unflavored gelatin
1 cup cooked potatoes, mashed
$^1/_2$ cup seedless raisins
2 hard-cooked eggs, chopped
6 black olives, pitted and chopped
1 teaspoon cayenne (I use more. Your call.)
Salt, sugar, cumin, and oregano to taste
1 egg, beaten
Oil for frying

Fry the onion in 1 tablespoon shortening. Add the meat and stir, separating it until it browns. Remove from heat and let cool enough to handle easily. Add the gelatin (dissolved in $^1/_2$ cup lukewarm water), potatoes, raisins, hard-cooked eggs, olives, cayenne, salt, sugar, cumin, and oregano and the rest of the shortening. Mix, taste, and refrigerate overnight.

TO FINISH
Roll the dough out to $^1/_8$ inch thick and cut into roughly 3-inch rounds (use a cookie cutter or jar rim). Brush each round with the beaten egg. Put 1 heaping teaspoon of mixture in the center. Fold each round over and

pinch the edges closed, making half moons, and seal with fork tines. In batches, fry in 375-degree oil until golden. Keep warm in oven until all are fried, then serve immediately.

FOUR

Border Crossings

(1969, 1999, 2004)

I pull on my *Thelma & Louise* T-shirt, sweet old thing, faded and shrunken despite the tag inside telling you how to wash it. I'm pretty sure that tag once was legible, if anyone had taken time to read it. No one had. And so, armed with a T-shirt that doesn't fit, an old friend, and a reason for going, I head for the Texas-Mexico border. Some people cross a border for lunch, some for life, some because they can't help coloring outside the lines. When I was a teenage Texas girl, getting laid in a border-town whorehouse was a rite of passage for teenage Texas boys. Today men cross the border to purchase Magic Penis Sticks — would I make this up? — or the more modern magic of Viagra, for which, in Mexico, one needs nothing so pedestrian as a prescription. There has been a great deal spoken, written, and filmed about magic and Mexico, although we all know magic doesn't exist except in the minds of children and fools. I'm going to Mexico for the magic.

It is the last spring of the twentieth century. I need a dose of magic. Mine feels used up by the harder facts of life. Oh hell, I'm depressed. Beth knows about depression, knows about facts, too, but she's strong, always has been; she just keeps forgetting. We are seasoned in each other's lives, Beth and I, our joys and sorrows woven into the tapestry of shared history. When we met, she had long dark hair and the face of an angel. I'm not sure I believe in angels. How, exactly, can one *know?* But I believe in Beth. She keeps her promises and my secrets, gets my jokes, and has given me unconditional love for all the years I've known her and all the times I didn't deserve it.

In 1969, my husband and I lived in Eagle Pass, Texas, across the border from Piedras Negras, Mexico. Our house twelve miles north of town on what had been a World War II radar base called — rather grandly, considering its postage-stamp size — the Eagle Pass Army Air Force Advanced Flying School. After the war ended, the army abandoned the base.

By the time my husband and I arrived, Maverick County was renting out the concrete-block officers' houses, arranged in a circle like a wagon train, two hundred yards from a dead runway, for $100 a month. Beth and Chuck rented the house next door. Once in a while, friends "fall in like" with as loud a thud as romantic partners fall in love. That was Beth and me. From the beginning, we knew we were in for the long ride. Our initial ties, along with being young, having babies, and making our first nests, were food — and life in a semiforeign environment. It was Beth who first taught me to recognize — even to seek — the connections between what I put in my mouth and the world around me.

Spring 1999. Beth and I rent a car in Brownsville — good name for it — and cross the Rio Grande into Matamoros, Mexico. We tell each other we are women of the *frontera*. Wild women. Thelma and Louise. Annie Oakley and Calamity Jane. Lucy and Ethel. Beth and Linda.

The excellent adventures of Beth and Linda.

In Matamoros, we check into the Gran Residencial Hotel, which sounds more *gran* than it is, but the rooms are clean and, because most guests are Texan, air-conditioned to the point of losing sensation in one's extremities — there is a swimming pool we can jump into to get warm. But we are on a mission at the moment. Hoping to find some of the genuine, meat-based regional cooking of northern Mexico, Beth and I drop off our stuff, strap ourselves into our rented car, and strike out for Los Portales, a restaurant we have been told is authentic. We will be the judges of that.

In the early seventies, after spending years in that country, Diana Kennedy wrote a cookbook introducing people to the pleasures of regional Mexican cooking. Well and good. I love it that I can go to Zarela's restaurant in New York and enjoy the complicated flavors of Oaxacan *mole* without first obtaining a boarding pass. As Thurber once noted, however, progress was okay, but it went on too long. Along came a gang of chefs who took what Diana Kennedy taught, twisted it, tortured it, and invented something called Nuevo Latino or worse, Nuevo-Mex. These were the chaps who decided pineapple and ginger might taste swell in a taco, or spinach in an enchilada. Repeat after me: Spinach does not belong in an enchilada, pineapple does not belong in a taco, and ginger does not belong in anything calling itself Latino. Go play somewhere else.

Fusion cooking. Phooey. Swedish meatballs with hoisin sauce. Stir-fried Irish stew. *Coq au vin* on a bed of kimchi.

Oh all right, once in a while it works. *Carnitas* is a traditional Mexican dish. In northern Mexico, pork is deep-fried — or as Mexicans sometimes put it, boiled — in its own fat, otherwise known as lard. If you plan on living forever you can skip the lard, simmer the pork in water or chicken broth, pull it apart, and put it in the oven until the edges are crisp. At Dos Caminos Soho, a Nuevo Latino restaurant in my neighborhood, they use lard, but they also add orange juice, coconut milk, and Coca-Cola. Fusion run amok, and still, Pancho Villa would love these *carnitas*. They are the same, only different. But oh how I would like to get my hands around the neck of the taste-bud serial killer who decided tortilla chips should be baked instead of fried, come in colors of dried autumn leaves, and taste roughly the same. Bet you'd find him in Southern California. Not at his stove. Chef Creepo is at his aerobics class, sweating up a new idea: How to roast pork without using a pig.

At the opposite end of the International Association of Mexican Food Manglers are the fast-food joints and chain restaurants that serve powdered refried beans — think powdered fried potatoes — fake cheese, preformed taco shells, and a kind of spaghetti sauce they call salsa. Let's not speak of black olives. People who will put a black olive on a tostada will do worse. Nevertheless, as I've already admitted to liking *carnitas* cooked in Coca-Cola, truth in advertising forces me to confess a major addiction to the Jack-in-the-Box Super Taco. The lettuce is limp, the cheese is a slice of ersatz Kraft, and the salsa is barely passable, but the shell is real — fried and greasy — which means it won't fall apart at first bite the way a baked, preformed shell always will do. The taco is a juicy, swell-tasting mess. Too bad there's no Twelve-Step program. *Hello, my name is Linda and I'm powerless over the Jack-in-the-Box Super Taco.* JITBST Anonymous. We'd be a large bunch in every way. No matter. I can cope as long as you don't tell me what the meat in that taco is.

What can one say about the invasion of those machines that cough up a Pepto-Bismol–colored frozen drink some people have the nerve to call a Margarita? Back when Beth and I went regularly to Mexico, a Margarita — Spanish for "daisy" — was a potent but simple drink in a *small* stemmed glass. Tequila, triple sec, and the juice of a lime. Easy as one, two, three: one part lime, two parts triple sec, three parts tequila. But those who cross borders must adapt to survive, and so, when Little Margarita reached the United States, she put on crimson lipstick and began to hang with a bad crowd. They took her daisy. They added fruits or food coloring, even club soda, and — the final blow — sweet-and-sour mix. They blended her or pulled her from a tap, like frozen beer, into a Manly Martini Glass. Sometimes a big iced-tea glass. One suspects it is necessary to reduce the amount of tequila to make this economically possible. But who would notice? In New York, "Let's go have a Margarita" is code for "Let's get bent." I think they get bent on the stuff that turns the Margarita funny colors. St. Patrick's Day Margaritas are big in my neighborhood.

"My name is Brian O'Brien. I'm high on a really big, really expensive glass of fake lemonade, green dye #44, and a thimbleful of tequila. Buy you one?"

You're a daisy if you do.

After passing several branches of

MacPollo, Beth and I finally find Los Portales. The Doors. Will there be posters of Jim Morrison? Will I have to ride the snake before I eat it? We order in Spanish. The more we speak, the more the waiter smiles. Our Spanish is laughable, but it is possible we aren't complete barbarians — have we not ordered enough food for six people and not once asked for that gringo abomination called "sauce on the side"? I believe he may have conveyed his hopes for us to the chef.

Dinner begins with a basket of home-made fried tortilla chips still hot from the frying, and a bowl of *pico de gallo,* beak of the rooster — a raw salsa of chopped ripe tomato, cilantro, fresh *chiles serranos,* onions, and the juice of a lime. There's nothing new about salsa. The Aztecs made salsa. Means "sauce." (In the United States, salsa now outsells ketchup. But be careful. If you're not vigilant you're apt to find mangoes, papayas, and grapes in your salsa or, if you mistakenly wander into the Gourmet Section of your local supermarket, in your ketchup.) We enjoy guacamole made with the little round avocados available only on the Mexican side of the border. Reason enough, when it comes to smuggling, to turn pro. We see our way through a plate of *queso fundido con rajas y chorizo* — melted stringy white cheese topped with roasted strips of fresh chiles and fried pieces of sausage made with pork and dried chiles.

A word about chiles and chili.

On his first voyage to the New World, Columbus ate a plant that made him cry. Having gone the wrong way to find China, he should have cried, but what brought tears to his eyes wasn't the fact he was directionally challenged. Columbus ate a chile. Familiar only with the black pepper imported to Europe from the Caucasus, he called this new plant "red pepper" because the pods were red. However, chiles, whether they are jalapeños, serranos, poblanos, habañeros, piquíns, anchos, or any of the dozens of other varieties that grow in the New World, are not related in any way to black pepper.

Chili is not a pepper either. Chili is a Texas dish — and the Jews are wrong: chili eaters are God's chosen people. Chili came about because cowboy cooks at home on the range fed folks with the handiest ingredient: beef. Because freshly butchered, unaged beef is not much tastier than spoiled beef, these cooks chopped it up and cooked it with water (or coffee) and chiles. The chiles added flavor to beef that was too fresh and masked the taste of beef that was too old. You will notice that countries incorporating chiles in their national cuisine all enjoy — or suffer from — climates where meat goes off rather quickly. There's a reason you don't find chiles in Norwegian recipes. A bowl of red is called chili or *chile con carne,* which means chiles with meat, but it is never called chile. Don't talk to me about putting beans or tomatoes in chili, and if you're from Cincinnati, where they put macaroni in chili, stay there. As for chili sauce, that's what you don't put in a Frito Pie.

Our waiter brings a brazier to the table. Chunks of *Cabrito al Pastor,* kid roasted on a spit country-style, are still sizzling. He brings us pinto beans that have been cooked, mashed, and then fried in lard. (Nothing is better for frying than lard. Nothing. Do not quote me on this.) *Frijoles refritos.* Refried beans. A misnomer. The beans are fried only once. The more accurate — in the nonliteral sense — translation is "well-fried beans." There's a disagreement about beans in Mexico. In some areas, serving cooked beans you've mashed and fried is akin to admitting you're fiddling around with leftovers. In other places, serving cooked beans before you've gone to the trouble of mashing and frying them shows you aren't really trying.

For three hours we eat as though we were still young and within chewing distance of the Rio Grande, and lives we haven't lived yet.

The Chamber of Commerce liked to refer to Eagle Pass as the place where "Yee-hah" and *"Olé"* meet. White settlers once called the country around there the badlands. Coyotes, lizards, Gila monsters, horned toads, scorpions, and rattlesnakes called it home. Because eagles flew overhead, the vicinity eventually came to be known as El Paso del Águila. The pass of the eagle. Borders are drawn by nations. The eagle recognized nobody's. For a while, neither did most people. Eagle Pass sprang up not too far upriver from an old smuggler's trail. It was not your proverbial sleepy little border town. They never are. Eagle Pass was a spicy *guisado,* a stew of Anglos, Mexicans, Mexican-Americans, black Americans, and Native Americans. Everybody had someone to look down on and, in one way or another, at some time or another, everybody went crazy. In the borderlands, insanity is a rational reaction to an insane world. If you saw John Sayles's movie *Lone Star*, you know Eagle Pass, for that is where it was shot, and the movie caught the soul of border culture. Watching it now evokes vivid memories of my young self. At the time, I didn't know I was young. You never do when you are. You never know as much as you think you do about anything. There was so much I didn't understand about borders.

When two countries touch each other, but one is rich and the other poor, there's bound to be more than a collision of cultures. What America had been to English, Irish, Germans, and Eastern Europeans, it was to Mexicans. Even if they were too smart to believe the streets were paved with gold, they lusted after what they regarded as the American Dream. We thought this meant democracy. They thought it meant a job. In 1969, Mexicans crossed the border like flour through a sieve. Those with green cards did so legally. Others told border guards they were crossing to shop for the day, and then stayed. Borders make liars of good people. We knew some — women who couldn't earn enough in Mexico to support their families. They crossed Monday morning, worked for Anglo and Mexican-American families until Friday night, and then crossed back to work for their own families. Beth and I paid the Mexican women who worked for us $15 a week. The other women in Eagle Pass, Anglo and Mexican-American, said we were ruining the gig; they paid $10. Beth and I remain deeply ashamed of how righteous we thought that extra $5 made us. These women made our lives rich. They taught us a new language and new stories. They gave us time out from our sweet but sticky babies. They gave us new ways of looking at life and death — and magic.

"*Cuidado.*" Be careful, they would say, wrapping our babies from head to toe in wool blankets, which, as it was 109 degrees in the shade, seemed odd to us.

"*Cuidado.* The baby will catch air."

"My baby will catch *air?*"

"*Los espíritos malos.*" The bad spirits. "The baby will catch air from the bad spirits and get sick. Everybody knows this."

Juanita and Carmela would shake their heads. We didn't believe in *los espíritos malos?* We didn't believe in magic? Clearly we were stupid. We didn't argue; some like to understand what they believe in, others like to believe in what they understand. If they believed in magic, possibly it was because magic was the only thing that might raise their families up from poverty. The women didn't seem to blame us, or their husbands, for their situation, although they often spoke of men as though they were necessary, if mainly useless, objects, but they said it with affection. They laughed easily, loved passionately, and treated life as a miracle that could turn on you, and so they lied to cross a border and believed in magic. For us, they *created* magic. Every morning when we went into our kitchens after nursing our babies, Carmela at Beth's house (and Juanita at my house), each stood in front of a hot *comal,* a rectangular cast-iron griddle placed over two of a stove's gas burners, patting out homemade flour tortillas, which then went onto the *comal.* By the time you sat down, the first tortilla was on your plate next to the butter and salsa. When you finished one, another appeared. Beth and I knew even then that no matter how much money either of us ever ran into, we would never be that rich again.

When we wake up at the Gran Residencial Hotel in Matamoros after our night at Los Portales, The Magic Mexican

Fairy we've appointed to watch over us on our journey has made us thin again in time for breakfast. We strike gold at a hole-in-the-wall café, consuming stacks of those perfect handmade flour tortillas we'd been privileged to eat when God was a lad and living down on the border disguised as someone named Carmela or Juanita. After breakfast we troll border shops, ignoring tacky machine-made pottery and cheesy Day-Glo paintings on bark or velvet. Elvis doesn't count. A painting of Elvis on black velvet is art. We pass on blankets in colors a drag queen would call over-the-top. We turn up our noses at blue-rimmed glassware called Margarita sets. But there are treasures to be had, if you know what to look for. The Aztecs used the cured pod of a particular orchid for a variety of purposes, including putting it in food. The Spanish named it *vainilla*. Little pod. In Mexico, *vainilla pura* is sold by the fifth, like booze, and is more flavorful than the vanilla extract sold in the States. We each buy one bottle. A fifth of vanilla tends to last. Mostly we look for the rust-colored pottery we used in 1969. Food cooked in that pottery tasted better. But the pottery was made with lead, so now it was unusable, which made it valuable and thus hard to find. Finding no life-threatening cook-ware, we head out of Matamoros on the road that runs along the Mexican side of the river. We see women cooking tortillas on grills over open fires. We smell chiles roasting on tin sheets and beans cooking in clay pots that probably contain the lead that makes the food taste better.

The best food was always across the river. When we lived in Eagle Pass, we regularly ate at a Piedras Negras restaurant called El Moderno. Didn't look like what you think of as Mexican — there were no sombreros on the walls — but they served a decent *Carne Tampiqueña*. A wartime offshoot of El Moderno was the birthplace of a dish that would cross the border to become an American classic. Make that an international classic.

It happened in 1943, a year before Beth and I were born. Rudolfo de los Santos, owner of El Moderno, also owned a place he called the Victory Club — it was war-time. One afternoon, several Anglo women whose husbands were stationed in Eagle Pass crossed the border, shopped, headed for the Victory Club, ordered Margaritas, and asked Rudolfo for something to nibble on while they got drunk. The cook was momentarily AWOL. Rudolfo told the waiter to go to the kitchen and come up with something. The waiter wasn't a cook. He didn't know how to make *antojitos,* the traditional small plates that went with drinks. The waiter looked around the kitchen for a way to save his boss's face and his own job. He grabbed a handful of tortillas and tore them into quarters. He deep-fried them until they were crisp. He grated yellow cheese and put that on top of the fried pieces of tortillas. He plated them, making sure no chip overlapped another, and put the plate under the broiler until the cheese melted. He sliced jalapeños into thin rounds and threw those on too. The ladies loved the result and asked Rudolfo what these tasty little thingies were called.

Pay attention. This is how history gets made.

The waiter's name was Ignacio Anaya. In English, someone whose name is Franklin is often called Frank. Joseph is called Joe. In Spanish, the short name for Ignacio is Nacho. Having no idea what to call the snacks Mr. Anaya had concocted, Rudolfo de los Santos told the ladies they were Nacho's *especiales.* Nacho's specials. The ladies went home and told other people about Nacho's specials. The dish became a hit at the Victory Club and then at El Moderno. The apostrophe got lost along the way. Nacho's specials morphed into nachos.

Later, Ignacio Anaya opened his own small restaurant on the road south of Piedras Negras. Mr. Anaya was an old man by then, but he made the world's best nachos. He told us he'd invented them. I don't remember whether we believed him. By that time, nachos had already migrated north of the border. Fast-food chains, ballparks, and cheap cafés had taken over from there. Today, you can get nachos at the Pittsburgh airport or a Knicks game at Madison Square Garden. They taste as much like real nachos as I look like Jennifer Lopez.

After his father died in 1975, Ignacio Anaya Jr. crossed the border to Eagle Pass and took up banking. Mr. Anaya is retired but still lives in Eagle Pass. I spoke to him on the phone. He told me that in 1995, Piedras Negras had declared October 21 the International Day of the Nacho. He said every year Eagle Pass and Piedras Negras threw a joint party, and that a bronze plaque had been installed in Piedras Negras in honor of his father. I said I might come down for the Nacho Festival. Would he accompany me? Mr. Anaya said he would, although he thought I might be disappointed in the nachos. Think I'll go anyway. How often do you get to meet the son of an international hero?

In the last spring of the twentieth century, Beth and I eat our final lunch in Mexico in the border town of Reynosa, at a restaurant decorated with live doves in filigreed iron cages. Texans love to take their guns to Mexico to shoot these tiny symbols of peace. Real good eatin', they tell you. We don't eat dove; we eat more ribs of barely born goats. At least they didn't keep them in cages in the dining room. After lunch I buy a couple of pounds of authentic *chicharrones* — fried pork rinds with bits of pork still attached — for the road, and then begin to worry about going to prison for smuggling a bag of heart attacks into the United States. The customs officer never sees the *chicharrones*, even though I have hidden them in plain sight. Beth and I return to Houston, where she lives. There is time for only one more meal before I leave for New York. We go to Felix's, where else? There is real Mexican food.

There is faux Mexican food (see spinach enchiladas). There is Taco Bell, owned by PepsiCo. And there is Tex-Mex.

Saved the best for last.

Tex-Mex is more than food. It's a way two different cultures began to appreciate each other, and nobody did more to foster that connection than Felix and Janie Tijerina. The son of Mexican migrant workers who moved back and forth across the border with the seasons until they settled outside Houston, Felix Tijerina was born in 1905. When he was thirteen, he went to work as a busboy. Felix didn't speak English. He learned; he taught himself. In 1933, he married Janie Gonzales. Felix drove a beer truck and Janie worked at a Five & Dime. Despite their beer income, Janie (the story goes) had champagne tastes and liked to gamble. Family lore says her boss gave her money to place a bet (for him) at a racetrack in the Houston area. Janie decided her boss wouldn't bet on a long shot unless he knew the horse was going to win. She pawned the family car, borrowed money from friends, and put $450 on the nag for herself. The nag won. She gave Felix the winnings, and after they got their car back and repaid their friends, she told him to take the money and start a

Felix Mexican Restaurant
904 WESTHEIMER   PHONE JACKSON-6214
HOUSTON, TEXAS

restaurant. She also promised to quit gambling.

They called it Felix's Mexican Restaurant. Back then we didn't call what they served Tex-Mex. We called it Mexican food, but it was Mexican food designed for Texas taste buds. Nothing too spicy or too *foreign*. The main ingredients were cheese, grease, and mild brown chili gravy, all basic food groups familiar to Texans. We ate ground meat and yellow cheese every time we ate a cheeseburger. We ate chili. Most of us, having come from families that came from the South, were no strangers to gravy or grease and we'd already learned from the Mexicans to eat *barbacoa*. After a while we called it barbecue and pretended we invented it. This was no great leap. Or was it? The Tijerinas' innocuous food introduced many a Texan to a culture — and people — that most of them distrusted. In the case of Felix's, it was a bridge built of cheese, for their *chile con queso* was like no other. At most Tex-Mex restaurants, *chile con queso* is a bowl of dip made by melting American cheese with a few pieces of red and green bell pepper thrown in for color. Not at Felix's. I can't tell you how they make theirs; over the years customers would plead for the recipe and every so often a Houston newspaper would publish what it claimed was the *real* recipe for Felix's *chile con queso*. It never was.

In 1949, my family moved to Houston, where we became regular customers at Felix's on Westheimer, which had opened a year before. I was four, which meant that if I lived long enough, one day I would be their oldest customer. I try to imagine it: Mrs. Felix — no one I knew called her anything else — is heading toward my table followed by Frank Barrera, the waiter who's worked there since the doors

138

opened. Frank is bearing a giant corn tortilla with one candle on it.

"This candle," says Mrs. Felix, "is because you're our oldest customer, Ellerbee."

She never called me anything else. That is, after she started calling me anything at all.

"And because of your loyalty," she says, "we've decided to honor you by building a room out back so you can live out your golden years close to the *queso*."

Felix's Mexican Restaurant was an icon of the fifties. Frank, the waiter, knew us all. When we were children, he knew that my friend Lona didn't want onions on her cheese enchiladas and that I wanted double cheese. He knew that Judy wasn't particular and that Carol wanted what I had. The four of us are still friends, still go to Felix's, and still order the same way. Although my parents are gone, when I'm at Felix's I'm certain that if I turn my head fast enough, I will see Mama doing one of those peculiar things she did, like ordering her guacamole with saltine crackers, or see Daddy swallowing a forkful of tamale, smacking his lips: Mm, mmm, *mmmm*. I go to eat the memories as much as the food.

Along with practically inventing Tex-Mex, Felix Tijerina changed a world across a border in other ways. He believed assimilation was the answer to poverty and prejudice. *If they get to know us, maybe they'll like us.* He worried about the dropout rate among Mexican-American schoolchildren. Anglos often said these children were dumb; after all, they couldn't even speak American. The Tijerinas were sure Spanish-speaking children would do better if they learned some English *before* they started school. In 1957, they paid a seventeen-year-old girl to teach a group of five-year-old Mexican-American children 400 words of English. The year before, half of all Spanish-speaking children in Houston had flunked first grade. The following year every child who had attended the Little School of 400 passed. The idea spread around the state, and then beyond; President Lyndon Johnson, the last real Texan to serve as president, invited Felix Tijerina to the LBJ ranch to discuss education. Which is how the Little Schools of 400, a project invented by two people who pretended to deal in tacos, became the inspiration for this nation's Head Start Program.

The Tijerinas continued to be active in Mexican-American politics in Houston. After Felix died in 1965, Janie kept up the tradition. The restaurant didn't officially open until 11 a.m., but if you knew enough to go there at 8 a.m., you might find the mayor and other assorted politicians making deals over tortillas and coffee. Normally, I do not think about politics when I'm at Felix's; however, I do remember asking Mrs. Felix what she thought about the presidential election in 1992. This was a brave act. She still scared me, as she did most people.

"I think," Mrs. Felix said, "that the American people no longer know what is good from what is not."

"You mean they can't tell a good politician from a bad one?"

"Worse. I've been visiting some of the other Mexican restaurants in Houston. Ellerbee, did you know they put black olives on tostadas?"

The Tijerinas raised their children in an apartment over the restaurant but never let them work in it. When Janie Tijerina died in 1997, however, at the age of eighty-eight, Felix Jr. and Sandra, his pretty, blond Anglo wife, took over, changing nothing about the food. Real Houstonians would have taken to arms if they had. In 2001, after working at one job for more than half a century, Frank Barrera died, and with him, as with Felix Sr. and Mrs. Felix, a little bit of my history too.

Today there is a Felix Tijerina Elementary School in Houston. I'm sure one day there will be a Janie Tijerina Middle School and a Frank Barrera High School. There are all kinds of borders. These people had crossed theirs, and the crossing made a difference.

Eagle Pass hasn't changed much. There's a mall now. The English-speaking movie theater is out of business. Our army-built identical houses still stand. Everything at the radar base is — other than being older and more run-down — as it was when our hair was long and straight and our jeans belled around the bottom. With one exception: None of the roads on the base had names when we lived there. Now there is a street sign on our old road, our memory lane, that place of such concentrated if unrecognized young joy. They named it Desolation Row.

I was pregnant twice in Eagle Pass. I don't think it was Mr. Anaya's nachos, although some people claimed they were so good they must be magic. But isn't all good food magic? I blame my perpetually pregnant condition on all that sky. The sky seduced me right along with my husband. The sky went on forever. Our time in Eagle Pass did not. My husband and I left for Alaska in 1970, where he left me. I moved to Dallas, got myself a job at the Associated Press, got fired, got a job in television, and managed not to get fired again. Chuck and Beth moved to New Orleans and then to Houston. In 1992, a brain tumor killed Chuck.

Beth survived Chuck's death as best she could. As the Mexican women who left their children and lied their way across a border in order to make a pitiful amount of money survived the best they could. As Janie and Felix Tijerina survived the prejudice they met on this side of the border. As Felix's Mexican Restaurant survived three wars, Bobby Flay, ballpark nachos — the death of the couple who began it — and that pulsating mass of constant change they call Houston, Texas.

As our friendship has survived.

I found the magic I went searching for in the spring of 1999. I'd gone to Mexico for a memory, one which, like Felix's *chile con queso,* was made up of specific, if secret, ingredients that, when combined, do create a kind of magic. I found mine inside chiles and cheese, inside me, and inside

Beth, who carries my memories along with hers because she was there. In the end, a border is an abstract concept. We all face and cross our own. If they are our limits, they are also our windows. On a recent visit to Houston, I went to dinner with Beth and Roberto. He is Beth's friend, perhaps more. Emotionally, Beth has crossed another border. Roberto is from Colombia. He took us to a Colombian restaurant. Not a single thing on the menu was familiar. We let him order. Beth and I smiled at each other in anticipation.

"Oh waiter? A brand new plate of memories, *por favor.*"

Linda's Real Texas Chili

SERVES FOUR TO SEVEN

Some eat it unadorned; others gild. This changes the serving size. So what? Freeze anything left over.

5 pounds beef chuck cut into $1/_2$-inch cubes (make sure the meat has some fat on it so it won't burn or dry out)

Cayenne pepper to taste (I start with a teaspoon or two and go up from there)

2 cups chopped yellow onion (two big ones or three mediums)

10 medium garlic cloves, peeled and chopped

2 tablespoons olive oil

$3/_4$ cup chili powder

2 tablespoons dried oregano

2 tablespoons ground cumin

5 cups beef stock (you can use canned; if you do, don't add salt to the chili)

3 tablespoons cornmeal or less, if needed, to thicken

Grated cheese, sliced jalapeños, tortilla chips, chopped cilantro, and sour cream, for serving (optional)

1. I prefer to make my chili in a cast-iron Dutch oven. Any deep-sided strongly made pot that will hold 4 to 5 quarts will do, but if it's not well-seasoned cast iron, you may want to add a little oil so the meat doesn't stick to the pan. Turn the heat to medium-low. Add the beef and cayenne. Cook uncovered, stirring, for 15 to 20 minutes. You don't want the meat to brown, because this will seal in the juices, which is not how good chili gets made. You just want the pink gone. When it's done, let the meat sit.

2. Cook the onions and garlic in the olive oil in a large skillet over a medium-low heat for 15 to 20 minutes, until they are soft but not too browned. Scrape them out of the pan and add to the beef, along with the chili powder, oregano, and cumin. Cook over medium-low heat, stirring, for 5 minutes.

3. Add the stock. Bring to a boil, reduce

the heat, and let the chili simmer, gently, uncovered, for at least 1½ hours. Stir when you walk by so it doesn't stick to the bottom.

4.   Taste the chili. Add salt if you think it needs it. Or more cayenne. If the chili is too thick, thin it with water. If it's too thin, thicken it by stirring in a little bit of cornmeal. You probably won't need all 3 tablespoons.

5.   Let the chili sit 15 minutes. Stir again. Serve.

6.   If you want, set out bowls of grated cheese, sliced jalapeños, tortilla chips, chopped cilantro, and sour cream (sour cream is especially helpful to those who find the chili too, ah, alert).

Dos Caminos's Carnitas

SERVES EIGHT

Ivy Stark is the inventive chef (at Dos Caminos Soho in New York) who created this improbable, inauthentic-authentic recipe.

3 pounds pork butt, cut into several pieces
1 14-ounce can sweetened condensed milk
5 bay leaves
10 whole black peppercorns
1 cup orange juice
1 can Coca-Cola
1 tablespoon salt
6 pounds lard
Flour or corn tortillas, for serving
Chopped fresh chiles, chopped onion, and chopped cilantro, for serving (optional)

1. Combine all ingredients in a big (preferably copper) pot.

2. Cook over medium heat 2 to $2^1/_2$ hours, until meat is very tender and shreds easily.

3. Remove the pot from the heat, remove the meat from the fat, shred it, and serve it warm, with heated flour or corn tortillas to wrap around the pieces of pork.

4. I put out bowls of chopped fresh chiles, onion, and cilantro to include in the wrap.

Felix's Mexican Restaurant
713-529-3949

Call them. They ship the real *chile con queso*. Tell them I said hello, and that I'll be back soon.

FIVE

Afternoon Delight

(1976, 2000)

My feet stumble on the stones of the old wharf like they think they're not supposed to be here. Smart feet. I promised never to set them down in St.-Tropez again. Indeed, because of how it was that other time, I have avoided all of France. But only for twenty-four years. I explain to my feet I've come to reclaim a country and maybe something else I left behind me. Back here. Back then.

Or . . . you could say I've come for lunch.

Really? Isn't it the most boring of meals?

Can be.

I'm not talking about cultures and customs where lunch is the main meal of the day, and fuel for labor still to come. They call that lunch "dinner." For most of us, lunch is a snippet of daily routine, like flossing, and every bit as thrilling. The Cup O' Noodles you eat at your desk,

150

trying not to drip on the keyboard. The nonfat yogurt in the locker room after that astonishingly awful All-Abs Class. A high-speed run to the cleaner's followed by a fast stop for a slice, double cheese. The Chicken Caesar Wrap in the food court at the mall. The handful of gorp you swallow on your way up the trail. The leftover breakfast your kid didn't finish. The business meeting over food about which you must pretend to be indifferent.

There is another, quite different kind of lunch, one where food is important to what is happening and what is happening presages something that might happen later. I'm talking, you understand, about sex. Dinner is sexier, you say? Candle-smeared eyes locked over charred beef and a glass of big red? Too obvious. The question too plainly put. Breakfast? Night-smeared eyes locked over hot croissants and juicy memories? Too late. The question — one of them, at least — already answered. Dinner and breakfast *work*, but it wasn't until a rainy day in Lyons that I caught on to the real thing. The Lunch Thing. Hormones at high noon. Testosterone at twelve. Madness at midday.

Yes, I said lunch.

The sexiest meal of all.

Maybe it's the timing. Not too early. Not too late. Not the point of no return but the halfway point in the story. Lunch is a question mark. Sometimes a dangerous one. It was August. The seventies. I was young. So was my husband. Everybody was young in the seventies. Our marriage, however, appeared to be dying of old age. It wasn't my first marriage either, but it was supposed to be my last, and so there were choices, all chancy. We chose to go to France, a journey meant to save the relationship — if nothing else, a hell of a tactical diversion — and apart from answering the question "Are you with the wrong man?" the result of this desperate trip would be the beginning of a lifelong love affair with a meal. I am here to speak on behalf of lunch — also sex and, possibly, redemption.

First we had to get to Europe. Of course we flew Icelandic. By its refusal to join IATA, the international organization that regulates airlines and, at the time, the fares they could charge, Icelandic Airlines became the cheapest way to fly to Europe, and a counterculture icon. *The People's Airline*. The catch was, the plane took you to Europe, but not to any part of it you really wanted to visit, and even then the flight wasn't direct; you had to layover in Iceland

152

before ultimately landing in the toy country of Luxembourg. To board an Icelandic flight without a guitar was suspect. We were still in recovery from the Great Folk Music Scare of the sixties. You no longer heard the stuff on the radio, but you heard it on Icelandic. *Puff the magic dragon,* sang half the passengers on our flight — and then did. Tie-dyed people with long hair and lazy smiles smoked dope in the plane's washrooms. Sometimes these were postcoital puffs. Women in Birkenstocks and Save-the-Whales T-shirts passed botas filled with red rotgut and said, "Outta sight." The correct response to this was, "I hear where you're coming from, man." Guys wearing close-fitting Qiana polyester shirts and pimp shoes said, when they wished to converse with you, "Let's rap."

Paul and I did not rap. We drank many small bottles of bad, cheap (redundant?) champagne. Because the stewardess kept offering them with what I took to be an example of old-fashioned Icelandic generosity, I thought they were free. I hadn't traveled much outside my own country, not counting South America and Mexico, which, as a Texan, I'd always considered my backyard only with better food. I'd never been to Europe. My parents had dangled the carrot: a year in Europe after graduation from college. When, at nineteen, I dropped out of school to marry the first time, my father, trying to save me from myself, offered to send me on that trip right then. Fool that I was, I had a ticket to ride and I didn't care. I said yes to the wrong man.

But this was another marriage, and at the moment it needed a paint job. Bad champagne worked, although I was surprised near the end of the long flight from New York to Reykjavík, during which more than one passenger had felt called to lead everybody in a few choruses of "Michael, Row the Boat Ashore," to discover they expected us to pay for our little bottles of cheap veneer. We paid — we had no choice — and got off the plane in Reykjavík already hungover and still drunk.

A two-hour layover? The airport appeared to be a large Quonset hut, the kind you saw in movies about World War II. I had attended classes in smaller Quonset huts planted on schoolyards all over America to make room for us, the many blossoms of war and postwar fertilization. There was a café inside the Quonset hut airport. Maybe food would bring me back to reality, even if at the moment it would not be my destination of choice. But what to order? It wasn't a question of where I was but when. Let's see. Left New York at 7 p.m. Been flying now for, oh, 289 hours. Breakfast? Supper? High tea? Barely in shouting range of conscious thought, I ordered a fried-egg sandwich. Nothing fancy. Slices of good white bread were toasted and spread with butter. An un-American egg was fried until its *orange* yolk quivered and the white edges were lacy, and then slipped onto toast as if bread and egg were engaged, needing nothing but salt and pepper to bless the union. Awright, it was only a fried-egg sandwich. But it was a perfect fried-egg sandwich. It fed me, gave me comfort and, improbably, hope. We reboarded, flew to Luxembourg, and struggled through customs.

Them: "Business or pleasure?"

Me: "Are those my only choices?"

After renting a car smaller than your average American bathroom, we did what everybody else did. We got the hell out of Luxembourg. In a country so efficiently designed for leaving it, this took less time than your average American shower. When I say shower, I'm being polite. We had a map and so, although we'd reached no decision about where we were going, we

155

knew where we were. Rather like our marriage. We were on a road somewhere in the Alsace-Lorraine, in the middle of a forest. Probably troll-infested. After a while we came to a village. Two-story, half-timbered houses with peaked roofs loomed over the main street like illustrations from *Grimm's Fairy Tales*. Windows sported glossy green-black shutters. Red geraniums and ivy overflowed boxes hung from the sills. Flowers outside a window would be good, I thought. I needed something to look at besides us. Paul had a different idea. It was, he said, time for dinner. How did he know this? My body was still somewhere over the North Atlantic mouthing the words to the fifty-second verse of "Kumbaya." We staggered into the village's only restaurant, surly from bad champagne, jet lag, and our sorry selves.

Early-evening light filtered through small windowpanes hung with lace curtains, splashed over white table linen, and danced off the ceiling and onto us. Another time, I might have felt blessed by such light. We sipped Lillet and said nothing. Not even with our eyes. Especially not with our eyes. Paul ordered for the two of us. *Truite bleue avec mousseline.* I come from the Gulf Coast, where oysters might still be alive when you swallowed them, but I'd never seen a barely dead trout with its head and tail curved that way. Fetal-like. The trout has been poached alive? I see.

Ummm. This water is nice. No, wait. Too warm. Water's getting hot! Arrggg. Help me, somebody. Please . . . ple . . .

I ate it anyway. Blame the *mousseline.* Who knew you could mix hollandaise with whipped cream? Paul smiled at me. I smiled back, but only with my mouth. Later that night I went into the forest outside the inn and burst into tears. I was crying for the fish, I told myself. Not even a troll came looking for me.

Smooth-talking and dressed in French-cut suits that fit his French-cut body, Paul was hot, a good dancer too, even if he wore what Billy Crystal would later describe as the white man's grimace. Once I had found that grimace sexy. Paul had the moves. Paul had the words. We'd come together a year after another man, on his way out the door, had told me I wasn't terribly bright, wasn't pretty or tall enough, and wasn't sexually attractive to him and what I did for a living was dumb. If you're not careful, that kind of talk can hurt your feelings. Paul said I was a woman of intelligence and uncommon beauty. I married him.

The first week, someone called my place. Fredrica, guardian angel of my household, answered the telephone as she always had.

"Ms. Ellerbee's residence."

Paul spoke sharply to Fredrica. "This is not Ms. Ellerbee's residence. This is Mr. ——'s residence."

I put down my rum and Diet Coke.

"Paul," I said, "did you think I was going to take your name?"

Please note I was such a wuss I didn't mention the fact it was *my* house.

"Not on the air," Paul said. "But television's not real life, is it, honey?"

Like I said. Smooth. Killing me softly with his song. Have you noticed? If a woman marries a man who is successful, maybe even a little famous for what he does, the world congratulates that woman on her smart choice and/or her good luck. If a man marries a woman who is successful, maybe even a little famous for what she does, the world asks him how he's coping. The way you'd ask a guy how he was coping since his dick fell off. He tried, but ultimately Paul did not cope well. And then he lost his job.

"Not my fault. My bosses are idiots," he said.

I agreed.

"Good thing your job pays well," he said. I agreed.

"Now I can write my novel," he said.

Life went on, but not as either of us would have wished. Paul resented my having a job when he did not. I resented not being able to stay home and write a novel. There was more, and the list was getting longer. We had arguments where we said too much, went too far. We bit off big chunks of our marriage, chewed them up, and spat the pieces at each other. But I wasn't going to give up. Not this time. Whatever was wrong, it must be my fault. The sum of my experience told me this. So did Paul. Right before we left for Europe, Paul said I wasn't terribly bright, wasn't pretty or tall enough, and wasn't sexually attractive to him and what I did for a living was dumb. France had its work cut out for it.

The year before, I had covered a story about Paul Bocuse, a revolutionary young French chef who came to the Four Seasons restaurant in New York to strut his stuff for one night only, preparing dinner for a dozen prominent women, among them Julia Child, Lillian Hellman, and Louise Nevelson. I had spent the day with Bocuse in the restaurant's kitchen, watching, making notes, and listening to him complain about agents of the U.S. Customs Service who, for no reason at all, he shouted, had impounded his French cream, butter, and foie gras. I couldn't be sure, but I believe he called them the bastard offspring of less than mediocre goats. We had no reservation at Bocuse's restaurant in Lyons, but I explained to the maître d' about that day in New York, how I knew Bocuse, how personally outraged I had always been myself by the ignorance of customs agents in general. I mentioned goats. The maître d' was less than moved. We were about to give up when Bocuse wandered out of the kitchen and saw me arguing with a man whose job it apparently was to keep people from spending money in his boss's restaurant. We ate truffle soup with a pastry crust so light it levitated over the bowl. We ate a Bresse hen so tender it melted off its little bones. We drank a bottle of *Le Montrachet*. Back then you could do that without mortgaging your firstborn. I chewed and swallowed and smiled at Paul. This time our eyes met. Outside, it began to rain. Bocuse brought a bottle of Armagnac and joined us for coffee, telling stories in his wretched English. They might have been good stories. I couldn't say. I was busy doing the eye dance with my husband. You know that dance. Signals were being sent, small silent messages that sparked across the table and then ignited. I caught my breath.

And everything old seemed new again.

The rain came down harder. Pumped by bad weather, bonhomie, and booze, Bocuse asked us to return that evening.

"Wait until you see what I can do for dinner," he said.

Wasn't going to happen. Sex was outside the dining room doing push-ups in the hall. We made it to the first inn we saw and fell into bed. All motions to adjourn were momentarily tabled. Lunch did it. Why had no one told me how sexy lunch could be, how under certain circumstances it might sharpen your senses and cloud your mind at the same time? Years later, I would watch the movie *Terms of Endearment* and get a kick out of the scene where Jack Nicholson and Shirley MacLaine meet for a lunch that has little to do with food and everything to do with sex. There would be other sexy lunches in my life, but that day in Lyons was the first. Afternoon delight? It made me forget — everything. The next day Paul and I were gentle with each other, trying to recapture whatever had caused us

161

to think we were in love, once. We retold old stories to bolster our belief in us, and pointed the little rented car south. There was nowhere to go but on.

Provence was a revelation. Basically ignorant, I had this idea Provence would be like the land of Oz, rolling fields of sweetgrass and red poppies. I was unprepared for granite. Had not anticipated pine trees clinging to cliffs. Was not ready for a light so clear it obscured reason. I liked that light. Reason had turned out to be useless — would a sane woman climb into bed with a man she was thinking of leaving simply because she had a decent chicken lunch? Reason couldn't save me. Maybe the light of Provence could. What a fool believes. After stopping in a village to buy provisions, we drove until we found the right glade. Pine trees shaded the ceiling. Pine needles softened the floor. Sausage never tasted so crude. Olives smelled of wild thyme and mountains. Cheese was barely hardened cream in our mouths. The crazy light sliced us like sharp knives, and the lunch thing happened again. Pine needles fell off us the rest of the day. But we still tiptoed around our hearts.

St.-Tropez. The Côte d'Azur. This was where we would find our way back to each other. The French Riviera would work its magic on us. I was hopeful. In any event, we'd reached the edge. Beyond St.-Tropez the only place south we could go was directly into the Mediterranean, an option I was not ready to rule out. We looked at a pretty inn away from the harbor; it had a garden with a big magnolia tree shading small tables and a price tag we couldn't afford. We settled for a small room in a not-so-nice hotel on the waterfront, a port populated by more yachts than fishing boats. There was wildness in the air. You could smell it. All around us risks were being taken. Brigitte Bardot had put St.-Tropez on the map, and those who still came wore their hedonism like cheap cologne, blasé about life in general and sin in particular. A resort town filled with the reckless and cynical. No wonder we felt at home. No wonder we began our stay with lunch. Why get off a winning horse or — in our case — the only horse?

At Le Girelier, an outdoor café at the harbor, we ate big bowls of *soupe de poisson*. I've never been sure if it was the taste of the sea in the soup or the garlicky *rouille* you stirred into it, but I was hooked from first slurp. We drank a bottle of Côte de Provence rosé. The only other rosé I knew was Mateus. This was an improvement. We drank another bottle. I was drinking as much as I could, as often as I could. *As much as it took.* Days followed nights followed days. We drank, ate, slept, and spent our afternoons in bed not sleeping. Sun filtered through the shutters. Stripes played across our sweaty bodies as if we were wearing cartoon prison clothes. One late night, we ended up drinking cognac at a waterfront bar and talking with the bartender, an old man whose English was better than my French, which I'd learned from teachers who had never been to France, possibly never even met a French-speaking person. We were his only customers. After midnight, I mentioned it was now officially August 15, my birthday. The bartender said a long string of words too fast for me to understand on my best day, and this wasn't. I shrugged what I hoped was the all-purpose Gallic shrug, the one that says, "I don't know what you mean, but it must be your fault."

He closed the bar — he did this by coming out from behind it and walking away — and motioned for us to follow. The old bartender led us to the far end of the harbor, where a plaque was set into stone. The words on the plaque said that on

August 15, 1944, American troops had landed here. The day I was born? On that day and on this spot men had fought for, given their lives for, *my* freedom? Their bravery made me cry. I didn't even have the courage to face what must have been obvious to the most casual observer. One, I was lousy at marriage. Two, I was fast becoming, if not already, a drunk.

One evening we had cocktails with an English couple we met at the beach. He was a retired major, a sandy-haired fellow with a thin mustache who gave the impression of being barely present. She was the unretired wife of the major — that is, she was always busy doing something for him. They seemed mildly pleasant, but really, how were we to know? Anybody who wasn't a serial killer seemed mildly pleasant compared with us. Mr. and Mrs. Major said they lived in a trailer. A caravan, they called it. They said they were traveling through Europe in their caravan so their children could be exposed to the richness of other cultures. We said that was great — had they tried the *soupe de poisson?* Mrs. Major said certainly they had not tried the "poison soup." You couldn't trust foreign food, she said, especially not French food. Mrs. Major ordered another gin and tonic for the major, protecting him from all that untrustworthy French wine.

"Nearly two hundred years after the Bastille and the French are still revolting," she said.

I took another swallow of untrustworthy French wine.

"Ha-ha," I said.

"Most people think that's very funny," she said.

"In that case, big ha-ha."

Mrs. Major removed the pointy end of the major's old school tie from his third gin and tonic.

"You laugh," she said (I thought I hadn't), "but have you been to the open-air market? Some vegetables still have dirt on them. They'll eat anything, these people. We brought cases of good, tinned English food with us. We have enough for all of Europe."

"Yikes," I said.

I finished my wine in a gulp and we made our exit before they could invite us back to their place for a bowl of Marmite. Next morning, Paul and I sought out the open-air market. There *was* dirt on the vegetables; they were that fresh. I wanted to hug the baby carrots and tell them that everything would be okay, any day now the

English would take their caravan of canned food and go invade Italy. We watched bees land on the pastries. No one swatted them away. French people understood the bees had first claim; they made the honey. We bought several pastries with tiny bee footprints on their honeyed tops and headed for a different beach. At this one, every other woman was topless. Paul asked me to take off my top. My pale Irish-American lady-things, having never seen the sun, would burn; I didn't want to take off my top. And I did want to. I didn't know what I wanted. I took off my top. By the time lunch arrived, my breasts were as red as my grilled lobster, which I ate with my fingers, wiping them on my bikini bottom, the only napkin I had. It felt like a diaper. I felt like someone's lost baby. Nevertheless, we barely made it back to the hotel. Sex was always safer. There would be time for the talk that had to come. Later. But we began to run out of August, and despite what I'd hoped, our time in St.-Tropez had settled nothing. Maybe we weren't trying hard enough. Maybe we were trying too hard. Maybe we were all tried out. Our marriage was a doorbell ringing in an empty house.

We headed north, to Paris. I wore blue. The Germans would have worn gray, if they'd won. Along the Seine, we pretended to be Gene Kelly and Leslie Caron, but we'd forgotten how to dance together. We would not always have Paris. We never had Paris to begin with. At the end of August, we left France. A year later, I took our dog and went to a house on Cape Cod, lent to me by a friend. I was going, I told Paul, to think things over. For a week I drank nothing and slept eight hours a night, rising with the sun to run three miles along the mudflats of the bay. I read, sketched, threw sticks for the dog, and grilled fresh fish on a hibachi I found under the kitchen sink. What I did not do was think things over, and I thought about that, driving back to New York. When I walked in the door, Paul was sitting at the kitchen table. He said hello.

I said I wanted a divorce.

There must be fifty ways to leave your lover.

For the next two and a half decades, my travels did not take me to France and I did not actively seek to go. But I never fell out of love with the lunch thing, even if for Paul and me, lunch hadn't done the trick (well, not in the long run it hadn't). There was just something about the meal. I don't mean I wanted to fall into bed every time I ate lunch. Most of my lunches are like most of yours — normal. But once in a while lunch would give birth to (or at least enable) desire, and over the years there were some fine ones, including a couple where the food was mediocre or even bad. The sweet afternoon the cameraman and I spent in bed at an old Colorado hotel right out of *The Shining*, following a lunch of Big Macs with double cheese. The time in East Anglia the journalist and I steamed up the windows of our rented car after eating whelks on a dock in a cold rain. Not that lunch must end with sex in order to be sexy. There is the flirtatious lunch you have with the much-too-young man. The lunch with your friend's father, the one who says you make him want to be seventy again. The lunch where you know that for maybe the only time in your life you are the prettiest woman in the room. The lunch you have with your editor after you write a best-seller. Grand lunches, each sexy in its own way.

Then there is the lunch you have with a former lover. Remembered passion leaves an interesting taste, but it doesn't necessarily mean you want another bite. Although my affair with Joe had ended years before, he still worked at the network that employed me, and I knew for a fact he had enjoyed other affairs with other women at that network. One was with a correspondent who also happened to be my friend. Their affair was over too, but she and I had shared stories. If you're keeping notes, write this one down: women *do* talk about these things. We decided to pull a whammy on Joe. We invited him to have lunch with the two of us. He accepted, having no idea either knew about his romantic interlude with the other. It was an elegant restaurant. Convenient to our purpose, the tablecloths fell almost to the floor. Joe sat between us. We ordered champagne and raised our glasses. Good times, we said. At a prearranged signal, I reached under the table and, continuing to carry on normal table conversation, placed my hand on the uppermost part of Joe's left thigh and began to stroke. Five minutes later my friend surreptitiously put her hand on his right thigh and began stroking. She and I kept on talking and pretended not to notice when Joe started to stutter, first losing his adjectives, then verbs and the occasional noun. His face blossomed, a red flower poking out of his bespoke English suit. His power tie seemed to be choking him.

"There must be something wrong with the air-conditioning," he said.

If he was clueless, he was also in what he may have considered to be a peculiar state of grace. The guy was being fondled by two ex-lovers. But what if one woman's hand brushed against the other's? Where might this lead? Two really pissed-off women? Or a threesome for dessert? No wonder he was sweating. Eventually there came the moment when he got it. He hadn't been stroked. He'd been had. Lunch ended with laughter, not sex. Perhaps we laughed more than Joe, but everybody knows girls have a strange sense of humor.

Now it is the spring of 2001 and I find myself almost by accident in St.-Tropez. I am no longer young, no longer drunk, no longer reckless. After Paul, I knew I would never marry again and I haven't. Like silence, marriage is not what I do best. I stop at Le Girelier, the waterfront café where Paul and I had our first lunch in the town where we ran out of hope. I order the same meal: *soupe de poisson,* extra *rouille,* please, and think about something I recently read. The author, whose name I can't recall, said soup and fish explain half the emotions in life. I can't figure out if this is right or just cute. It is true that on more than one occasion a lunch of fish and soup — or fish soup — has sparked a fearsome lust, and isn't lust an emotion, if one of the less applauded? Although I had not understood it at the time, I now think the decision to quit the marriage — to quit all marriage? — was not made one sober week on Cape Cod. It was made here in France, in St.-Tropez, probably after a lunch of fish soup. I lost parts of me in that marriage. Some important bits were buried here in St.-Tropez, but the losses mostly were of my own making, the result of an alcohol-informed arrogance, which assured me that, with determination and one more drink, I could fix everything, the world would dance to my tune, and we would all be people we were not.

But there is this: I've come to believe that if we can't be other people, we can be better people. Crushed dreams, broken promises, lost loves, and unhappy endings needn't leave us hard. They can leave us human. Human is always better. I raise my water glass to the memory of that young woman and her solid, basic instincts, which she kept hidden even from herself for so long.

"To lunch. The sexiest meal of all."

The waiter smiles at a woman alone toasting an invisible companion. I wink at him, pay my bill, and walk to the end of the harbor until I find the plaque commemorating the landing of the Americans on the day I was born. Do I now think I could be that brave? I know only this. I am braver than I was the night I first saw this plaque.

In the garden of the Hôtel Les Palmiers, the hotel Paul and I couldn't afford, I drink tiny cups of espresso at a small table under the same giant magnolia tree. Birds sing. The afternoon passes slowly. The sun lowers enough to be seen and not felt. The breeze rises. Dried leaves from the magnolia tree fall around me. When I glance up, I see that the tree can spare them. Despite the not inconsiderable number of leaves that have shriveled and fallen, the tree is green, still alive, still growing.

The Perfect Fried-Egg Sandwich

MAKES ONE SANDWICH

A perfect fried-egg sandwich depends on only a few variables: good bread, a good egg, good butter, and your attention span. Start with the bread. You want egg bread or any fresh homemade loaf bread available to you. The loaf shape is important because the bread should be approximately the same size as a fried egg. Today it's actually possible to buy farm eggs. Go find them. Their yolks are golden yellow to orange and they taste like eggs — almost a lost flavor these days.

Salted butter (I know, but for this salted works better)
2 slices bread
One large egg, freshest you can find. Make friends with a farmer.
Salt and pepper to taste

THE TOAST

1.   Add 4 tablespoons butter to a skillet big enough to hold two slices of bread. Turn the heat to medium. As soon as the butter has melted, add the bread, and cook until golden and crisp. Transfer the bread to a plate in a warm oven. (If you toast only one side of the bread, the untoasted side will cling to the egg, making a mushy middle inside a crispy outside. Or if you prefer, you can turn over the slices in the pan and toast both sides.)

THE EGG

1.   Use another pan — a 6 to 8-inch skillet (I use cast iron). Put it over medium heat. When it's hot, add a tablespoon of butter. When the butter has foamed and the foam begins to subside, break the egg and slip it into the pan.

2.   Reduce the heat to low and cover the pan. Cook until the white is firm and the yolk has begun to thicken but isn't hard, about 3 minutes. Baste the top of the yolk with a little butter by tilting the pan and spooning up the pooled butter from the edge.

3.   Slide the cooked egg onto the un-

175

cooked side of a piece of toast. Season with salt and pepper. Put the other piece of toast on top, cooked side up. Ease the sandwich onto your plate, or eat standing at the stove. If you're only frying one egg, who's there to see?

SIX

Like a Rhinestone Cowgirl

(1962, 1998)

It was Craig who first called us the Rhinestone Cowgirls. Craig owns the general store in North Egremont, Massachusetts. Discounting the B&B across the road and the restaurant next door, it's the village's only commercial establishment: grocery, deli, post office, newsstand, liquor store, bait shop, video rental outlet, general emporium, and source of all information about the village and its residents. Carol, Judy, and Lona were up from Houston for a summer week in New England. We'd come to the store to buy Dr Pepper. Craig got a kick out of my girlfriends and what he considered their strange ways. Being Texas women in good standing, they were grounded in big hair, big shoulders, and big jewelry. Carol was wearing a T-shirt that had "Texas" spelled out in stones that sparkled. People in New England tend not to wear clothes that sparkle.

"I'm going to call you the Rhinestone Cowgirls," Craig said.

Carol shot back at him, "What makes you think these are rhinestones?"

A relatively short time ago, "girlfriend" meant the companion of a boy or man, a sweetheart. But there it is, the third reference in *Webster's New World Dictionary*: the woman friend of a woman. To women, girlfriends aren't a luxury. They're a healthy necessity, like good skin or good hair, or love. A girlfriend represents a thing in us not born until she arrives. I'd known these women since we were five. Girlfriends. I liked the sound of it. Liked the sound of us too. I'd lost my thick Texas accent — a combination of a drawl and a screech — somewhere along the way, but when I was with them it came back. Our voices collided like a nine-car pileup on I-10 and it didn't matter that we were women who knew things, who did things, women who wrote, produced, sold, nursed, nurtured, managed, computed, invested, coped, and survived — when we were with one another we were girls; we giggled in high C.

Sitting on the front porch their first night in New England, surrounded by wisteria and memory, they spoke of turning fifty. The birthday cards had been the worst. On the outside, one popular card had said, "There was a time when we didn't trust anybody over 30!" Inside, it said, "Now we don't *know* anybody under 30!" We hated that card. Besides, it wasn't true. We knew lots of people under thirty, even if most of them were our children or employees. I was certain my reality must be different from theirs. I hadn't stayed in Houston, as they had. Lona said she might have liked to leave, but she'd never traveled enough to know where else she might have liked to live. Judy said she and John had traveled and sometimes thought about moving, but never got around to it. Carol said she'd always wanted to travel and would still like to live somewhere else, like New England without winter, or Austin without summer, but she'd stayed in Houston too — mainly, she guessed, because she was supposed to. It was home. I had lived in a commune in Alaska, opposed the war in Vietnam, and plotted the overthrow of the United States government by any means necessary (well, I thought about it, but I could never figure out what to do about my parents, whom, though obviously the enemy, I loved). I had worn beads and a headband, for goodness' sakes. If I was *there* then, how could I be *here* now? Fifty? How could *I* be fifty?

We'd gone to our thirtieth high school reunion. The music was loud and silly. *Tonight the light of love is in your eyes. But will you love me tomorrow?* And what about all those middle-aged people? Okay, maybe a little more than middle-aged. We were forty-eight, and how many people do you know who live to be ninety-six? I couldn't place half the faces, and the print on their name tags was too small to read without squinting or putting on my glasses. People didn't show one another pictures of their kids anymore. Kids were grown and flown. Nobody asked, "Where's your husband?" or even "Are you married?" although we did notice some male classmates brought wives who weren't born the year we were graduated from high school. Oh yes, we did notice that.

Among the four of us, we had had nine marriages. Three of us were grandmothers. Two of us had survived cancer. All of us had buried parents. One had buried a husband. We were no stranger to grief, joy, or hot flashes and were sure of only one thing: Ours had not been the lives we were raised to live.

The class of '62 was nothing if not hip deep in 1962. If I open my high school

The Rhinestone Cowgirls:
Lona, me, Carol, and Judy.

yearbook and look at the pictures, my first thought is how clean we were. My second thought is how white we were. Most of our parents had come to Houston after World War II to seek their fortune and many had found it. The rest of us, if not rich, were comfortably settled in the middle-to-upper-middle class of a city on the make. When we had entered Mirabeau B. Lamar High School in 1959, the best-selling book in America was Vance Packard's *The Status Seekers*. Even if we hadn't read it, we were not unfamiliar with the principle. Ours was a high school with fraternities and sororities, invitation-only dance clubs that held formal affairs several times a year, and May Fête courts with elected Queens, Princesses, Duchesses, and Ladies-in-Waiting. The summer camp we attended, assuming that one fine day each of us would be voted royal, somewhere, taught us how to contort our ten-year-old bodies into something called the Coronation Bow. Arms held gracefully at a 45-degree angle, head held high, and one leg tucked behind the other, you sank into a near-lotus position, dipped your head until it touched the floor, and then rose again — *without anyone helping you in any way*. The same camp gave us rifles when we were eight and taught us how to use them too.

If we were meant to be pretty and proper — and armed — well, we went to the right high school, in the right city; Lamar, with its beautifully manicured grounds, faced a beautifully manicured street called River Oaks Boulevard. At the other end was the River Oaks Country Club. It was said, back then, that it was the only street in Houston with a country club at each end. We drove up and down the boulevard in convertibles with the top down and the air-conditioning going full blast. Fuel shortage? The fuel came from oil. The oil came from Texas. The fuel was *ours*. And the cars were fabulous. We drove the Great American Automobile. *Genuine* Heavy Metal. Big steering wheels, fins, chrome. Two-toned Chevys, metallic-green Oldsmobiles, and baby-blue Buicks cruised a raw new city under an old Gulf Coast sun. Thunderbirds still looked like Thunderbirds and not like Fords. A certain candy-apple-red Pontiac convertible, its Indian Chief hood ornament pointing the way, could take seven of us to the beach fifty miles away in Galveston. They don't make cars like that anymore. They never will. We got our drivers' licenses at fourteen. I believe the state took the attitude it was so big we probably wouldn't run into anything important.

Sometimes we drove or were with drivers who were drunk. Booze and cigarettes were the drugs of our time and the drugs of our parents, whom we emulated in other ways. At fifteen, we girls dressed more like our mothers than the large children we were. We wore torturing undergarments called Merry Widows, strapless corsets de-signed to squeeze our waists to a perfect Scarlett-sized seventeen inches. If you could breathe, your Merry Widow wasn't tight enough. We wore girdles, elastic armor to ensure no part of our newly developed bodies could be seen to move. We sat in the sun lathered in a mixture of iodine and baby oil, which was said to enhance tanning (if you had skin that tanned; otherwise it enhanced burning). We sported frosted lipstick and teased our hair and our boyfriends, but when it came to sex, we said nice girls didn't. Some of us lied about that. As girls — we never once thought of ourselves as young women — our major interest was, and was expected to be, boys; therefore, if you were smart, you were encouraged to conceal the flaw. *That silly old A+ in chemistry? I got lucky.* Lona was lucky that way; of course she studied harder than anyone I knew, always had, and got incredibly frustrated when she couldn't do something well. It was how we first met. Lona was crying because she couldn't draw a cat. I couldn't add. A deal was struck. I still can't add and Lona still can't draw, but that's not much of a price to pay for a lifetime friendship. Carol and I met at Sunday school; mutual boredom blossomed into mutual attraction. Judy was our landlord's niece and the only little girl I knew who talked back to her parents. I became a lifelong fan the day her mother told her to go to wash the dishes and Judy said, "Later, maybe."

In twos, threes, and fours, we played together, went to the movies together, and slept over at one another's houses. My house was especially popular. I don't fool myself; my mother's fudge pie was better than hanging a lamb chop in the window when it came to attracting friends. Mama was always willing to make a pie. We were always willing to eat one. The smell of her fudge pie baking is one of the nicer memories of my childhood. Even Lona loved it and she hated what she referred to as "weird foods." Like vegetables. Almost everything else too. Our mothers kept peanut butter and jelly around so she wouldn't starve. In the final tally, my biggest culinary contribution to the world may be that I taught Lona to like olives.

Carol's family had a vacation house in Wimberley, outside Austin in what we Texans like to call the Hill Country, but only because even a Texan would be hard-pressed to call these hills "mountains." Her mother would load a bunch of us girls in the car and then spend the weekend — or a week — watching us swim in the river, giggle in the night, and wait for our breasts to grow. When we were twelve, she took us to see Elvis Presley and when we screamed like three-year-olds, she did not leave us to find our own way home. And she made ice cream. The best. Gallons of it. The kind you hand-crank. I expect the effort she expended in cranking kept her from killing us. Mama's fudge pie and Carol's mother's ice cream. And wasn't that future enough? We thought so. We were auditioning for the lives we thought would be ours, protected by our husbands' money so we wouldn't have to go to work to support ourselves, much less our families, protected by society from divorce, and protected by the great state of Texas from everything else nasty and too, ah, real.

We were in high school when the world around us underwent a sea change. The fifties became the sixties. John Kennedy was elected president. The Berlin Wall went up. Castro came down from the mountains and captured Cuba. Rachel Carson published *Silent Spring*. Black Americans agitated for rights guaranteed them in the Constitution of the United States. If our minds were more on dating than current events, if we were more interested in luau parties where local white boy bands covered R&B hits than we were in the struggle for civil rights, if we preferred *Peanuts* to the front page, if we thought the universe revolved around us, well, we were lucky. We were teenagers who never had to worry about classmates bringing guns to school — although many of our classmates had guns. We didn't have to choose between sniffing glue and dropping acid. We didn't go home to empty houses or mean streets. We were safe in our school and our insulated, ignorant existence. We should have been blindly happy. I wasn't. The pressure to be popular was fierce. In order for there to be people who are in, there must be people who are out. I thought that was always going to be me. In third grade, when I was not invited to a certain birthday party, I went home and tried to cry on my mother's shoulder. It got me nowhere.

"But Linda Jane," my mother said, "why would you want to go to a party where you're not wanted?"

In fifth grade I was dropped from the car pool because we'd moved and one of the mothers didn't want to drive the extra mile. As nobody told me this, I blamed myself. The not-popular kid will not be picked up tomorrow morning. Even Wimberley was a land mine. If I didn't make the cut for a particular weekend, well . . . Carol must not love me anymore. In sixth grade several girls formed a secret club. I wanted to join. They told me I had to pass an initiation test. We met on a Saturday at the house of one of the club members. They put a blanket over my head and told me to remove anything I was wearing that I could do without and still feel comfortable walking down Main Street. I took off my scarf. This wasn't the right answer. I took off my belt and shoes. Eventually I took off my skirt, and then my blouse. Would I be comfortable walking down Main Street in my cotton panties? I would not. But if I had to . . .

It was a trick test. I was supposed to take off the blanket.

As we got older, I took my confidence from being, if not popular, then successful, but I continued to envy my friends. I envied Lona, who was beautiful and sweet and never had to go to work and leave her children in order to keep them. I envied Judy's indomitable courage and her contributions; as a nurse, she made the world a better place. I envied Carol her passion and the sense of humor that kept her sane, most of the time. Of course, I loved them for the same reasons. But still I could get caught in the trap of our history. We continued to love and to hurt one another over the years, at different times in our lives drifting apart and then finding one another again. When Lona, a bridesmaid in my (first) wedding, did not invite me to be in her wedding, I cried. Many years later, Lona told me she'd felt bad about that ever since, and wanted to apologize. I lied and said not to worry; I really hadn't given it a second thought. When Judy and I stopped being close during high school — my doing — it hurt her. But at that age I was too obsessed with being liked by everybody to be a good friend to anybody.

I brought this up to the Rhinestones that first night on the front porch. How I had always felt like an outsider knocking at a door everyone else had a key to.

"But it was like that for all of us, wasn't it?" Lona said.

I almost fell out of the porch swing. How could it have been like that for Lona?

"When I would leave the room," Lona said, "I was sure the rest of you were talking behind my back."

Carol told us how it was when she'd gone to the University of Texas and been blackballed by sororities.

"I wanted to drop out of school after that. I didn't. I did the right thing; I flunked out."

She tried to make the porch swing move by pushing on the ground with her feet, but they didn't reach. "I did my share of rejecting too," Carol said. "There was a Saturday night at college. Someone had set me up with a blind date. The reception desk at the dorm called me when he arrived. I went downstairs and there was this total dork. He asked if I was Carol and I said I wasn't but I would go look for her. I went back upstairs and spent the evening playing bridge with Lynda Bird Johnson. She and I often spent Saturday nights without dates."

"What *was* all this business about popularity?" I said. "Like we had to be rated the way they do beef? Prime. Choice. Dork."

"Why didn't we understand that everybody felt left out at some time?" Lona said.

"Well, shit, could it be because we never talked about these things back then?" Judy said.

Being a nurse, Judy gets to the obvious faster.

The week we came together in North Egremont, we talked about those things. Talked about all kinds of things. Asked questions we'd never asked.

"What do I cling to? I cling to what my parents wanted for me," Lona said. "I cling to the me they saw in their eyes, not mine."

We were sitting around the kitchen table in shorts, T-shirts, sweats, whatever passes

190

for jammies now, finishing off another fudge pie. Glasses that had held wine or iced tea or Dr Pepper were beginning to make sweat rings on the wood.

"Give us an example," Carol said.

"My whole life," Lona said. She picked up her glass, took a paper towel, and began blotting, then rubbed the table, wiping out all traces of damp and polishing the wood, after which she carefully folded the paper towel and put it under her glass. "I wanted to be a doctor."

And I had thought Lona had enjoyed the perfect existence, the life she wanted, at least until her husband of thirty-something years (to whom I had introduced her when we were in junior high school) left her for a younger woman.

"What do I think my life would be like if I hadn't married?" Carol said. "I would have missed having my children, but I would have trained myself to do work I loved and not have to have spent all these years in one *job* after another."

Carol stopped. Laughed her contagious belly laugh. Carol is always giving us laughter. It feels like getting flowers.

"Aw hell, I hated school and studying. I probably would have made the same choices. But I'm still looking to get married again. So there."

Marrying again at our age seemed to me to be either very foolish or very brave. But we were brave women. Hadn't we shown courage that week when we bared our thighs in order to go swimming (except for Lona, who was having a good hair day)? Generally speaking, our thighs were not a pretty sight. I had found better living through chemistry and it wasn't baby oil mixed with iodine. Self-tanning lotion had come a long way since Man-Tan. I showed off my bronzed legs. Carol said brown fat was better than white fat. Lona said she would never put anything like that on her body; you don't know where it's *been*. Judy lifted her Margarita to toast the best bottle-tanned legs. Or the best white legs. *Whatever.* I said she didn't understand. Being able, finally, to have tan legs was a peak experience. Judy said a peak experience was the first time you worked in ER and they brought in a body with his brains coming out his ears.

"Can we talk about sex?" Carol said.

A couple of days later, we did. We were back on the front porch; our best talks were on that porch. Judy told a story about going to Las Vegas with her husband.

"We were in our hotel room. John was

drunk. There's a knock on the door. I open it. There's a hooker standing there. John comes up behind me. Naked. I pushed him out the door and locked it. The next morning, John, sober and pretty damn sorry, says, 'Uh, honey what are you going to do today?' I said, 'I'm thinking of going back to Houston and when I get there I'm going to own that little oil company of yours.' And John, who was, as you know, kinda stingy, threw his platinum card on the table and suggested I find something else to do."

We laughed at the picture of John in the hotel hall, naked and keyless. Judy told the best stories. And she thought her thorns hid her heart. John had died of cancer in 1991.

"I think real intimacy," Judy said, "is that look you give each other, where you both know what you're thinking — and that it's not going to come back at you. We had plenty of those moments. If John could be alive again for just one hour, we'd find that look. And he wouldn't need any hooker to tell him what to do next."

What would Carol do if she had found her husband in bed with another woman? She said she wasn't sure. Okay, what if she had found him in bed with another man?

"Oh, that's easy. I would have asked them if we could become Peter, Paul, and Mary."

The talk turned more graphic and more private, and when it got too graphic and private, we switched to imaginary sex. Lona and Robert Redford. Judy and Robert Redford. Carol and Robert Redford. Steve McQueen was dead and I hadn't made up my mind yet about Russell Crowe, but I said I enjoyed looking at Brad Pitt and imagining. Also Daniel Day-Lewis. Even Keanu Reeves, though not until he grew some muscles and began to speak in near-sentences.

"In real life," I said, "society looks askance at a relationship between a woman and a man twenty (or more) years younger than she, but in my dreams — how nice to discover being older doesn't prevent me from spinning young fantasies, sexually speaking."

Judy said I was full of shit about this too. Her crap detector was constantly set on high and her mouth followed her machine. Some people said Judy was sharp-tongued. I don't know why.

We tell one another our mothers didn't talk this way. We don't believe we're aging the same way our parents did. We believe our parents "acted old." We believe we don't. When I asked for a show of hands on who actually *felt* old, only one hand went up, Carol's, but Judy reminded us Carol knew what a dental dam was, so she couldn't be feeling *too* old.

Rolfe drove up to join us the last night the Rhinestones were in North Egremont. He grilled Monster Steaks. One day several years before that summer, I was standing at the counter of Mazzeo's Meat Market at Guido's, the best little grocery store in western Massachusetts, waiting my turn, when I noticed Mark, the butcher, cutting the biggest steaks I'd ever seen.

"What are those monsters?"

"Rib cuts with the bone in."

"They're three feet tall."

"Nah. Only three or four inches."

"Close enough. Why haven't I ever seen them in the meat case?"

"We cut these for ourselves."

"What do you call them?"

"Monster Steaks."

"I'll take two."

Monster Steaks had become tradition. Rolfe grilled them, basting constantly with my daddy's homemade steak sauce, which, because he cooked it at a high heat for a fairly long time and refused to cover the pot, Daddy was for a time forbidden by my mother to make indoors. I thought Daddy's sauce was wonderful then and still do, and I manage to make it without needing to repaint the kitchen. Rolfe grilled the Monster Steaks until they were black and crusty on the outside and blood-rare on the inside. It was his tour de force and he would brook no interference. His rule was one person, one black-and-blue Monster Steak. If you said you didn't want your steak black-and-blue, he said that was your problem; you could put it back on the fire. If you said you wanted only half a steak, he said you weren't really trying. I've never been able to eat a whole Monster Steak at one time. Most people can't. But the leftovers make great steak sandwiches for the next week, or year. We made a Caesar salad to go with the steaks. I chopped the anchovies into tiny pieces. Maybe Lona would think they were olives.

After dinner we finished off still another of my mother's fudge pies. A happy accident. At the beginning of the week we had talked about that pie, the smell, the taste, the perfect texture — its place in our collective childhood. I said how much I missed it. Lona said I had given her the recipe years before, but it never tasted right. I said this may have been because I made up the recipe, having lost Mama's. I said I felt awful that I'd never asked my mother for another copy. Now it was too late.

"Linda," Carol said, "I have your mother's fudge pie recipe. I've been making it for years."

Girlfriends.

We made fudge pie every day after that.

Monster Steak Night was the climax of our week together. The next morning Rolfe decided to make a picture of us before my friends left North Egremont. Actually, I asked him to. How was I to know it would be like herding cats?

"My eye shadow's not right."

"Are you going to wear that T-shirt? It clashes with mine."

"Worry about your thighs, not my T-shirt."

"How long is this going to take? My moisturizer is melting."

"Stop brushing the lint off me. I like lint. Lint and I are old friends."

I said goodbye to them in our driveway. We cried and decided to make the Rhinestone Cowgirls an annual event. We would celebrate ourselves at a different location every year. Several months later, Judy wrote an e-mail to another friend; she was tired and out of sorts and said some un-kind things about Carol. By accident, when she sent the e-mail, she copied it to Carol, who felt deeply betrayed and then realized you're probably not going to meet a whole bunch more people you can be friends with for more than fifty years. She forgave Judy — but not for a while. Others took sides — for a while. Junior high all over again.

I still believe in the Rhinestone Cowgirls. I need to. These women are like songs I can't get out of my head. When I look at us, I don't see what you might see. I don't see our lines, our wrinkled necks, and our sagging lady-things. I don't see our thighs. I don't see our ridiculous spats or insecurity hangovers — or our everlasting inconsequential differences. I see us then and now, little girls and not-yet-old women stirred together in a friendship soup, and still bubbling over to scald someone once in a while. But we no longer have to explain ourselves; we are who and what we are and have learned to love our friends for their sakes rather than our own. You don't get to that place easily. It takes time and work. I am reminded of what Sherman said of Grant.

"Grant stood by me when I was crazy,

and I stood by him when he was drunk, and now we stand by each other."

We're not always going to get along, and our lives turned out to be harder and more complicated than we'd imagined or planned for, but we're still young enough to hope. And we go on dancing, together and separately. *Will you still love me to-morrow?* The answer is yes. Carol was right that day in Craig's store. We aren't rhinestones. We're the real thing. We always were.

Mama's Rescued Fudge Pie

2 squares unsweetened Baker's chocolate
1 stick butter
1 cup sugar
$1/4$ cup flour
2 eggs
1 teaspoon vanilla
$1/4$ teaspoon salt

1. Preheat the oven to 400 degrees.
2. Put the chocolate and butter into the pie pan. Melt them (microwave).
3. Add the sugar, flour, eggs, vanilla, and salt. Stir it all together.
4. Bake 25 minutes. Let cool for as long as you can wait. If you can't wait, vanilla ice cream helps cool a slice of pie on your plate.

Daddy's Repaint-the-Kitchen Barbecue Sauce

MAKES ABOUT THREE CUPS SAUCE

My way, you don't have to repaint the kitchen. This sauce will keep in the refrigerator for weeks if you don't add the butter until you're ready to use it — otherwise, only one week.

36-ounce bottle ketchup
10 ounces Lea & Perrins Worcestershire Sauce
1 cup brown sugar
1/2 cup cider vinegar
1 tablespoon Tabasco
2 tablespoons butter

1. Put everything but the butter into a sturdy saucepan. At this point, Daddy would turn the burner on high and watch the sauce spatter as it reduced.

I turn the heat on low and let it simmer for two hours, giving a stir when I pass by.

2. Allow the sauce to reduce to about 3 cups. It will be the color and consistency of a thick chocolate sauce.

3. Remove the pan from the stove and whisk in the butter until it is absorbed and the sauce has a velvety texture. (It will keep for a week in the refrigerator. Let it come to room temperature and then stir it again.) Use the sauce to baste steaks liberally while grilling. Serve any extra on the side.

SEVEN

No Shit, There I Was . . .

(1992–1998)

I am not supposed to be here.

It is — and I am — cold and damp. Gray sky. Wind. Wet. Don't know if it's raining, don't care; so much river water coming over my head, what's a little more wet? I could be in a warm, dry office in New York City or lollygagging on a Caribbean island, not crouched in a rubber boat ankle deep in 48-degree water, watching a bearded stranger row us down the Colorado River. The river bends. Lee's Ferry, our starting point, disappears. Two weeks? I'm already miserable.

"Bail," says the bearded stranger.

Twenty-four and one-half chilly miles later we make first camp. As soon as I set up my tent, it blows up and away and might now be half the distance to Canada but for a big man who jumps into the air like Michael Jordan and catches it. George from Georgia. Quit the navy at thirty-eight and figures if he lives frugally, he won't need to look for a job until 2001. Meanwhile, George is seeing the country. Having recently hiked the Appalachian Trail, he's doing the canyon now. Doing the river thing. I ask George if he's scared of the rapids. I am.

"Nah. You only live once."

What is it I say when I talk about having had cancer?

"Smell the flowers. Take chances. Live as if . . ."

I wonder. Do people know I might be lying?

Right after I was diagnosed with breast cancer, I did make time for flowers and chances, and it was then I discovered the woods, a gift that apparently had been waiting years for me, a Gulf Coast gal with a centrally air-conditioned past. I fell in love with being in the woods, and with the pleasure of getting from here to there on my own two odd-looking feet. That I should not have discovered so consequential a piece of information about myself until I was forty-seven confounds me. Or perhaps the information would not have been correct until then. I was not raised to sleep outdoors, or to *walk* places. I was a

Texan, not a Girl Scout. When I moved to New York, a city whose traffic often encourages going on foot, I learned to love walking, but on pavement. The woods remained something one drove by or flew over.

Cancer had made me realize I liked being alive; I began to consider what I might do to increase my chances of staying that way. Exercise was high on the list. I decided I would go to the gym during the week; on weekends in the Berkshires, I would walk around the "block" — four miles. Soon I began to feel like a donkey on a track: every day the same four miles. The woods were there — I could see them — but it was foreign country, and so I did what I have done all my life when I needed to learn something: I read a book. Next I took a small hike on a trail that didn't go straight up, at least not in the beginning. It was summer. Sunburn, even in the woods, seemed a possibility. So was heatstroke, I reminded myself, climbing what I must have thought (hoped) would be a flat hill. I climbed on, swallowed by green. Birds sang at me and flowers bloomed my way. A breeze gentled me. The earth smelled rich and rare. Suddenly I was at the top, and I was hooked. It wasn't just the beauty.

There was this feeling of competence; I could do more than I thought I could. *I could learn a new trick.*

My hikes and hills grew. I found my way to the Appalachian Trail, which runs from Maine to Georgia and crosses Massachusetts near Huckleberry Hill. I began to hike parts of it. Autumn came. New England did its thing. My woods turned red and gold, the sky a blue to break your heart. Some days I walked in soft silver rain. Some days I made footprints in snow sprinkled like sugar on dead leaves. Once I hugged a tree, put my arms around it and pressed my face against rough bark that was warm from the autumn sun, and squeezed. I can't tell you how glad I am nobody saw me hug a tree. I bought a sleeping bag and a tent, a lightweight cookstove, a pot and a cup, a knife and some maps, and moved from hiking to backpacking, discovering I liked sleeping outdoors and, although I always set it up, never used my tent unless the weather turned foul. I played as though I were a child, following animal tracks, climbing trees, skipping stones in a brook. Sometimes I sang out loud, once coming upon a Boy Scout troop with knives out, *being prepared* for whatever beast was making that godawful noise. Another time I took off my clothes and played in a waterfall. I slid down a hill on purpose and again by accident. I slew a dragon with my walking stick, drew magic circles in the dust, and told myself stories about fairies and Indians. I threw leaves into the air, talked to squirrels, laughed at nothing at all, and ate dessert first. If I did not wear my underwear on my head, it's only because I wasn't wearing underwear. Always I walked, hiked, climbed, hour after hour, touched by beauty for which I had no words.

In a *TV Guide* cover story about my having had cancer — "TV's Joyful Survivor" — I said I was fifty and had not made up my mind whether to have a face-lift or go on an Outward Bound expedition. The following week I got a call from Outward Bound.

"Don't have the face-lift."

I was sure they must be kidding. All I knew about Outward Bound was that they plunked people down in the wilderness and left them. I was unclear about what was supposed to happen next, but decided I didn't care and said yes. The night before the Outward Bound expedition, it got tense at my house; this felt like going to camp for the first time, only much worse.

"What if," I said to my son, "I can't keep up with the other kids? What if they don't like me? What if I've brought the wrong clothes? What if I fall? What if I'm too slow, too fat, too old, too tired? *What if I'm too scared?*"

Not much sleep. The next morning I came downstairs in search of the slightest excuse to call in sick. On the bottom stair step I found a note from my son.

"Dear Braveheart," it began.

I grabbed my backpack and was out the door.

Imagine a sunny day in June. Another river. Not the Colorado. A wider, slower piece of water. Five canoes. Ten women. The youngest of us was forty-six. The oldest was fifty-five. I was forty-nine. We were none of us Wonder Woman, but we had, we discovered, what it took to climb a rope ladder, carry a heavy pack across slippery mud-bottomed streams, set up tents in the rain, sleep in treetops, and sing Broadway tunes around a candle. (Later I would be asked if we'd participated in any of those "bonding" exercises and I would explain that most women didn't need exercises to bond. Put ten women in an elevator and by the time it reaches the top floor you know what each woman's favorite position is.) Now we were in canoes. I was eating Grape-Nuts sprinkled over cold spaghetti with a wooden spoon of my own making. First night out, the Outward Bound leader had said to us, "You want utensils? Make some." We were paddling down the upper Potomac River, the final stretch of our trip. On one side were the mountains of Maryland, on the other the mountains of West Virginia. We wore swimsuits, T-shirts, and baseball caps. We were wet, bitten, scratched, sunburned, dirty, right tired, and really ripe. We'd not seen another soul for many a day. Two men came up the river in a motorboat — a couple of good ole boys out for a day's fishing. We glided by them. We waved. They stared. As the last of our canoes passed, one good ole boy scratched his forehead.

"You think those guys are 'merican?" he said to his pal.

I was, I understood at that moment, truly outward bound.

Although I didn't know it then, that canoe trip was my basic training for the Colorado River. Well, not the river itself. I met the Colorado as most people do, unprepared but for a world of inexperience. I came to the Grand Canyon meaning to see it as woods with no trees and the Colorado as a slightly louder river with no Bubbas. Uh-huh.

So here I am, day two in the big ditch, cold and wet and frightened of big rapids before I've even seen one. There will be more white water today, they say. I thought about the guy sitting across from me on the plane to Flagstaff. On the back of his T-shirt, it read: *Face your fears. Live your dreams.* I couldn't read what was printed on the front; at the time, he was bent over, throwing up. My shin is bandaged. On this morning's hike, I pulled a piece of the Cambrian Period down on it. Hurts, but I won't let on. I'm facing my fears. Only, make this rain stop. Please.

I am not supposed to be here.

Someone asks if I would like to try the paddle raft. There are five boats, all rafts. In four of them, the boatman rows while four passengers, uncomfortably seated front and back, ride, talk, look at rocks and river, and every so often hang on for dear life. In the fifth and smaller boat, six people paddle to the commands of a seventh, the paddle captain. The trouble with the paddle raft is that there's nothing to hang on to and you can't hang on anyway because you have to paddle, to go through big hungry water leaning out and shoving a stick into it at regular intervals. Counter-intuitive, someone says. Suicidal, I say, but not out loud.

"Sure, I would like to try the paddle raft."

I have checked the map; there are no giant rapids today. We come to a small rapid. I manage to stay in the raft and keep my paddle in the water. Whee! I like the rush, I want a bigger rapid. We get one. Again, victory. Give me more!

And then we are blessed. The rain stops. Yellow sun dances on green water, bounces off red canyon walls and shoots back up into blue sky. A crayon day. Feels like falling in love. It has taken a while for the river and canyon to grab hold. But they have. I wake in the night to catch the Big Dipper grinning six feet above my head. *Gotcha.* Hours later, warm in my sleeping bag, the predawn air cool on my face, I say goodbye to the morning star. So much beauty. So little time. Canyon, fill me up.

Our travels are not always the voyages of discovery we say we seek. Often they are rituals of reassurance.

"Yes, the Eiffel Tower looked exactly the way it does in photographs."

"That cruise was as relaxing as we'd thought it would be."

"I don't like sushi in Chicago and I didn't like it in Tokyo."

This was different. This required you to take not just physical but emotional chances. It wasn't only the river. It was the *people*. But then, isn't one of the gifts of travel the possible discovery of yourself through other people? At seventy-three, Wini is a retired professor and beautiful woman, smart and prickly. She does not suffer fools, period. This is her fourth trip down this river. There is an afternoon when Wini gets sick on a hike. Too much sun? Too little water? John, the trip leader, asks if she needs to be lifted out of the canyon by helicopter.

"No," Wini says. "I don't."

The subject is closed.

The next day I remain by the river when the others go hiking. Wini has also stayed behind. She stops by my camp, says she's come to realize this is the last time; she will never make this trip again. I ask what it is like to do something for the last time. She says she's finding out as we speak. I want to cry for Wini.

That night it rains again. We are camped on a rock ledge so narrow we must sleep lined up like sardines waiting for the can to be sealed. Our guides manage a decent meal in spite of a lack of space, but after a day on the Colorado, everything — any-thing — tastes great. Tonight is Spicy Thai Chicken with rice — many steps up from cold spaghetti with Grape-Nuts. There is a bowl of what I take to be red soup — I eat it, assuming it is meant entirely for me. I've no idea why I assume this. The river has snatched my reasoning powers. I'm wiping my mouth after finishing the soup when one of the guides points out what she considers to be a relevant fact.

"You just ate a bowl of hot sauce meant for twenty-one people."

Well, it wasn't *that* hot.

I'm now in the paddle raft every chance I get. I like the thrill, and find it less frightening to be involved in my fate than to watch someone else row while I hang on and try not to notice a twelve-foot wall of water coming straight at me.

Horn. Granite. Hermit. *Crystal.* The rapids that people talk about in hushed voices. The big guys. Boat killers of the Colorado.

"You can do it," says Julie, paddle captain and hero.

You should see Julie. No matter where we sleep, she sleeps higher, curled up on some rock or another. Mornings, Julie comes down lightly, leaping from boulder to boulder, boat to boat, sure-footed as any other wild creature. On the water her voice is gentle, teaching us to work together, turning a group of inadequate paddlers into a team able to pass through rapids and come out thinking they did it by themselves. But today, when we climb ahead to scout the first of the really scary-sized rapids and I look down, my stomach falls away. Oh dear God I can't paddle *that*. I will panic. Fall out. Drown. Worse, I will chicken out. I will drop my paddle and cling, sniveling, to the boat. I *can't* . . .

Julie says I can.

Thus begin the days of big water. One boat flips, tossing its occupants into the current. People in the other boats pull them out of the cold water — 48 degrees year round — downstream. They are shivering, teeth chattering, humbled. Our paddle raft shoots through the white water, rapid after rapid, as though it were greased. I am flying. I feel strong and competent and nineteen. *No.* I feel strong and competent and fifty-two.

Can't wait to tell people back home about *this.*

Julie asks if we know the difference between a fairy tale and a river story.

We say we don't.

"Well," she says, "a fairy tale begins, 'Once upon a time . . .' and a river story begins, 'No shit, there I was . . .'"

Now there are long easy days of play, water fights and waterfalls, skinny-dipping alone in a turquoise pool up a side canyon and then napping in soft grass next to it, sun and sunrises, and sunsets; days of climbing cliffs I once thought too tall, of walking ledges I once thought too narrow. There are crude drawings on canyon walls, graffiti left by the ancient ones who disappeared. The nights are littered with stars. Do the stars know where the people who made the pictures went? One hot afternoon near the end of the trip, drifting toward more rapids, medium-low ones, Julie tells us the reason we're a good paddle team is that we do what she says when she says it. We nod in pompous agreement. Teacher's pets.

"And that is why," Julie says, "I want you to put down your paddles, jump in the river, and swim the next rapid."

I could have argued — haven't we spent two weeks trying to stay *out* of the river? — but I am too busy jumping into the Colorado.

Whoooosh. The cold knocks the breath out of me. Whoooosh. Breathe out at the top of the wave, that's what John said. Breathe in at the bottom of the trough, that's what Julie said. Swallowing and swallowed by the river. The world tumbles up and over. I see sky, water, sky, water, sky, water until it's all one thing: skywater. The wave train subsides. Julie helps us into the raft. We are wet and slithery and loud. We are invincible. I start thinking how great it would be to be a boatman (even women guides are called boatmen); how fine to live each day mindful of the world immediately around you, focused on river, boat, passengers, wet and dry, hot and cold, food and drink, sun and sand and sleep. Life 101. I'm ready to quit my day job when Eric, a real boatman, points out a reality I've not considered.

"Every year," Eric says, "I make less money. I'm sort of working toward a cash-free existence."

This has a certain appeal. It's a life, a good one. But not mine. Not this time around. I go back to New York and tell river stories.

"No shit, there I was . . ."

August of that same year. Near the Massachusetts-Vermont border.

I'm three days into what I've come to think of as my annual birthday hike. Each year I walk a little farther, stay out a few days longer. When you wake up in wilderness on top of a mountain you've climbed, carrying on your back everything you need to survive, when you make your tea and salute the sun as it rises, whatever age you are about to be doesn't feel old. Time on this year's trail has been hot, hard, and happy, but getting to the top of this particular mountain is wearing me out.

And now this old man.

I think it's surprising I'm here until I meet him. He looks like anything but today's backpacker, who is often outfitted in clothes composed entirely of chemicals and toting a pack large enough to house many pounds of high-tech gear, including the latest — the backpacker's espresso machine. The old man carries a small canvas rucksack like the ones kids use to carry schoolbooks, and an army canteen. He wears work pants, a flannel shirt, and a pith helmet with mosquito netting. He has on boots but no socks. Assuming him to be a determined panhandler or an elderly gentleman who set out for a stroll and got lost, I ask where he started.

"Georgia."

The Appalachian Trail is a footpath that begins on top of Springer Mountain, Georgia, and ends on top of Mt. Katahdin, Maine. In between are roughly 2,150 miles and more than 400 mountains big enough to have names. The trail doesn't skirt the mountains; it goes up and down them. Those who thru-hike — walk it end to end in one big bite — usually start in early spring and finish in late September or early October. Every year around 2,000 start. Around 200 finish. The first thru-hiker was a Pennsylvanian named Earl Shaffer, back in 1948. Mr. Shaffer was twenty-nine. I'd seen photographs; he looked to be in great shape, but in his written report to the

Appalachian Trail Conference, he said words failed to describe the hardships of the hike.

"Gradually the trail became a seemingly endless adventure so that I was probably the most amazed of all when I finally reached Trail's End. I often pondered whether the difficulties provided me with the impetus to carry me along."

Sometimes on my own hikes I had thought of Earl Shaffer's words in the context of literal hills, and in the broader context of life. Instead of obstacles being things to overcome, was it the hard stuff that kept me going? Was there something about struggle that was necessary to survival?

The old man in my path is three-quarters of the way to Maine. I ask, politely, how old. He says seventy-nine. I ask if he's having a good time. He says he's not (his eyes say he might be lying about that). Why doesn't he quit? He says because he started. Why did he start? He says it's the fiftieth anniversary of the first time he did it.

"You made this trek fifty years ago? That would be in, ah" — arithmetic is not my best subject — "1948?"

He nods. Talkative as the Tar Baby on

Quaaludes, the old man is.

"Wow. Then you must have known . . ."

I stop. *No way.*

"Ah, sir, what is your name?"

"Earl."

"I see."

I tell him that a few months ago I'd read Earl Shaffer was planning to try it again, but I'd thought the story was hype. I mean — *seventy-nine* years old? Two thousand miles of mountains? And without a tent, it turns out. Or a sleeping bag. Without the backpacker's espresso machine. Without *socks.*

"What do you eat?"

"Fig Newtons."

"What do you sleep in?"

"A blanket."

"Why don't you wear socks?"

"To much work to wash them out. Too much weight to carry extras."

"Don't your feet hurt?"

"Two months before I started, I put sand in the boots and walked in them until the bottoms of my feet toughened up."

"Where's your weather gear?"

He points to the pith helmet.

"What if it rains?"

"I get wet."

"And if it snows?"

"I get wet and cold."

I tell him that running into him is the best birthday present. He walks on up the trail, in the direction of Maine.

I have another thought. I call out to his back.

"What's been the worst part of the hike this time?"

Mr. Shaffer answers without stopping or turning around.

"Reporters and their silly questions."

Weeks later, back in New York City, a phone rings. A woman, someone I once wrote a story about, has died from breast cancer. It was the treatment, which was new, and risky, that killed her. I celebrate her courage, mourn her death, and, sorry to say, am relieved it wasn't me. I put down the phone and go back to work. That night, lying in bed, troubled by death and overwhelmed by life, I shut my eyes and whisper.

"Take me there," I whisper.

The song begins. The woods beckon. The trail goes on forever. Gold light slides down a red canyon wall. A green river sings. I am a shining thing in a shining place.

And I belong here.

Incredibly Interesting and Easy Thai Chicken for 21 Possibly Wet People with Enough Hot Sauce for Linda or, If You Insist, to Share with All

$1/4$ cup vegetable oil
$1/4$ cup soy sauce
12 whole chicken breasts
7 teaspoons sugar
6 tablespoons rice wine vinegar or white vinegar
2 cucumbers, peeled, halved lengthwise, seeded, and sliced on an angle or chopped
$1/4$ cup grill seasoning (Emeril's Chicken Rub works well)
6 cups fresh bean sprouts
4 cups shredded carrots (these are available in pouches in the produce department)
12 scallions, sliced on an angle, or chopped

2 cups chopped peanuts
1 bunch chopped basil leaves
1 bunch chopped mint leaves
1/4 cup sesame seeds
Salt
Cooked rice for serving

1. Heat giant skillet (or do in batches) over high heat. Wait until pan is smoking. Add oil, soy sauce, and chicken breasts and sauté 6 minutes on each side. Do not be tempted to turn the chicken breasts constantly. Take off the heat. Let the chicken rest and then shred it.

2. In a big bowl, mix the sugar and vinegar. Add the cucumber, grill seasoning, sprouts, carrots, scallions, peanuts, basil, mint, and sesame seeds. Season with salt to taste. Add to chicken and toss. Add chicken and vegetables to the cooked rice or put it on top of the rice. Serve with sauce on the side.

SAUCE

You don't make this. You buy it. *Sriracha* sauce is actually Vietnamese (see Vietnam chapter), not Thai, but it is what was served with the Thai Chicken and Rice. It's made from sun-ripened chiles, which are ground into a smooth paste along with garlic and packaged in a convenient squeeze bottle. Many regular grocery stores and all Asian ones carry it. Or you can order it online. It's available in 17-ounce and 28-ounce bottles. Which one you get depends on whether I'm invited.

EIGHT

The Man Who Hated Picnics

(1986–FOREVER)

The movie *Picnic* came out in 1955. I was eleven, but when I saw Kim Novak get on that bus to follow William Holden, who had nothing but a torn blue work shirt and a two-hour head start on a fast-moving freight to nowhere, I knew she was making a mistake — and that I would have done the same thing.

I have always known too much and not enough about men. In a world where you can't open a newspaper without reading about the shortage of men for women who are over thirty or make more than $200,000 a year — or won't ever make $200,000 a year — or women who are too tall, too short, too dark, too light, too fat, too thin (maybe you don't hear this one much), too quiet, too loud, too close, or too far away, I never felt shorted. A boyfriend tree grew outside my window. Call it luck. I was not beautiful and rarely sweet.

But if one boyfriend went away, or I did, all I had to do was reach out the window and pick another. You think you know what you want because you think you know who you are.

I would never have picked Rolfe.

We met in Washington in 1975. I was a correspondent for NBC News. Rolfe was a cameraman for ABC News. We were friends who often worked side by side and kept up with each other at other times. Rolfe left ABC to direct for PBS's *Smithsonian World*. I went to a screening of his documentary about the Battle of the Little Big Horn. He had taken an event that occurred before there were moving picture cameras to record it, and made it come to life. No small trick. At the reception, Rolfe was uncomfortable with the attention. His pale Norwegian face was red. With black hair and beard, the guy looked like a bashful pirate. But you would never catch him in a torn blue work shirt. Rolfe was not the type. Not my type.

In 1986 I was living in New York. Having written a funny book about my twelve years at NBC, only to discover my employers didn't share my sense of humor, I had moved to ABC News to write and anchor *Our World*, a new prime-time series about recent American history. When I signed with ABC, I had it written into the contract that I could start my own production company; ABC would have first option on anything my company produced. I had no clear notion of why I wanted to do this or why it might matter, and the network honchos didn't take me seriously. I was a news correspondent — what could I know about producing, much less running a production company? In this, they were more right than wrong. If I was going to make this work, I needed a partner, somebody smarter than I. I asked my pal Rolfe, also now living in New York and back at ABC to produce and direct for *Our World*, if he'd be interested. Rolfe said the timing was good; cable TV was exploding. They couldn't keep airing Joan Crawford movies, infomercials, and reruns of *I Love Lucy* forever. Cable networks were going to need original programming. There would be a place for a production company with journalism credentials. Rolfe had ideas *and* business skills. We shook hands. He asked what we should name our company.

"Lucky Duck Productions," I said.

"Silly name."

I agreed. We named it Lucky Duck Productions.

Our World went on the air in early September. Critics thought it was swell. Viewers stayed away in large groups. It didn't help that we were on opposite *The Bill Cosby Show.* Rolfe and I worked at keeping *Our World* on the air, and on making Lucky Duck real. We were together a lot. One night we went to Café des Artistes to have dinner with a mutual friend who was flying up from Houston. Café des Artistes is a romantic place. The smoke-fogged murals help. Rolfe ordered a bottle of champagne. We waited for our friend and talked about work, and when we tired of that, began to talk about other things, including ourselves, not a subject we'd discussed much before this night. Time passed. The two of us had salmon four ways: tartare, smoked, gravlax, and I forget the fourth. After another while, we shared *pot au feu,* which Rolfe enjoyed. Far as I'm concerned, no matter how fancy the name, it's still boiled beef and a lousy end for a self-respecting steer. We waited another hour. Rolfe ordered glasses of port with slices of pears and Stilton. This combo was new to me. Flavor followed flavor as naturally as sentences in a well-written paragraph. By closing time it was clear we'd been stood up. Rolfe waited with me on Columbus

Avenue while I hailed a taxi to take me home. A cab pulled over. Rolfe opened the door. I got in the back seat and looked up to say what a fine evening it had been anyway.

My friend Rolfe bent down and kissed me.

After *Our World* was canceled, we quit ABC News to concentrate on Lucky Duck Productions. We had moved in together not too long after that first kiss. Nobody we knew thought we were a good match. I was loud. He was not. I was effusive. Compliments didn't come easy to Rolfe. Neither did small talk, the only kind I was any good at. Rolfe was a computer geek. I was a natural-born Luddite. Rolfe was a news junkie, read six or seven papers a day, and owned a shortwave radio so he could listen to the BBC while he slept. If allowed, I could go days — years, possibly — without looking at a newspaper or listening to all-news radio, but I was into music: Ellington and Ella, Coltrane, Janis, Bruce, Mozart, Bach, The Dead, Sondheim. Rolfe liked the Beach Boys.

The first summer we were together, Rolfe bought a house in the Berkshires. I bought two bicycles and a wicker picnic hamper with linen napkins, flowered china, and tiny salt and pepper shakers too cute for words. I saw us reclining on an antique quilt by a gurgling stream, passing pâté and making eyes at each other. Rolfe's vision was different.

"I don't like picnics," he said.

At first I thought I hadn't heard right. We were still sort of new together, but how could I not have known this? Not like picnics? *The man didn't like picnics?*

"What is wrong with you?"

"I don't like salad bars," he said.

"It may be I'm missing something here."

"If I'm paying money to eat out, I ought not to have to make part of the meal myself," Rolfe said.

"Speak slowly and avoid big words," I said.

"Why go to an outdoor concert when I have a better sound system at home?"

"And this has to do with picnics because . . ."

"Why eat outside," Rolfe said, "when we have a perfectly good table and six chairs inside?"

My introduction to Rolfe's Salad Bar Theory of Life.

I loved Rolfe, but I also loved picnics; therefore he had to change. All summer, I tried. I packed the hamper with cold poached salmon, dilled yogurt, and aspar-agus vinaigrette. Curried chicken salad with walnuts and apples. Garlicky sausage, crusty bread, and a runny cheese. *Peanut butter sandwiches and Twinkies.* Rolfe said the food was good except for the Twinkies, but . . .

When I was a kid, my father and I always went on a Fourth of July picnic. Mama was thrilled not to be invited; picnics were not air-conditioned. Daddy would bring a small charcoal grill on which he would burn a piece of cow. We didn't always set fire to the campground. If my father's annual outdoor food firestorms left me with the notion that anything could happen on a picnic, they also, once I thought about it, helped me to understand Rolfe's attitude. It's not that men don't enjoy eating outside; it's that men don't enjoy eating outside unless they can char some animal flesh. Perhaps it has to do with gender history, survival of the fittest, and so on. Or maybe it's that cooking meat over flame is the only acceptable way big boys get to play with fire. I don't know, it could be the cute long forks. At the end of our first summer together, I gave away the wicker hamper with the terminally darling salt and pepper shakers and bought Rolfe a set of tools for the stone grill we had built on the patio. He promised not to wear an apron with a motto.

Although we have never married, in 2006 Rolfe and I will celebrate twenty years as partners in work and in life. Every year at the end of September, we take a trip to mark the beginning of our journey together, the weekend two friends became lovers. In the beginning I saw these anniversary trips as a way to persuade Rolfe to travel with me. It wasn't that he disliked traveling, he merely felt he'd done enough time in the unfamiliar; now his favorite trips were to places he'd already been, as his favorite new foods were those he already liked.

One year we went to New Orleans for our anniversary trip. The perfect solution, I thought. Our friends Kit and Billy lived there; we would stay with them. What could be more familiar? Kit and I began to plan. In New Orleans, sensible people arrange life around eating. We'd start out Friday night with spicy boiled crawfish at Frankie & Johnny's. Saturday lunch we'd have Oysters Foche at Antoine's. Saturday night, Crab Imperial at Arnaud's. Sunday brunch, Eggs Hussard with extra hollandaise at Commander's Palace. Sunday night we'd eat at Kit and Billy's. She would make her gumbo. Monday lunch meant red beans and rice at Mother's, with an order of fried chicken on the side, just to be sure. Later we'd stop by the Acme Oyster Bar for an oyster po'boy on the way to the airport. Maybe get a couple of extras for the plane. Between meals, we'd prowl the antique markets on Magazine Street.

Monday morning, Rolfe collapsed.

"It's too hot here, I hate antique stores, and all this rich food is making me sick."

"But it's New Orleans," I said. "You've got to like it. What about Mother's? What about the red beans and rice?"

"Dine without me."

Dine without him? We were a couple on an anniversary trip. Could I eat while he did not? Could he stay at home while I went out?

I could and he could and we did.

The year after New Orleans we went to California for our anniversary. A chef who had worked at a restaurant one block from our house in New York (Rolfe ate there at least three times a week) had moved to the Napa Valley and opened his own place. There would be no surprises; Rolfe already liked his cooking. Didn't hurt that the chef's name was Thomas Keller and people were saying his restaurant, the French Laundry, might be the best in America. When we got to Napa, Rolfe said it was time to visit vineyards. I couldn't think of anything I'd rather do less. A previously injured disk in my neck had kicked in. Rolfe took me to the emergency room, where a doctor gave me painkillers that didn't kill the pain but did make me dumb as a box of dirt. He dropped me off at the inn and headed for the vineyards.

"Never mind. I'll be fine in time for dinner," I said.

I'd better be. We'd made our reservation two months before. Come evening I dressed through pain, and brain fog, and rode to the restaurant cradling my left arm and shoulder. There was whimpering, but I was brave. I'd had babies. The French Laundry is a small two-story stone house surrounded by herb gardens and blooming flowers and looks as if it were somebody's country house, although at one time it truly had been in the business of getting clothes clean. That was in the nineteenth century. Now it was a hotshot restaurant serving what food critics described as Contemporary American with French Influences. They talk that way. Thomas Keller's cooking was all the description we needed. Keller believes any dish loses its flavor after three bites; therefore, he gives you three bites of many dishes. I made it to the second bite of the third dish, an eggshell filled with the freshest pea soup short of God's own kitchen. It was the color of spring. So was I. Because I am a civilized human, I made it to the restroom before unloading pea soup on my shoes. Still a very pretty green, I noticed. Hurting, queasy, sweaty, and clammy, I returned to the table.

"Rolfe, I'm sick."

"I'll call you a taxi."

Rolfe remembers Napa as one of our best anniversary trips, the same way I think of the weekend we spent in New Orleans.

Couplehood is not my best subject. I'd always believed if you loved somebody, you were supposed to eat out of the same spoon. Rolfe showed me a different way to be together. He said we didn't have to like the same things, or learn to — or pretend to. He said we could be separate people with separate tastes and still live happily ever after.

But I'm stubborn. I kept on trying to interest the guy in picnics. I got sneaky. One September, Rolfe agreed to spend the day with me in a canoe. An easy float down a curvy little New England river — what better way to celebrate an anniversary? It was a Saturday morning, not really cold, but there was a breeze. Rolfe and I wore jeans and flannel shirts. We met the man who rented canoes at the put-in point on the Housatonic River. From there we would paddle to Ashley Falls, 25 miles downstream as a stoned crow flies. I had made the arrangements over the telephone, but now Canoe Man talked only to Rolfe, the way guys do.

"Excuse me," I said, basically to establish my existence, "are there obstacles in the river, anything that might not be marked on this ten-year-old map you've given us?"

"Linda," Rolfe said, patiently. He says things patiently a lot when I'm around. "This is the Housatonic, not the Colorado."

"If the captain of the *Titanic* had only had better charts . . ."

"Lady," Canoe Man said, "it's early autumn in the hills of western Massachusetts. Won't be iceberg season for a while yet."

He passed Rolfe a Sluggo look. Girls. Phooey.

We arranged to meet Canoe Man at the take-out point, pushed off in our rented canoe, and pointed its nose downriver. In sync. Well, mostly. I was in the bow of the canoe. Rolfe was in the stern. I reminded him I had more experience in canoes. I should be in the stern. He pointed out he was the better driver. That this was not a car he regarded as irrelevant. The wind picked up. Rolfe shivered.

"Paddle harder. You'll warm up faster," I said.

"I'd warm up faster at home," Rolfe said.

Trees bent over the dark water. Most leaves had not yet turned red. Some, already blown off the trees, never would. Cornfields lined the river, their stalks the color of pale straw. Everywhere you looked, yellow was beginning to overtake green and the sky was more white than blue. There had been big storms that summer; we'd been moving dead branches out of our way all morning. I was starting to get hungry. Rolfe didn't know it, but in my backpack were a hunk of cheese, half a cold chicken, an apple, and a chocolate bar. Of course I wouldn't call it a picnic.

We came to some ripples in the river.

"Watch out for the rapids," Rolfe said.

"Those aren't rapids," I said. Ms. Great Outdoors has seen real rapids.

The rapids that weren't real took my paddle and ran off with it.

"Rolfe," I said, waving my arms about, and pointing, "my paddle is going downstream without me!"

"Be still. You're going to flip the canoe."

"Am not!"

An intelligent response, I always think.

"Are too!"

We are alike in the important ways.

Eventually we caught up with the paddle. Rolfe was sweating.

"This is not fun," he said.

"I thought the last ten minutes were thrilling," I said.

"You weren't paddling."

"Might have been the best part."

"I'm hot and cold at the same time," Rolfe said, "and it looks like rain."

"It does not look like rain. It's cloudy is all."

Please don't let it rain, God. He'll never get in a canoe again.

"It would help if you'd paddle *with* me instead of leading," Rolfe said. "I'm in the stern. I should set the stroke."

"You're not paddling as hard as I am," I said.

"What is this, a contest?"

"What is *this*, a fight?"

"*You* wanna get in the stern?" Rolfe said.

"Yes!"

"Well, you can't."

"Lighten up," I said. "It's our anniversary."

"I think I'm catching a cold."

We continued downstream, silently battling our own headwinds. The river narrowed. And then we saw it. Hard to miss, actually. A tree about three feet in diameter had fallen, part of its roots still attached to one bank. The trunk lay across the river, and a foot above it. For our purposes, the river was blocked.

"Would you call this an obstacle?" I said.

Rolfe ignored me.

"We could call it a Popsicle and wait until it melts," I said.

"Awrighty, Ms. Great Outdoors, what do you suggest?"

"We paddle up to the log. We climb onto the log; it's plenty wide enough. We haul our packs up, and secure them. Then we lift the canoe up and over, lower it into the water on the other side, put our stuff back in the canoe, climb aboard, and off we go, no problem."

Rolfe sighed.

"I know what's got to be done," he said. "I just don't want to do it."

"There will be lunch on the other side," I said.

His face brightened. "A riverside café?"

"Not exactly."

Bright face dimmed. "You are shameless. You've brought a picnic, haven't you? Let me see if I have this right. After we get over the log — if we get over the log — I'll have to get my feet wet pulling the canoe up on some bank and then sit on a bunch of moldy leaves, swatting insects off my food in the rain."

"It is not going to rain," I said.

"And there are no obstacles in this river."

We sideslipped the canoe up to the log, which turned out to be smooth and slippery and without any bark on it, meaning it had been lying across that river for at least one full season. Thank you, Canoe Man. You piece of shit. This was going to be tricky. Rolfe took charge, telling me to hold the canoe steady while he climbed onto the log. I passed up our paddles and gear. He tied everything to the remains of a branch sticking out from the log.

Now it was my turn. Rolfe held the canoe in place. I could sense him tense up. We both knew the real obstacle here wasn't the log. Although Ms. Great Outdoors brags about liking to hike, swim, paddle, ride, and sleep outdoors, she is not the most coordinated kid on the block. The last time I'd gone skiing with Rolfe, he beat me to the bottom of the mountain because I came down the last part strapped to a stretcher. On Nantucket, we rented motor scooters and it was going well right up until my machine and I fell over sideways twenty feet from the garage. My clumsiness is a family joke and it doesn't matter that I can in fact walk and chew gum at the same time. What people remember is that not too long ago I twisted my ankle when I tripped on a french fry. I moved to the middle of the canoe, where it is most stable, rose up slowly, and when I could, swung a leg onto the log. Rolfe reached out and grabbed my hand to pull me the rest of the way up. I could have made it on my own, but guys like pulling girls up. Makes them feel all Harrison Fordish.

So far so good.

Rolfe instructed me in detail how we were going to lift the canoe out of the water, over the log, and back into the water on the other side. I still thought I knew more, but who argues with Indiana Jones? We lifted and strained, managing to keep our feet and other parts dry and — whaddaya know? — the canoe was on the downstream side of the log. Rolfe told me to get in first. This wasn't gallantry; if I slipped and turned the canoe over, at least the gear and Rolfe wouldn't get wet. I crab-crawled down the log, which might as well have been made of glass. As carefully as a bomb squad guy deciding whether to clip the blue wire or the red one, I chose what I sincerely hoped was the right spot and slid my body into the canoe. Not even a wobble. I made my way to the bow and smiled at Rolfe. I knew what I wanted to say, but do grown-ups say, "Nya-nya-nya-nya-*nya*-nya"?

"Hand me the gear and paddles," I said.

He untied our packs and passed them down. He gave me the paddles reluctantly, as if the idea of being up a creek without one while I was downstream with two had just now crossed his mind. I stowed the packs and paddles the way packs and paddles are supposed to be stowed. His shoulders relaxed. I hadn't screwed up. Yet.

"We're almost there," he said. "All you have to do now is to keep your balance while I climb into the stern. Do not move. Do not tell me what to do. Do not turn around to see how I'm doing. Do not ask me if I'm having fun yet. Do not say, 'Rolfe, look at the awesome sky!' Do nothing at all. Quietly, if such a thing is possible."

"Yes, darling."

It wasn't Rolfe who'd slipped on a french fry. Besides, he was not enjoying the day and I felt responsible. I loved him. I wanted him to be happy. Certainly I didn't want him to be testier than he already was. I held on to the gunwales. Balanced. Ready. *Silent.*

Rolfe stepped confidently into the stern.

The canoe performed a perfect 180, rolling over, tossing our packs — and us — upside down and into the river.

Took all of two seconds.

I came up, sputtering. So did Rolfe. We were standing in five-foot-deep water. His black hair was plastered to his pale forehead. More water dripped from his beard.

That's when it started to rain.

Rolfe looked up at the sky. There was no expression on his face. And then he began to laugh, the one that comes from someplace deep inside. It grew bigger and louder until the laughter broke his face wide open and my heart with it. Two fools neck deep in a cold, muddy river and the kind of love that lasts.

We lifted the canoe over our heads, drained it as best we could, set it upright, and climbed back in. For another hour, chilled, wet, and grinning, we paddled on down the river — completely in sync. At the take-out point, Canoe Man was waiting to drive us back to our car. Every time he asked how our trip was, we giggled. The back seat of his car was going to take days to dry out.

Once home, we jumped into the hottest shower we could stand. It took a long, long time to get clean. Or something. We got into dry clothes. Soft sweaters. Woolly socks. Rolfe built a fire. I put the kettle on the stove and rummaged through the pantry. I hadn't been to the market; this would be a make-it-up-according-to-what-is-on-hand meal. I found some dried porcini and a box of Arborio rice, put the mushrooms in a bowl of water to soak, and the pan on the stove to heat. When it was hot enough, I added the olive oil and the rice, and then I made myself a cup of tea. Rolfe poured himself a hefty snifter of his best cognac. When he put the snifter down on the counter, I poured some of his best cognac into the rice. I dumped in the now-reconstituted porcini and canned beef broth, and began stirring. Every time I could see the bottom of the pan, I added more broth and more cognac.

We ate out of old yellow crockery bowls, sitting on the floor in front of the fire. His hair was damp, his cheeks were pink, his eyes were blue, his heart was pure, and he was no more necessary to my life than, say, air.

"What do you call this?" Rolfe said, scooping out the last bite.

"We call this the River Risotto."

"We do?"

Rolfe smiled that way he can, the way that makes my heart stop, back up a beat, and do a little flip.

"Honey, I'm sorry about your picnic," he said.

"Rolfe," I said, smiling back in a way that I hoped made his heart do something too, "this *is* a picnic."

"It is?"

"Finest kind," I said.

"I like this kind of picnic. Can we do it again?"

"Depends," I said.

"On what?" he said.

"The obstacles."

"But we're at home," Rolfe said.

"That's one."

A few years later, I actually persuaded Rolfe to go on another outdoor picnic. Tanglewood is fifteen miles from Huckleberry Hill. The Boston Symphony performs outdoors there every summer. Tonight there would be no Mahler, no Wagner, no *sturm und drang*. Tonight was the James Taylor concert. We both liked James, as did those of our family and friends who were visiting from out of town. Five of us went early in order to reserve a great spot on the Great Lawn. We parked in the main parking lot. Rolfe and the rest of the group came later. Acting on the advice of his pals at the Castle Street Café, where he often ate when I wasn't in the Berkshires, Rolfe parked in the lower lot.

"You get out much faster this way," he said.

A James Taylor concert at Tanglewood is a roll-your-own picnic. Some people brought candlesticks, white linen, and cold lobster; their women wore pearl earrings and flowered skirts. Some people brought beer and Ritz crackers; their men wore gimme caps and hairy backs. Some people brought jug wine and joints; they wore happy, blank smiles. We brought fried chicken, potato salad, bread-and-butter sandwiches, bread-and-butter pickles, salami, smoked oysters, cheese, grapes, chocolate cookies, and homemade lemon bars. We wore loose-fitting clothes.

The concert was a blast from all our pasts. Near the end, it began to drizzle. Nobody minded, not even Rolfe, because James was singing "Sweet Baby James." When he got to the part about the Berkshires seeming dreamlike, the crowd levitated, arms joined, singing along, swaying to music and memories. Pretty purple clouds and gentle rain blended into the song, and we all knew we were in the right place at the right time.

At first I thought the ear-splitting crash came from cymbals. The next thunderclap was simultaneous with the lightning that knocked out the sound system and stage lights. What followed could not be called rain, not precisely. I believe it is usually referred to as hail. People ran for their cars. My group got back to the house within twenty minutes. It was hours before Rolfe and the people riding with him, who'd gotten trapped and then quite literally stuck — in a muddy parking lot with two hundred other cars — made it home. Rolfe walked over and put his hand under my chin. He looked into my eyes. He smiled his sweetest smile. Was he going to kiss me? Had I, despite everything, finally sold him on the romance of picnics? Were we about to eat from the same spoon at last?

"Repeat after me. It will be a cold day in hell . . ."

I don't give up.

There are picnics in our future.

Just not anytime soon.

The River Risotto

3 tablespoons butter
1 large onion, chopped
$1^1/_2$ cups Arborio rice
$1^1/_2$ ounces dried porcini mushrooms
    soaked in $1^1/_2$ ups water for 20 minutes
3 to 4 cups beef broth
$^1/_4$ to $^1/_2$ cup cognac (or more)

1. Melt the butter in a wide saucepan over medium to low heat. Add the onion and cook until golden.
2. Add the rice, the porcini, the water the porcini have been soaking in (strain this water if it seems gritty), $1^1/_2$ cups of the broth, and half the cognac.
3. Boil. Reduce heat. Stir. Every time you can see the bottom of the pan, add more broth and cognac and

keep stirring. Simmer until creamy
and the rice still has a bite.
4. Bite it back.

NINE

The Fly on the Beluga

(1986)

It would be both the shortest and most expensive trip I would ever take, but I wasn't paying. Malcolm Forbes was. We were up to our necks in the decade of greed. Specifically, it was the summer of 1986 and New York City was preparing to celebrate, on the Fourth of July, the one hundredth birthday of the Statue of Liberty, a party the likes of which the city had never seen. Everybody knew the best seats in the house would be the wet ones. Anyone who had a boat, a kayak, or a really large rubber duck was planning to take to the water, to spend the great day in the harbor, where the statue was and, therefore, where the action would be. The best seat of all would be on board *Highlander V*, the yacht belonging to publisher Malcolm Forbes, laissez-faire capitalist and probably permanent head of the New York chapter of the no-government-is-good-

251

government society. I had read that the guest list would be short. You had to have enough money to buy your own country, or at least rent one for the summer. Forbes was nothing if not a showman, however: a select few members of the press would also be invited along for the ride. The guy from *Sports Illustrated* said on the telephone that he thought it would be swell if I was one of them and then wrote about it for his magazine.

"Being rich is a sport now?" I said.

"I'm looking for color. Filthy Freebooters at Play. Masters of the Universe on Parade. Wretched Excess. Silly People," he said. "You know what I mean."

"You mean a hatchet job," I said.

"You'll be our fly on the wall."

"Who will invite me?"

"Malcolm Forbes," he said.

"Why would he do that?"

"You'll ask him nicely."

I didn't know Forbes, but I called him. Journalists are always calling strangers to ask unreasonable questions, nicely. I had no idea why he said yes.

Independence Day in America. Dawn over Manhattan. Me at Chelsea Piers. Alone. I hung around the dock trying to appear as if I were doing it on purpose. I could see *Highlander V* tied up at its berth on a pier about fifty yards away. Once I had gone for a ride on a cigarette racing boat, a fancy, fast thing. Forbes had one too. His was on top of his yacht next to the twenty-three-foot Donzi, two tenders, two BMW motorcycles, and a Bell Jet Ranger III helicopter. The guy liked to be prepared. Maybe he was a Boy Scout before he was an über-capitalist. I knew about this yacht because I'd done my homework; that is, I'd read the press kit somebody from *Forbes* magazine had sent. It told me that *Highlander V* was the fifth Forbes yacht (well, duh). The first *Highlander*, a former warship, had been launched in 1955. The second, in 1957, was bigger. The third was bigger still, until 1980, when it caught fire and burned up. Or down. I guess the fourth hadn't been big enough. Forbes had replaced it in 1985. *Highlander V* was practically brand-new. He'd probably built it just so one day I could come aboard and say wow. I knew about him too. The third son of a Scottish immigrant who'd founded *Forbes* magazine, Malcolm Stevenson Forbes espoused free enterprise and competition and the best man winning, the way you can when you've inherited Daddy's store. But Forbes had taken what he'd been given and pushed it into bigger, rounder numbers.

If he liked to make it, and he obviously did, he also liked to spend it, ride it, and stay in it. The yacht. The private jet called, what else, *The Capitalist Tool*. The collection of Harley-Davidson motorcycles. The hot-air balloons. The château in France. The palace in Morocco. The Fabergé eggs — I didn't know what you did with those, other than gloat over being able to afford them. He was flamboyant. He was legendary. He was my host for the day. He was still nowhere in sight. After another twenty minutes, the stretch limos began pulling up. One, no more than two, people stepped out of each, a reverse of the old circus routine where twenty-four clowns climb out of a car the size of, say, a Fabergé egg. Most male guests wore their sailor suits: white slacks and dark-blue blazers. Female guests wore designer duds and high heels, and carried overnight cases with little V's printed all over them. They'd brought a change of clothes? I'd brought a windbreaker. Would this count as a change of clothes?

Forbes appeared at the top of the gangway to welcome his guests.

I couldn't wait to hate the man.

Forbes shook my hand and told me to make myself at home, we'd talk later. I wandered down the Grand Staircase past the Jean Cocteau and the Toulouse-Lautrec and kept on going until I got to the Main Salon. On the walls were photographs of other *Highlander* guests over the years. Kings, presidents, prime ministers, big-time Wall Street crooks. A buffet had been set up. I ignored it; I planned to be *at* this shindig, not part *of* it. *Highlander V* gently and almost silently began to move away from the dock. There must have been about sixty people on board, not counting us few journalists, our host, his family, and the who-knows-how-many minions who worked on the yacht.

Now my host was coming — what? — downside?

"Morning again, Mr. Forbes," I said. "Nice boat."

"Call me Malcolm."

I thought not.

You had to admit that, at sixty-nine, Malcolm Forbes was still easy on the eyes. He was tall and in good shape. His silver hair was combed back off his face. It didn't look styled, and although he might be losing a little, he did not, as Donald Trump had already begun to do, attempt anything as incredibly dumb looking as that push-it-forward-like-a-pompadour-

and-then-spray-it-with-all-you-got comb-over. His eyes were clear and looked straight into yours when you spoke.

"Hiya. Glad I found you." He smiled at me.

He was a good smiler. I almost believed him.

"I want to show you something," he said. "Follow me."

We went below to the master stateroom. Inside the door, he stopped.

"I wanted to show you this," he said.

More cushy sofas. Good lighting. The polished wood chest built to house the state-of-the-art TV, VCR, and stereo. The giant bed. Artwork that looked, but by definition was *not,* priceless.

"Yep," I said. "Like Oscar Wilde, you are a simple man, satisfied with the very best."

"Not the stateroom. I meant I wanted to show you *this.*"

He pointed to his bedside table. On top of a copy of Tom Clancy's *Red Storm Rising* — gotta keep that profitable Cold War fear going — was a copy of a book I'd recently written. I picked it up and opened it, feeling the binding. The book had been read. You can always tell. Okay, he could read. So what? Schmoozing wouldn't change what I was going to write.

"I asked you down here because I wanted to talk to you about some of the things you say in your book. Too many people above to have a real conversation."

He sat on the sofa next to the wall of windows and motioned for me to join him.

"I agree with you," he said, "that the mistake most of us in the media make is to underestimate the intelligence of our readers, or viewers, whatever," he said. "But how do we go about changing this —

I mean on a big scale? What are your thoughts? Whaddaya know?"

My first thought was that he didn't give a damn what I knew, but what did I have to lose by speaking my mind? What was the worst he could do? Throw me overboard? By now we must be in the middle of the Hudson River, a body of water so polluted I suspected I could walk back to shore. I said I thought rich white guys who owned and ran the media were a bunch of arrogant sons of bitches who had no idea what a dozen eggs cost or how smart the guy eating his, scrambled, standing over the kitchen sink on his way out the door to his minimum-wage job, might be.

"Eighty-seven cents," Malcolm said.

"Beg pardon?"

"Eggs are eighty-seven cents a dozen at Dag's," he said. Dagostino's was a local supermarket chain.

Was this true? Or something he'd read somewhere?

"How do you know this?"

"Bought a half-dozen yesterday."

"I still say you're out of touch. All you fat cats. Even if you once knew what the real world and the people who live in that world were like, and I doubt it, you've long since forgotten."

I was being rude to my host, but I was in a rude mood.

"Are you saying that by the time we've made it, we've had it?" he said.

Ah, yes. *The Sayings of Chairman Malcolm*.

"I'm saying by the time you guys have made it, *we've* had it. In the rear end, for lack of a better description."

He laughed.

I was in the bedroom of a multimillionaire's yacht telling the owner that he and his kind were full of shit, and he was laughing as though I'd said something smart. I couldn't help it. I started to laugh too. We stayed on the sofa talking for the next half hour. He was funny. He was articulate. He thought before he spoke. And he was a good listener; he gave you 100 percent of his attention. I had met only one other mover and shaker with that kind of focus and it had been every bit as flattering when Fidel Castro had turned it on. Malcolm and Fidel, the best listeners I'd ever met. There was a thought.

I looked at my watch.

"Isn't it about time for the festivities to commence?"

"Right you are," Malcolm said, leaping to his feet. He grinned as if we were parties to a secret. "Let's go check out our position."

While we had been below, *Highlander* had sailed down the Hudson, and then dropped anchor. I looked around and caught my breath. New York Harbor was filled with boats of every kind and size. You could step from one to another. All of them were jockeying for place. *Highlander* was not jockeying. *Highlander* was nose to nose with the Statue of Liberty, not counting the liquid freeway between the statue and us, up which the tall ships would sail. We were curbside at the biggest parade in town. How had Forbes arranged this, I wondered, and then stopped wondering because the answer was obvious.

The USS *Iowa*, with the president of the United States of America on board, was coming down the Hudson River, daring any craft to get in its way. When the great gray beast of a boat passed by us, several women leapt from their deck chairs and rushed to the rail of the yacht looking as if they'd taken a direct hit from an Adolfo cluster bomb.

Do you think they can see us?
Yoo-hoo! Nancy!
Walter sends his best!
They called out. To a battleship.

The *Iowa* parked next to the Statue of

Liberty and more or less directly across the water highway from us. Someone had saved her a place too.

I strolled casually around the deck, enjoying the morning, which was glorious, and the sights, which were just as glorious, listening to my fellow travelers. Mostly they seemed to be talking about business: mergers, takeovers, buyouts, white knights, green knights, junk bonds, and arbitrage. *On a day like today?* I watched Forbes circulate and circulated behind him, eavesdropping. He inquired after people's families, getting all the names right. He listened to the answers. He told witty stories. Seemingly without trying, he made businesspeople forget business. I decided to introduce myself to some of his guests. Maybe I was wrong about them. The first guy I talked to told me the Dow was going to top 1800 this year; he was excited by the prospect and seemed to think I ought to be too. Forbes appeared from nowhere, took my elbow, and making a polite excuse to Dow Guy, led me away.

"Sorry," Forbes said. "He's ten of the most boring men in the city, that one."

Forbes asked if I wanted anything. There were cold lobster sandwiches on the buffet downstairs, he said. I said I would pass.

The fly on the wall doesn't fall for the old cold-lobster-sandwich trick. But a few hours later he said the magic word. Twenty-three tall ships from all over the world had just floated by, their sails billowing their stories, when Malcolm Forbes came over and said it was time to go below for some beluga.

You hear people say caviar is an acquired taste. I acquired mine the first time I met some. Caviar tasted the way I thought the sea might taste if it burst inside your mouth. A passion was born, especially after I discovered the real thing in Chicago in the early sixties, when, playing grown-up, I went to dinner with a man twice my age. He ordered caviar. When they served it, I told him in a twenty-one-year-old confident whisper that he should send it back; the eggs were *gray*.

"This is beluga," he said. "Give it a try. If you don't like it, we'll see if they can find some caviar that's black."

To his credit, the man never cracked a smile.

My only problem was supply and demand. My demand for beluga exceeded my supply of ready cash in approximately the same proportion the national debt exceeded the national income.

There was, however, a moment.

In the seventies, journalists returning from the shah's Iran often carried in their suitcases a couple of kilos of caviar — Iranian beluga, the best there was; it was cheap, and we did right by it. A former lover tells of waking up one night and not finding me next to him, getting up to look, seeing a light on in the kitchen, and when he investigated, discovering me standing in my jammies, holding a tub of caviar and a spoon, eating beluga by the light of the refrigerator. The supply train ended when Iran threw out the shah, and then the American journalists. My passion for fresh caviar did not.

I didn't run over the elderly lady in front of me on my way downstairs, but it was close.

Forbes pulled me aside.

"Like caviar, do you?" he said.

"No. I like shoving little old ladies out of my way."

"You know the only way to serve it?"

"I do," I said, assuming he meant caviar and not little old ladies. "Plain. No chopped egg, onions, capers, sour cream, or any of that crap. Toast points. Maybe a little unsalted butter, but even that's gilding the fish egg. Use a spoon made of horn or mother-of-pearl. Metal will corrupt the flavor."

I was proud to know so much about a food I couldn't afford to eat.

"You're almost right," Forbes said.

A man wearing a kilt and carrying a set of bagpipes stepped into the room and began to play. When he did, men in white jackets entered bearing little bowls of caviar set in big crystal bowls filled with crushed ice. Until this moment I had regarded bagpipes as the Wagner of musical instruments; they had to be better than they sounded. I revised my opinion as I gazed, covetously, at mounds of fresh beluga coming our way accompanied by the wonderfully horrendous wailing of a bagpipe.

"This," Forbes said, grinning at me, "is how you serve caviar."

I had met my enemy, and he had won.

This round.

I ate my caviar. I may have eaten everybody's caviar. Forbes kept stopping by my table.

"Want some more?" he would say.

"Got any more?" I would say.

And I thought Scots were stingy.

There was more to the lunch than caviar. I let other people eat it. I concentrated on what was important.

Forbes was everywhere. His energy never lagged, or his manners. I couldn't say the same for everybody on board. We passed the afternoon sailing up the Hudson River, then turned around and headed back to New York City. Dark was closing in, but we could see some of the six million people who were lining the shores. Most were cheering. It was a day for cheering. I was standing on the fantail deck, I think it was called, next to a well-known Wall Street hotshot and his wife, a former stew who, after her marriage, had donned a mental tiara as part of her everyday wardrobe.

"Look at them," she said. "They may be the little people, but they are *our* little people."

We parked in another part of New York Harbor — the place where you would get the best view of the fireworks. Steaks were served, each guest having been consulted as to how he or she would like it cooked. I said I'd pass; I was back on track, back on the job. Forbes came over to the table where I sat, steakless, bent down, and whispered.

"Maybe you'd like a little more caviar instead?"

Oh, all right.

After the fireworks ended, *Highlander*

powered her way back to her mooring at Chelsea Piers. The rich made their good-byes before retiring to their limos, which were waiting, all in a row. I headed for the gangway, shook Malcolm Forbes's hand, and thanked him for the ride. He smiled that good smile, the one I liked so much more than I wanted to, and made a motion with his hand. A steward handed me a gift-wrapped package. I knew what was in it. Another journalist on board, a society reporter, had told me. It was traditional, she said: a model of *Highlander V,* a deck of cards with the yacht's insignia on each card, and a pillow inscribed, "There's no way to move without making waves — Chairman Malcolm."

"Take this with you," Forbes said, indicating the box.

"Don't think so," I said. "I'm not brib-able."

"I know. Take it anyway."

I took the box. Would have been bad manners not to, under the circumstances. I could give the souvenirs away. In a taxi on the way downtown, I thought about the day. I had found everything *Sports Illustrated* sent me to find. So many of the people on that yacht represented so much of what I despised about the eighties: the belief that making money was what life was all about, the smugness, the assumption that they were real and everybody else on the planet was not. We weren't just the *little* people. We were *their* little people. My story would be a piece of cake to write.

When I got home, I opened the package. There was no toy yacht, no cards, no pillow. Only a kilo of beluga and a note.

"I know we disagree on many things, but I like passion. People who aren't carried away should be."

Another saying from Chairman Malcolm.

Yeah. My story would be a piece of cake to write.

Except for one thing.

I liked Malcolm Forbes. It wasn't the caviar. It was the guy. He was kind; I'd seen it a dozen times that day — a gentleman, he was — and smart. I'd seen that too. And something else. Malcolm Forbes was more *present* than most people — when he was there, he was all there. You could feel sparks fly off him. He laughed loud and often, loudest of all at himself, and he wanted everybody to have as much fun as he was having. On occasion I had wondered, as we all do, what I would be like if I were rich, and when I wondered this, I was always reminded of Dorothy Parker, who said, "I don't know much about being a millionaire, but I'll bet I'd be darling at it." Malcolm Forbes was darling at it. He did what I like to think I would have done — after, of course, I bought world peace and fed all the hungry children: enjoyed my money and invited my friends to join me in doing so. Maybe I would have hung out with a different crowd. Maybe I wouldn't have bought a yacht, a hot-air balloon, motorcycles, or those silly eggs. But I sure would have bought a jet and kept that sucker in the air taking me and mine to all the places I hadn't been to, eating anything and everything I wanted.

There was this too: Malcolm Forbes was no dummy; he knew how things worked. He knew the Statue of Liberty Birthday Voyage on board *Highlander V* was no sports story, knew why *Sports Illustrated* had sent me and what it expected me to write — *the man had read my book* — and still he invited me to come aboard and treated me as if he didn't know I was there to trash his party. I couldn't do it, couldn't write about what I had seen without insulting my host, a man I'd come to think of as a nice guy, and I was afraid that if I wrote that, if I wrote what I've written here so many years later, I would be accused of having gone soft, or worse, having been bought off. Journalists are supposed to have scruples. I'd compromised mine when I'd assumed I knew what my story would be before I covered it. The next morning I called *Sports Illustrated* and said, sorry, guess I wasn't cut out to be a sports reporter after all.

A fly landed on my desk. I killed it with one swat of my hand.

I never saw Malcolm Forbes again, but four years later, when he unexpectedly died, I was sad. A unique light had been turned off and the world was a poorer place for it. John D. Rockefeller said it's not the money — it's what you do with it. For too many people on that yacht, on that glorious day in New York Harbor in 1986, celebrating the first hundred years of a statue meant to represent all kinds of opportunity to all kinds of people, it *was* the money, and for all they had of it, not many seemed to be happy. Except my host. He was happy. He was having a good time. Nobody ever had a better time than Malcolm Forbes. He was wrong about one thing, though. That night, getting off his yacht, when I'd said I couldn't be bribed and he'd said he knew that? He was mistaken. I *can* be bought. But even Malcolm Forbes couldn't afford that much beluga.

Texas Caviar

This recipe, basically a dip, comes courtesy of my friends Kris Yettra and Joel Gordin at Cowgirl, a restaurant near me in New York that serves genuine Texas food despite being way north of the Red River. It's not real caviar, but it's real good eating, and so cheap to make that you can use what you saved in money to get yourself a decent secondhand set of bagpipes.

3 fresh garlic cloves, pressed or minced
$1/2$ bunch parsley, chopped
1 tablespoon dried oregano
1 tablespoon Tabasco
1 tablespoon Worcestershire sauce
1 cup olive oil (maybe $1^1/2$ cups, but no more)
3 (16-ounce) cans black-eyed peas, drained
    and rinsed

1 small jar chopped pimientos, juice included
1 red onion, chopped
1 teaspoon black pepper
1 teaspoon salt
1 jar jalapeño chiles, chopped, juice included
    (juice part optional)
1 firm, ripe tomato, seeded and chopped
1 green bell pepper, finely chopped
Saltines or corn tortilla chips, for serving

1. In a food processor combine the garlic, parsley, oregano, Tabasco, and Worcestershire sauce. Process to a fine puree. Slowly add the olive oil.
2. In a large bowl, mix the "vinaigrette" with the other ingredients. Refrigerate at least 2 hours (or overnight), so flavors can marry.
3. Serve with old-fashioned saltine crackers or with corn tortilla chips.

TEN

Take Small Bites

(1998)

I've known what it is to be hungry, but I always went right to a restaurant.
— RING LARDNER

Tasha sits on the curb sweating. She holds Patik and Felicia close, pulling their heads to hers and singing the Barney song.

I love you . . . you love me . . .

In July in Baltimore, the heat from the street will melt your eyeballs, never mind a fuzzy purple dinosaur.

Tasha's two older children are helping women lay out boxes of doughnuts and sandwiches, and loaves of bread. They put them on a folding table set up on the sidewalk of a hard-luck street in what white liberals like to call an inner-city neighborhood. This is code. Inner-city means black. Some of the food is fresh. Most of it you would have preferred to have met when it was young. The food is for giving away to people who are hungry. It has been donated to an organization that does this and more; for four days, Tasha and her children have been staying in a shelter operated by the same organization, but only because they have no place else in this world to go.

More than half the city of Baltimore's population is black, and more than half the blacks in Baltimore live below the poverty level. The poorest of the poor are homeless. Having no home robs you of your dignity. Having no food robs you of your life. The people who come for free food are mostly black. The food donors are mostly white. The organization that operates as middleman is made up of people who are black and white and all the shades in between. Everybody trips over their good intentions. And their racism. The kind you like to pretend doesn't exist. Today there is a group of white women here. We are mostly from New York City. We are middle-to-upper-class. We have come to Baltimore to see poverty up close and personal. We have come to learn as much as we can about lives so different from ours they might as well be being lived on another planet. We have come for half a day.

They call it a soup kitchen, but there is no soup. I don't know why. I'm ashamed to know so little, embarrassed by my ignorance and by my well-fed-and-housed self. Exactly what is it I'm supposed to learn here — that being poor is no fun? This just in?

The oldest of Tasha's children is careful as he lays out the boxes of food, gentle with his hands and in his face. He stands taller than his age would suggest. He is eight. His name is Honree.

"I was thirteen," Tasha says. "I didn't know how not to have a baby. What did I know about spelling a French name?"

Baltimore was never a French colony. A second-tier icon of American freedom forever trapped geographically and historically between the white-marble multimonolith of Washington, D.C., and that red-brick national birthing room we call Philadelphia, Baltimore's claim to fame came *after* the American Revolution. The city had a harbor and in that harbor it had Fort McHenry, which had been attacked by the British during the War of 1812, an historical fact that might have gone unnoticed by all but historians, had not the battle inspired a local fellow to write a poem about a flag that — despite being shot at, battered, beaten, and ripped to pieces in what one might describe as the first sail-by shooting — did not, would not, fall, or fall apart. Francis Scott Key called his poem "The Star-Spangled Banner." From that moment on, Baltimore went its own proud, damaged way.

East Baltimore was the first center of black Baltimore. Frederick Douglass was born there. Following the Civil War, more blacks migrated to the city from the South. Baltimore grew — expanding, as every city on the East Coast did, westward. And so it went with Baltimore's blacks, who began to move out of East Baltimore and into West Baltimore, where, and I know you will be as surprised by this as I was, white people already living there tried — by ways legal and not — to prevent this migration. They lost. West Baltimore turned solidly black. Thurgood Marshall, the first black American Supreme Court justice, came from West Baltimore.

Have you been to Baltimore? Then you know about row houses. We are in a neighborhood of row houses today, but not the mellowed, aged-in-the-barrel-of-time, high-priced ones people buy, renovate, and fill with antique furniture and paintings of someone else's ancestors. The bricks on the front of the buildings around us often are not real — just that fake half-brick that is multicolored and comes only halfway up the front of the house. Above that, wood — or asbestos siding. You see a lot of that. See a lot of boarded-up windows and abandoned row houses too. You don't see too many folks carrying gym bags on the way to their aerobics class. Around here, people carrying gym bags are often burglars on their way to work. Or thugs who need something to carry their arsenal in. Or drug dealers who carry them because they can afford to, and like the look.

Honree asks if he can have a pair of the thin white plastic gloves we white women wear to handle the food. We say of course. We are knowledgeable; we have read about empowerment. I want to find a hole for well-meaning assholes and crawl into it.

Next time someone approaches the food table, Honree is ready. You would think we've given him a pair of handmade Italian leather gloves, so proud is he of his disposable, cheap plastic hand covers.

"May I help you, sir?" he says.

Like he's a waiter.

"Watcha got?" says the man.

Like there's a menu.

"You can have a sandwich, a doughnut,

and three loaves of bread," Honree says.

He glances at his mother. She sends him one of those mother looks, the kind that says, "Where are your manners?"

"May I get the food ready for you, sir?" Honree says.

The man grumbles something that might be taken — or mistaken — for a yes. Honree gathers a dry ham sandwich — nothing but boiled supermarket ham and bread, no butter, mustard, mayo, lettuce, tomato, or cheese — one chocolate-covered doughnut, and three loaves of stale bread. In the heat, the chocolate has begun to melt. Honree looks at his chocolate-stained gloves. I see his dismay.

"Don't worry," I say. "We have plenty. That's what disposable is all about."

I do not mention the obvious. There are more gloves than there is food.

Honree hands the man his box of food along with a slip of paper from the organization.

"Will you sign here, please, sir?" he says.

The man throws Honree a hard, ancient street look. What's the catch here? Signing things is not smart. He looks at us. White people are never a good idea. But it's food. He's hungry. He signs the paper.

"Thank you," Honree says, putting the

slip of paper precisely on top of a pile of other slips of paper. I look where the man has signed.

"Fuck Me," he has written.

Good name. Wish I'd thought of it first.

The man to whom Honree has given the box of food reaches with his free hand and takes a second sandwich.

"I'm sorry," Honree says. "There isn't enough. You can only have one."

Although he is shorter and younger, the boy faces the man down with nothing but his dignity. After a couple of beats, the man hands the second sandwich back to the boy. The heart hurts for them both.

What do I think I'm doing here? My experience with hunger has been limited to running out of gorp on the last morning of a five-day backpacking trip. Or dieting. My memories of food and Baltimore have chiefly to do with the glorious comestible for which this city's restaurants are best known: crab. Steamed crabs. Crab soup. Soft-shell crab sandwiches. Crab bisque. And the biggest Baltimore treat of all: crab cakes. Usually at Obrycki's. I have been responsible for the death of many a poor crustacean at the city's most famous crab house, which is in East Baltimore, the first-but-no-longer black part of town. The property Obrycki's is built on includes the original Goodwill Industries Building. You could run over from where we are right now and get two backfin-crab cakes at Obrycki's for maybe $25. Or feed Tasha and her children for a week.

Honree runs the free-food table all afternoon. He is courteous but firm. He gives what he has. When no one is wanting food, he plays with his brothers and sister. If someone approaches the table, Honree rushes to put on his food-handler gloves. He wants to do it right.

Oh hell, the whole damn city wants to do it right. Look at Baltimore today. The other Baltimore, I mean. The Chamber of Commerce likes to describe it as a new travel destination. There's old stuff: the ships, the museums. There's not-too-old old stuff: Pimlico racetrack where they run the Preakness Stakes, the second leg of thoroughbred horse racing's Triple Crown. There's the new stuff: Baltimore's Inner Harbor. It's been revitalized. Generally this means old buildings get torn down and new buildings designed to look like old buildings get put up. To "revitalize" a city, you must build a new convention center. Baltimore did. It hosted a big food-service convention a few months ago: three separate seminars on portion control and profitability. You must also have a retail and restaurant complex. Baltimore does. At Harborplace, you can buy a model of Fort McHenry, a new pair of running shoes, or a plate of crab cakes not overburdened with crabmeat. Then you can stop by Baltimore's National Aquarium and see what the crab looked like before it was a cake. Honree has never seen the Inner Harbor. Never tasted crab. Never heard of an aquarium. When I tell him about it, he thinks it's funny. The city built a house for fish to live in? A homeless kid considers this.

"Do they feed them?" Honree says.

"Feed who?"

"The fish."

"Yes," I say, quietly. "They feed them."

"That's good," says Honree.

Tasha has laid Patik down for his nap. Patik sleeps on a blanket on the sidewalk. His sweet baby face carries in it all the possibilities. No one has explained to him yet how limited his are. A taxi pulls up carrying a woman and a little boy. The boy is crying. The woman apologizes for the way her face looks. She says her husband came home from a bar drunk and found her too high on drugs to take care of her son. She says he hit her because he said she wasn't supposed to ever get too high to take care of *his* son. They go inside the shelter.

Tasha answers the questions of the nosy white women who have come to help distribute food only to find an eight-year-old boy does it better.

"My children's fathers?" she says. "Two are dead from drugs. The other two, they don't do anything for the kids. Nothing at all."

We shake our heads in sympathy. *Men.*

"My own mother was a junkie," Tasha says.

Okay. *Some women.*

"My mama been clean for six years now," Tasha says.

We nod our heads in approval.

"She made me go to parenting classes for a year," Tasha says.

One of the women looks a question at Tasha but says nothing. Plain speaking does not always come easy to those who know all the words. Tasha answers the question the woman doesn't ask.

"Yeah, I did drugs," she says. "But I'm in the program now."

Tasha looks at Felicia, her daughter, who, at four, is already beautiful.

"Got to do what I can do to make sure

her life is different. Don't want her to be thirteen and make the choices I did — or only have the choices I had," Tasha says.

She pushes a small sticky curl off Felicia's forehead. The humidity is palpable, the heat debilitating. The pavement burns my bottom. My toes sweat.

"But it's hard," Tasha says. "I can't get a good job because I can't get my GED."

More than half a million adults in Baltimore have no high school degree. For every unskilled job there are at least two unskilled applicants.

"Well, why don't you just knuckle down and get that darned old GED," one of us says. She makes a go-get-'em gesture with her arm and clenched fist. "I mean, surely there are night classes, adult education programs . . . and then you can find a good job . . . you know . . ."

She doesn't know. None of us knows. We cannot even imagine. Tasha explains it to us. Slowly. Like we're Felicia's age.

"I can't get a GED because I have no child care. I can't do anything until I work out the child-care thing. And I can't do that until I find a place for us to live."

Tasha and her children had been sleeping on the floor of a relative's apartment, and when that opportunity expired, in an abandoned building. The shelter is a temporary solution. Nobody *lives* here.

More people have shown up. Seeing us, some are sullen, taking their food and leaving as quickly as possible. A skinny woman with no teeth looks at us as if in some odd, unfamiliar way, we might be human. Then she looks at Tasha.

"Girl, you got yourself a place to live yet?"

"I may be getting a place to live next Monday," Tasha says. "The social worker called and said we'd go look at it."

Tasha laughs out loud and Patik wakes. She pats his tummy, humming. He dozes back off, making little baby snores. Tasha speaks quietly so as not to wake the baby again.

"*Look at it?* I told her I don't have to look at it. If it's got a roof and walls, and locks on the door and windows, and a toilet that flushes, I'll take it."

The skinny woman grins a toothless grin. Honree hands her the food. She signs for it and unwraps the dry, dead sandwich.

"Just like my mama used to make," she says, and wanders off down the street chuckling.

The sun has lowered. If you had an egg, you could no longer fry it on the sidewalk. If you had an egg.

Robert, the second oldest of Tasha's children, and Felicia sing a song about a rabbit and smile at everybody. Their smiles could light this city without turning on a switch. When they finish singing and smiling, we applaud. They hug us. Not because we are worth hugging. They hug because they have been hugged. I know plenty of people who could take parenting lessons from Tasha. One wants to do something — something that will give Tasha the opportunity to give Honree and Robert and Felicia and Patik a chance. But where to start? You want to live as a human being in this world? You want to raise a family? You need a safe place to live. You need enough education to find work to support you and your family. You need a sense that in the scheme of things, you count.

You need food.

Fresh, healthy food and enough of it.

Every day.

I think of politics. Politicians take too long. Tasha, Patik, Felicia, Robert, and Honree don't have too long.

Two wasted old men approach the free-food table.

"I'm sorry. The sandwiches are all gone," Honree tells them.

Tasha hands the old men two sandwiches she has put aside for her children.

"Here," she says. "Take these. My kids got fed last night. They're not as hungry as you."

On our way back to New York, we don't talk much. The steward in the first-class car on the Amtrak train, a black man, walks down the aisle handing out menus.

"Try the Crab Cakes Baltimore-Style," he says. "Everybody likes them."

But nobody is hungry.

America's Second Harvest is the largest supplier of food to food banks across the United States. Second Harvest accepts monetary donations and large-scale food donations. Small-scale food donations should be brought to your local food bank. Second Harvest can tell you where your local food bank is.

America's Second Harvest
www.secondharvest.org
35 E. Wacker Dr. #2000
Chicago, IL 60601
Phone: 800-771-2303,
312-263-2303

ELEVEN

Divorced Eggs and Ham

(2001)

"Sixty percent of the people who move here," Charlotte says, "come for a cheap house and a cheap maid."

She turns in her chair. White hair and cheekbones catch the sun, her key light. Liza, her daughter, interrupts. They do this, the two of them.

"San Miguel is a good place to do nothing," Liza says. "A good place to be yourself."

Her mother interrupts back.

"Or reinvent yourself. When people move here, they decide who they want to be. Then they pad their parts. Or at least embellish their pasts."

Charlotte clearly disapproves.

It's April and I'm chatting with, mostly listening to, Charlotte and Liza, in the garden of Casa de Liza, the B&B they own in the Mexican hill town of San Miguel de Allende, where, they tell me, days are warm and nights are cool. It is Semana Santa. Holy week. Celebrating a familiar holiday in an unfamiliar place can be a wonderful sidebar to traveling, or the chief reason for going.

I have come to San Miguel for Easter celebrations, which are bound to be different from my memories of standing on the lawn in back of our church, wearing the pastel dress and straw hat with matching ribbons my mother has bought especially for the day, holding a paper-petal Easter basket in my hand and thinking Christian thoughts like how much I really hate the sticky little boy who found the gold egg. I've come for other reasons too. I plan to explore the city a little, and then rest a lot. Didn't Liza say this was a good place to do nothing?

San Miguel is an antique and a national monument, which means no buildings in the central district that don't conform to the Colonial style, no neon, no traffic lights, no parking meters, and no billboards. Once it got its wealth from silver. Today San Miguel survives on tourists like me — and the eight to ten thousand expatriates, mostly from the United States, who, like Liza and Charlotte, came and stayed.

Liza arrived in 1989.

"I sold my house in Virginia, and because I am a Jewish child with medical problems, of course my mother moved here two years later."

Mother and daughter are beautiful women with big eyes, carved faces, and silvery to pure-white hair. Charlotte was once a John Robert Powers model. Liza worked in interior design. Together they created Casa de Liza, a B&B that is not one house but a walled compound of several houses surrounding what can only be called a private park. Lush doesn't begin to say it. I like the place instantly, which is surprising, not because I had chosen and booked it on the Internet, sight unseen, but because I'm not a B&B kind of girl. I've done my time in them — done my time in Motel 6 too, but I'd rather think I'm not that kind of girl either. It's not that B&Bs are cheaper than (and therefore not as good as?) small luxury inns, or big-ticket hotels with copious concierges. It's not about money. I've slept in three-sided wooden huts I liked better than your average B&B, which is stifling and stuffed with cute. Why is nothing allowed to be itself? Excuse me, I can't find the toilet paper. *Under the Scarlett O'Hara doll in the hand-crocheted dress? The one she wore to the Wilkes barbecue? How sweet. I would have looked there next.* What is this canopied bed fetish? If I want to spend the night with cloth over my head, I have a tent. Why do they think my breakfast of choice is pancakes drenched in chocolate syrup with a side of oat bran muffins? Last time I wanted oat bran I was much younger and given to pretending I was a horse. Who are these other people at the table with me? If I want to eat breakfast with strangers, I'll do it at dinner.

Casa de Liza is not like that. My room is comfortable, and although done up with Mexican folk art, it's not overdone. I know this because when I'm in it I can still breathe. The toilet paper is where it should be and looks like what it is. When I go to sleep I can see the ceiling. I can see out the window. I can wake to nothing but my inner alarm and have breakfast when I want it, outside on my terrace, alone except for birdsong and blossom. My first morning I do right by a plate of *Huevos Divorciados,* two fried eggs with clashing sauces: a red chile sauce and a green chile sauce, separated on the plate. Divorced eggs. Maybe I should lie down, give the eggs a chance to reconcile inside my stomach while I rest and consider what makes people choose to live in a country not their own. I must ask Liza and Charlotte more questions. *Exactly why did they come here?* Gotta be more than cheap houses, maids, and meds. Do people really reinvent themselves here? And why do I care? Am I thinking of moving to San Miguel, or simply unable to stop being a journalist, even on holiday? I head out to explore town. Maybe I'll run into the Easter Bunny.

El Chorro, the natural spring around which San Miguel was founded, is across the street from the Casa de Liza compound. Mexican-Indian women wash their laundry in cold spring water that drips from faucets set above a stone trough. Their strong brown faces are all intersecting planes and angles, their eyes obsidian pools that swallow light like the sinkholes you sometimes find in jungles. The women talk to one another while they work and the sound of their voices is like music. My Spanish is not good enough to catch all they say. I wonder if they are embellishing their parts.

The Jardín, the plaza, is a five-minute walk up the hill. The stone and stucco-fronted buildings on both sides of the old, narrow street reveal nothing. Houses here face inward. Fountains sing their songs in secret tiled courtyards where exotic flowers bloom — where a person like myself might learn to sit around hamming it up, sipping from a tall glass of something cold and pretending to be someone I'm not? No one invites me in to try. I keep on climbing the hill. Sidewalks are so narrow two people cannot pass. When you meet people coming the other way, everybody looks at everybody else's shoes to gauge who is best suited to step off the sidewalk and onto the unevenly cobbled, ankle-breaking street. I'm wearing hiking sandals. I have to step into the street a lot. I come close to getting run over once or twice, but I don't break anything. I do notice I'm sweating in unladylike amounts. This nights-are-cool, days-are-warm business apparently does not apply to April, when, as I've discovered in the last twenty-four hours, nights are warm and days are hot, even at 7,000 feet. Near the top of the hill, I make a wrong turn, but eventually I find the Jardín. Rather like going to New York and saying, "Eventually I found the Empire State Building." If you can't, it's time to go back to Dallas and rethink your map-reading skills.

The Jardín has been the center of town

since 1737 or time began, depending upon whom you ask. It's across the street from the Parroquia de San Miguel Arcángel, the parish church, whose provenance is disputed, but everybody seems to agree the final builder based his design on the ultra-modern buildings he copied from European postcards in 1880. In the Jardín, I buy a cold soda and look for an empty bench. People pass by, around, and through the plaza, where, along with benches, there are pathways and trees and, of course, flowers. They are everywhere in San Miguel; flowers grow on bushes and vines and stalks, bloom in pots and jars and gardens, cascade down old stone walls, and hang from trees. People sell them on the streets, in the markets, and outside the churches; they are clumped in vases on tables or in windows, or pinned in the hair of young women. San Miguel de Allende is a good place to stop and smell the flowers.

For the next few days, I work at being myself while I explore, climbing only a few hills — no need to overdo — sit in parks and browse the markets and the many art galleries and craft shops. I introduce myself to Mexican locals — merchants, priests, waiters, old women in black, and exquisitely coiffed ladies who speak several languages, organize garden tours, and sell real estate. They are welcoming and polite. Courtesy is a national habit. I also seek out people in the expat community. There are so many and they are so everywhere. Some are retired. Some are artists. Some just say they are, and having seen their work, I think they should stop saying it. Expats with enough money tend to live in the big houses of the gringo ghetto in the hills surrounding town. Those with little or no income live like natives in the barrio. Others live in circumstances somewhere in between. San Miguel is said to be a place where Mexicans, Anglos, Indians, hippies, yuppies, dopers, drinkers, rich people, poor people, religious people, atheists, widows, the newly divorced, people of varied sexual preferences, priests, painters, posers, and perverts coexist without wanting to kill one another. My kind of town.

Certain expats I meet who've moved here from the United States seem unduly proud of what they've done, as if nobody else was ever quite as clever as they. But when I ask them where to eat, nobody tells me about the Mexican café with the *sopa de ajo con crema,* a cream-of-garlic soup that will rearrange your molecules. I'm directed to the newest French, Italian, Continental, Argentine, Thai, or Nouvelle Whatever restaurant, all of which flourish basically to serve the expat community. Although a divorcée from Phoenix, who says she moved to San Miguel in search of her inner child, tells me it's fabulous, I do not care to try the town's new sushi bar. I have not come to Central Mexico to eat raw fish. Instead I do what they tell me not to do. I buy goat tacos from street vendors, hold the wasabi.

Early in the week I go to the *mercado* for a few goodies to keep in my room to ward off starvation between meals. Mainly spicy peanuts. *Cacahuates*. Fun to say. Try it. Kah-kah-*what*-tays. Next time a New York cabbie tries to run me down, I'm going to shake my fist and yell, "*Cacahuate* this." Give some Pakistani a good laugh while he mentally measures the distance between us and floors it. I also buy *cajeta*, a caramel candy made from goats' milk and sugar. Sometimes *cajeta* is made into a dessert sauce called *dulce de leche*. Vanilla ice cream streaked with *dulce de leche* is now one of Häagen-Dazs's most popular flavors in the States, and a big seller here too. Many expats tell me they like it better than the real thing. It's not that they don't like indigenous food — several expats tell me they have given a copy of the *Betty Crocker Easy Mexican Cookbook* to their Mexican cooks. Stephen and Spik used to teach elementary school in San Francisco. Now they run an art gallery and hold "openings" where they serve wine from the Napa Valley and tiny cornucopias of baloney filled with Philadelphia Cream Cheese.

"I was always the adventurous type," Stephen says.

So many seem to want to go somewhere without leaving home, which also may account for the new two-plex that shows recently released U.S. movies in English with Spanish subtitles in what, last time I checked, is a Mexican hill town. I visited the home of an expat couple from Chicago. They came for the climate, they said, and to experience life in a culture completely unlike their own. Their house was newly constructed and centrally air-conditioned. Most of the walls were glass. The most colorful objects in their living room were the gray upholstered Castro Convertible sofas, the brown Barcalounger, and the black satellite-TV remote. Didn't want to miss an episode of *Sex and the City*, they said.

Angie is a different kind of expatriate —

an ex-patriot, perhaps, despite her wide-open, all-American face, the for-spacious-skies blue eyes, and a grin Huck Finn would envy. A fortysomething woman who dresses in bright clothes that look handwoven and comfortable, Angie is a real artist who makes her living painting, and deserves to. She tells me her story. Two months before graduating from "a small, private, rich girls' high school" in Coconut Grove, she ran away to get married, ran away from him, met someone else, ran again, always working in small jobs and living the Bohemian life. When she discovered it got cold in Greenwich Village, she moved back to Florida.

"But at twenty-four," Angie says, "I realized the American Dream didn't do it for me."

It is Angie who finally introduces me to the cream-of-garlic soup. We are eating our *sopa de ajo con crema* at a mostly empty (of North Americans) and unfancy restaurant away from the Jardín. People might tell you anything after a bowl of that soup. Angie says she moved to Haiti in 1971 and then to San Miguel in the early nineties, when the Organization of American States — led by the U.S. government, with whom she carries on a lifelong philosophical dispute

— imposed an embargo on the poorest country in the Western Hemisphere. I nod, but all I can think about is the soup. It is the soul of garlic. If the kitchen has enough, maybe we could FedEx some to Haiti.

"One morning," Angie says, "I found four bullet holes in the living room wall of my rented house. It was time to move on."

Since then, she has lived in San Miguel, which, she says, she's fairly sure the United States has no immediate plans to invade, not officially, that is; after all, there are the expats to consider. Angie offers to accompany me to the remaining Semana Santa festivities. So far during Holy Week I've seen some fireworks and a few parades, and even though they attract tourists, it has been clear that these events are not put on for tourists — or expats. The people who take active roles in Semana Santa are permanent residents who have always been permanent residents. Put another way, they are Mexicans. Angie finds us a spot where we can sit on the curb, eat chunks of cold melon sold by more of those germ-spreading street vendors, and watch the Good Friday procession. It's getting dark when Mexican centurions in Roman costume ride their horses down the narrow street, followed by perspiring groups of men who carry on their shoulders life-sized statues of saints whom, not being Catholic, I don't recognize. Jesus — the crown of thorns is a dead giveaway, so to speak — is carried in a glass coffin. Of the hundreds of people in the procession, everyone but Jesus and the centurions wears black. We watch for more than an hour. Evening turns to night. The only light comes from candles carried by those not carrying statues, and except for a solemn drumbeat, it is silent. I've shut up too. Even if I don't get it, I get it.

I get something else while watching the parade. These expats who've come to a new place and tried to make it like the old place? Isn't that what the Spanish did when they got here? Look at the buildings on both sides of the street. They look Aztec to you? And didn't the early Christians do the same thing when they spread out from Rome? Look at the centurions with their brush-plumed helmets. Look at the robes on the statues. In San Miguel by way of Spain and before that Rome and before that the Middle East. Is there something in us that can never really let go of where we came from, no matter how far we travel?

"Angie, what do you miss?"

We are walking through the Jardín after the procession has ended.

"I miss a certain kind of wit," Angie says. "A certain kind of laugh. People here are lovely and generous, and still I miss that American belly laugh."

She pauses.

"Then again, I don't really drink much anymore."

Saturday Angie invites me to see her apartment. She lives on the third floor. As there are no buildings in the center of San Miguel taller than three floors, let's call it a penthouse. Her small roof terrace is crowded with potted geraniums. An even smaller inner courtyard overflows with plants and vines. The inside of Angie's apartment is like her paintings, suffused with light and infused with the colors of Mexico. Blankets in stripes of raspberry and ruby and lime and turquoise and lavender and lemon are thrown over unmatched sofas and chairs. Mexican art books with Technicolor dust jackets are stacked on low tables next to pieces of decorated pottery that feel good to touch (cream-of-garlic soup would be right at home in one of these bowls). Her paintings cover every piece of wall that isn't covered

299

by photographs of friends and family. Visiting Angie's apartment is like falling into a rainbow.

"Would you ever go back?"

"I can't afford to be an artist in the United States. I'd be forced to live in a ghetto and eat cat food. I *have* to live in a Third World country."

Angie smiles. It's a private smile. I can tell. Journalists are trained observers even when they're resting. For instance, I have noted a purple bowl full of spicy peanuts sitting on a side table. An involuntary sigh and I part company. Angie reaches for the bowl and offers some peanuts. I grab a handful and urge her on. What has she learned living as an expat?

"Being an expat *is* about learning something," Angie says, "but it's mostly about looking for something. I wanted a place that's cheap, and where people know your name, and I have that in San Miguel."

I nod and wait for her to say more. Good interview technique. Also, my mouth is full of spicy peanuts.

"But there is no place," Angie says, taking a few peanuts in self-defense — they are almost gone — "I call home anymore."

Come Saturday evening I'm resting at a tiled table in the flower-flavored courtyard of Casa de Liza, exploring the moonlight, tasting the night, listening to a cricket and more of Liza's take on why folks switch countries.

"Every American should live here for two years and every Mexican should live in America for two years," Liza says.

I do not remind her that Mexico is America too. Instead, I think about moving to San Miguel for two years. Could I do that? Live surrounded by beauty, wonderful eccentrics, and a few self-indulgent twits? Wouldn't be that much of a stretch. I'm already crazier than most of them. Liza gets up to go inside to find her mother. After she's gone, I realize I still haven't gotten a good explanation from either of these two women about their own decision to live here.

Easter Sunday morning I go to the Jardín to watch the Judases blow up. Life-sized papier-mâché dolls have been strung up and hang, twisting in an otherwise indiscernible breeze, from wires stretched between the tops of trees in the Jardín and the wrought-iron balconies on the buildings across the street. Fireworks are wired to the Judas figures, who aren't Judases from the Bible — they're effigies of whomever the Mexicans of San Miguel decide

Exploding Judases

they dislike most at the moment, generally local politicians, although I do manage to make out a George W. Bush doll. A few expats mumble about the ingratitude of *foreigners*. A few volunteer to light the fuse. The first Judas spins wildly and then explodes, the bang amazingly loud, the smell of cordite overpowering. Children rush in to grab a papier-mâché hand or — most prized — the head, which has fallen intact into the street among other, less recognizable body parts. More Judases are blown up. Crowds cheer. More heads and hands are taken. There isn't an Easter Bunny in sight.

Monday, the day before I'm to leave, I go

back to the garlic soup restaurant. I've eaten here almost every day, and every day I tell myself I will order something different, and then order the cream-of-garlic soup. You never outgrow your need for cream-of-garlic soup. I hadn't known this before.

"Hello, Marie," I say to the owner, a large redheaded European-looking woman of a certain age who must have been a beauty once; now there's a softness around the chin and a hardness in the eyes. "How are you today?"

"I was in San Miguel six weeks," Marie says, "and someone said to me, 'You don't speak Spanish? How rude. Why are you here?' "

I haven't been here six weeks, but I try.

"*¿Porqué está usted aquí?*" Why *are* you here?

I had heard stories. That she came from Austria. That she was a former *fille de joie* from Marseilles. That she was a refugee from the Soviet bloc. That she was born to a family with a minor Italian title (the way she orders her waiters around, I would have said a minor Greek title). That she was rich by mysterious means. That she'd had many lovers in San Miguel — that they were always younger men. All week I have tried to find out Marie's story and, naturally, the recipe for the soup. So far she has evaded my questions. Today Marie agrees to at least sit down with me. I order a bowl of *sopa de ajo* to show my gratitude for her appreciation of authentic Mexican cuisine. Surely this will make her want to spill her secrets to a total stranger. We're outside. The tables are shaded by large flowering trees and yards of white openwork cotton spreads (like your grand-mother's tablecloths), which are draped from one tree to another to catch the blossoms when they fall. I tell Marie how fine I think her restaurant is. Journalism Rule #42: Begin a hostile interview with a compliment, even if it's true.

Marie lights a cigarette, shrugs, and says the restaurant is for sale.

"So," I say, ignoring the question of why the restaurant might be for sale. That will come later, once I've loosened her up. "Where are you from, Marie? Sounds like someplace in Europe."

My job would be so much easier if people would interview themselves and let me get on with my eating.

Another shrug from Marie.

Okay. Cut to Journalism Rule #65: If someone doesn't want to talk to you, talk to them.

"You know, Marie," I say, as though it had just occurred to me, "this town must be an interesting place to live. I mean, for someone who probably grew up in, say, Europe?"

Marie stubs her cigarette out. "I'm done here."

At first I think she means she's done talking to me, which she can't be because so far all she's said is ten words. Then I realize she's speaking in the larger sense; but I'm flexible. We can skip ahead.

"Why are you 'done here'? Don't you like San Miguel anymore?"

"You want the cream-of-garlic soup recipe?" Marie asks.

"Only a little less than I want to live forever."

"It's all you're going to get from me."

My winning interview technique apparently has lost its erection. Journalism Rule #14: If all else fails, give up. I turn to a blank page in my journal, ready to start writing down the recipe, which she passes on to me in a way that plainly says I'm a fool not to have known it already, not to have grown up making perfect cream-of-garlic soup, but what can you expect from a nosy North American broad who goes around asking people about things that are

305

none of her business and isn't going to buy a restaurant?

I should be satisfied with the recipe. But I continue to wonder about Marie, where she came from, why she came, where she was going, and why, at her age, she insisted on going again. Would the next be her last stop? Would she try to make that place like this? Or was she lying about leaving, putting on an act for my benefit? Some expats I have met in San Miguel seemed to regard truth as a relative concept. Once upon a time I planned to grow up and be an artist, until I found out most don't make enough to eat regularly. Maybe if I moved here, I could reinvent myself — be the artist I wanted to be, or pretend that I was. I could tell people my paintings were world-famous in Bryan, Texas (where I was born). Maybe I could buy Marie's restaurant. How hard could it be to run a restaurant? I would sit at my own table every day, reading books and eating cream-of-garlic soup. I would speak with a Mid-Atlantic accent and hint at having been born the illegitimate daughter of an English duke who'd dallied with an American debutante. Or I could move here and write true stories that I would make up, beginning with the one about having to leave the United States because I bludgeoned a B&B owner in Nantucket to death with the miniature wooden lighthouse hiding the soap dish.

Or I could . . .

Marie is a mystery, I tell myself. This is all I know and all I will ever know.

On the last morning of my stay, there is time for one final plate of divorced eggs in the garden with Liza and Charlotte, two women who look as if they would be so much more content living within shouting range of Saks. I'm sopping up the last remaining bit of a no-longer-wedded egg when I think I get a peek behind the ladies' stylish personal veils.

"I was the oldest person at my health club in Tyson's Corners," Liza says. "At *forty.*"

She grimaces and lifts her chin, and it's as if a light goes on inside; she looks almost regal, caring but formal, removed from the rest of us. Her eyes take on a fierce brightness as she surveys what she has created for herself.

"Here," Liza says, "I am a *queen.*"

"So is everyone else in San Miguel, darling," her mother says.

Charlotte hands me a linen napkin without mentioning the wee glob of green divorce sauce stuck to my lip. Royalty never stoops to rudeness.

I leave San Miguel having rested often and explored some. I have witnessed people marking Easter in ways beyond my ken. I have met interesting people along with a few dullards. I have heard entertaining tales, some of which might even be true. What more can one ask of a familiar holiday spent in what — because of the number of my compatriots who have moved here — turns out to be a not-so-unfamiliar place after all?

A few months later, an expat I met in San Miguel e-mails me in New York. He says that not too long after I left, Marie tore up the account books for her restaurant and fled the country, leaving a long trail of debts. He says the restaurant has reopened under new ownership, a couple from Milwaukee. He says the cream-of-garlic soup is as good as ever. The new owner told him it's an old German recipe.

Sopa de Ajo con Crema, aka Cream-of-Garlic Soup, aka Liar's Soup

SERVES FOUR

When I made the soup according to the recipe Marie gave me, it turned out she'd lied about that too. With the help of Brigit Binns — friend, professional chef, and cookbook author — we managed to untangle her directions in order to replicate as best we could the world's best cream-of-garlic soup. And that's no lie.

$1^1/_2$ sticks (6 ounces) butter
1 cup sliced garlic (about 30 medium cloves)
1 large onion, finely chopped (about 2 cups)
$^1/_2$ cup all-purpose flour
5 cups chicken broth, preferably homemade
5 medium garlic cloves, pressed or minced
$^3/_4$ cup heavy cream
Salt and cayenne pepper
2 tomatoes, peeled, seeded, and finely diced

1. In a heavy pan, melt the butter over medium-low heat and sauté 1 cup sliced garlic with onion gently until softened, 5 to 7 minutes. Stir in the flour to form a paste. Cook, stirring, for a couple of minutes, until frothy. Do not let it brown.

2. Whisk in about one third of the chicken broth, then pour in the remaining broth and stir occasionally over low heat for 10 to 15 minutes, until slightly thickened. Add 5 pressed or minced garlic cloves and simmer for 5 more minutes, stirring occasionally.

3. Add the cream and return to a simmer. Stir and cook for 8 to 10 minutes, and season to taste with salt and cayenne. Stir in the tomatoes and remove from the heat. Let stand for 10 minutes and then serve.

TWELVE

Home for the Holidays

(1944–PRESENT)

Why can't we get all the people together in the world that we really like and then just stay together? I guess that wouldn't work. Someone always leaves and then we have to say good-bye. I hate good-byes. I need more hellos.

— SNOOPY

Sometimes you must go a long way to get back home. Inside the house was the lingering scent of a wood fire, of cinnamon and apples, garlic, baked ham and coffee and toasted pecans, the pungent smells of autumn indoors. Outside, the world was swept clean, spare and without smell, unburdened by grass, flowers, or leaves, a no-frills beauty, and everything a New England Thanksgiving ought to be. Except for snow. There was none. Cousin Shirley was disappointed. Cousin Billy was not. He'd seen snow; once was enough, he said. Now they were an hour gone, my Texas relatives, and I was still standing on the porch. Maybe still waving goodbye.

Growing up, we always spent our holidays together. There were more of us then. Our parents were alive. So were their parents. All the uncles and aunts, nieces, nephews, and cousins were alive, which meant there was love enough to go around. Also enough slammed doors, raised voices, and tears. We were family. When it comes to fighting, no one does it better. All you need to know about the past insanity of the Civil War or the perpetual insanity of the Middle East is that both were ("are" in the Middle East) *family* fights.

Time passed. We grew up. Parents and grandparents died. Cousins, nephews, nieces, aunts, and uncles moved, and not to other towns — to other states and once in a while across oceans. We were like American families everywhere. Our big bunch of relatives broke up into small nuclear families that went away. At first I welcomed the change. A holiday without family was a holiday without emotional explosions — and *with* choices: Turkey or goose? Tree or no tree? A fake tree if *I* wanted. Over the years, however, my memories of those loud, occasionally rancorous family holidays grew rosier, rosy enough finally for me to urge my cousins to bring their families to our place in New England for Thanksgiving. We would see what happened.

Maybe we were on our best behavior, that or we'd actually learned something. Our squabbles were minor and concerned only food. My cousins had brought a turkey with them. It was a Texas turkey, you see. When I offered up a sturdy New England pot of beans slowly cooked in the oven, the cousins said they were not as good as a pot of pintos slowly cooked on top of the stove. When I made stuffing with walnuts and apricots, the cousins said cornbread dressing with celery and onions was better. When Alvin said he was going to make his barbecued shrimp, I pointed out you cannot barbecue anything in an oven. Alvin comes from Louisiana, where they may be loose about what they call food but not about cooking it; he told me to shut up.

"It would be a sin against nature," he said, not to love a recipe that begins: "First you take two pounds of butter."

We went into barns by the side of the road and poked at old furniture quite like the old furniture in our grandparents' houses, only now they called it antique and wanted money for it. We brought home apple cider and made long, warming fires to fuel conversation. We talked, teasing one another, telling the old stories, remembering, and knowing that given the same set of circumstances we would make the same choices, and because of that, still go our separate ways. But we missed what had been lost, a closeness that begins, although it certainly does not end, with geographical proximity. The kind of closeness our parents and their families had. The kind we had as children. The kind our children had not had. Would not have. When my cousins left, we said we really must do this more often.

Cut to Labor Day the following year.

"Mom, I won't be coming home for Christmas."

My twenty-five-year-old daughter goes on, rushing, as if her speed will make the words mean something else.

"We were thinking we'd like to have Christmas at our house in Seattle. With our friends."

She continues, but I can't hear her. What I hear is myself at twenty-five.

"Mama, I don't think I'll be coming

home for Christmas this year. I want to go skiing."

"Oh Linda Jane, where did we go wrong?"

My daughter has stopped talking. She is anxious about what I will say.

"Vanessa, when I was your age I told my mother I wouldn't be home for Christmas and she behaved as if I had driven a stake through her heart. I promised myself that I would never do that to my kids. Now I'm called on to keep my promise. Not easy, but here goes. Enjoy Christmas in Seattle. I'll miss you."

I take a deep breath. "But I understand."

Vanessa says nothing. I think she may be in shock.

"What I *don't* want," I say, "is to have to go through this every year. Me wondering: Is she coming home this Christmas? You wondering: What will Mom think if I don't? We deserve better. And so I have an idea. We'll have family Christmas every other year. On the odd years, Rolfe and I will go traveling. You and Josh can do what you want. Nobody's feelings will get hurt, because everybody will know we'll be together the next year. What do you think?"

"Mom . . . it's so . . . *rational.*"

She sounds surprised I can be rational. We go to tell her brother how we've solved at least one of the holiday problems that bog families down.

"In principle, I approve," Josh says. "But maybe I want to have the family Christmas *this* year. Why does Vanessa get to decide when we start?"

The alternate-year theory of the stress-free family holiday was dead on arrival. What changed instead was my definition of family, which over time has grown to encompass relatives, old friends, new friends — the regulars, semiregulars, and fresh meat. Now it comes down to this. If it's a holiday and you're here, you're family.

My two favorites are Thanksgiving and the Fourth of July.

Thanksgiving because it is our only national holiday dedicated to food. We sometimes spit-roast a baby pig for Thanksgiving. We also smoke a turkey that has been brined in water, sugar, soy, and ginger; and roast a goose stuffed with quartered apples and onions, and then basted with maple syrup for the last ten minutes. On the years we don't do a pig, we add a horseradish glaze to an already baked pepper-coated ham. When a dozen or more people travel, some a long way, to get to your place, you want to make sure you have enough food for two dozen. One time we were invited to a buffet dinner at the house of a woman who ran out of dinner the first hour. I mentioned to my hostess, who seemed shocked at this embarrassing turn of events, that we had, all of us, been *invited*.

"Yes," she said, "but I didn't think you'd all come."

I will never be that woman.

Thanksgiving 2002 was typical. We had fifteen holiday-defined family members and enough food to feed the 101st Airborne.

Everybody helps. This way I don't feel as if I'm my mother, stuck in the kitchen and too tired by the time we sit down to enjoy meal or company. I say if the gang's all here, the gang can all *do* something. Along with three meats we had three gravies and a large bowl of our friend Henry's Essential Mashed Potatoes (Henry Meer, owner and chef of the restaurant City Hall in New York, taught me how to make them) to act as primary conveyor of gravy to mouth. David was, as usual, the chief chef at my stove, which is something to give thanks for; David is a good friend who also happens to be a jazz guitarist — and a professional chef. The rest of us just like to cook. Well, most of us. My pal Nadine, David's wife, doesn't cook. She eats. Food, like art, needs someone to appreciate it.

But try not to get in her way.

David made the mashed potatoes and two kinds of stuffing (one was cornbread), roasted some beets and yams, composed a corn pudding and — midmorning — whipped up a batch of almond cookies to keep the other cooks cooking.

I made the goose cabbage. Rolfe used to say he didn't like cabbage, but that was before he tried it shredded, sautéed in goose drippings, and finished with a little bit of chicken broth and a lot of pepper. We had Brussels sprouts too, because Majda, who had traveled the farthest, coming to New England from the Greek island of Santorini, insisted. Most of my family rates Brussels sprouts up there with spit, but Majda performed some magic in which a great deal of garlic was involved, and even those who claimed to hate them were seen eating them.

Carol blanched green beans, tossed them with olive oil, pecans, sliced pears, and goat cheese, and drizzled on a small amount of balsamic vinegar. Carol had traveled from Houston to meet up at our house with Carolann, her daughter, a flight attendant based in New York. Carolann made a green salad. Rebecca, Josh's wife, made the vinaigrette. She also made the big yellow pine table beautiful, setting it with white china, linen napkins, and the good silver; and then she scattered the table with votive candles, dried leaves, and shot glasses stuffed with blossoms, everything in colors of late autumn: crimson, burgundy, umber, faded orange, and pale yellow. A gorgeous professional garden designer who is smart and funny and cooks? No dummy, my son.

For dessert, I baked apple and pecan pies the way Willie Pearl had taught me so many years ago. Jim made a pound cake — and cranberry relish, for which people seemed pathetically grateful, possibly because not caring for cranberries, I always managed to forget to serve them.

Rolfe was responsible for port, pinot noir, Armagnac, and champagne.

To be sure people don't go away hungry before dinner, we opened the feast hours earlier with platters of Tids & Bits. You don't know what Tids & Bits are? Yes, you do. They are anything edible that someone brings, or you already had on hand, or might happened to have ordered from a food catalogue — as long as you can eat it with your fingers.

We put out the spiced pecans Carol had brought from Houston. We served Parmesan aioli (left over from two days before, when I'd used it as a dip for asparagus) spread on grilled slices of French bread and broiled until some bubbles showed up. We put out the little pastry cups filled with creamed spinach that had come from the Neiman Marcus Holiday Catalogue. (I used to order the pepper-coated baked ham from their catalogue every Thanksgiving, until one year the catalogue didn't offer it and Neiman's wouldn't give me the name of the supplier, no matter how nicely I begged. Don't say no to reporters. If *you* want the best-tasting, juiciest water-free, pepper-coated baked ham available anywhere, you too can order one by calling the supplier to Neiman Marcus, Ham I Am! in Plano, Texas, at 800-742-6426. Tell them I sent you. Some secrets are meant to be shared.) The Tids & Bits are accompanied by champagne. It was the champagne that got me in trouble at the 2002 Thanksgiving and I never drank a drop.

I asked Buddy, our favorite Big Blond Broadway leading man, to set up the champagne glasses, bucket, and bottle. To get him started, I filled the bucket halfway with water — if you use ice only, you can't get the bottle in deep enough to do any good — handed it to Buddy, and turned back to the sink to help Rebecca wash bowls. Not everybody volunteers for cleaning chores throughout the day; only those who want to eat. When I looked back, Buddy had dumped out the water, filled the bucket with ice, and was struggling, manfully if unsuccessfully, to stuff the bottle into it. I like to think I maintain an even strain, that our holidays are not like my grandmother's, or my mother's. Ours, I tell myself, are a stress-free zone, no tears, no fuss. I also like to pretend I'm not a controlling bitch. Sometimes it leaks out.

"Buddy, you ass! You threw out the water? How could you be so dumb?"

It was half an hour before I noticed Buddy was missing. When I asked other people what had happened to him, they said *I* had.

"Was I rude?"

"Worse," they said. All of them.

I found Buddy on the living room sofa, contemplating a retreat to his house in Pennsylvania. I told him to ignore me — I was a world-class fool; everybody knew that. I begged him to stay. Being a gentleman as well as a good friend, he agreed. No wonder certain unsavory holiday traditions are hard to shake. We breed them.

Christmas was mild. There were only seven of us: Rolfe and me; Josh and Rebecca; Elizabeth, Rolfe's mother; Casey, who once had lived with us in the New York house (and you would know as Legate Demar in one of the *Star Trek* series); and Brigit, Casey's pretty lady, a writer of cookbooks and oh joy oh joy — a chef herself. What could go wrong? I remembered Thanksgiving and cut my coffee intake by half.

Mama always cooked the exact same big-deal meal for Christmas that she'd cooked barely four weeks earlier for Thanksgiving. Christmas at our house is simple. You get roast tenderloin, a potato gratin, and Caesar salad. Steak, baked, and salad. Maybe some sautéed mushrooms with the beef and a hot fudge sundae made with peppermint candy-cane ice cream for dessert, but the theme remains: big flavor, small work. I had Christmas dinner down pat. It was the other stuff that got to me around Christmas.

1986. Mama had died three years before, at sixty-nine. My children and I were spending Christmas in the city. Cousins Billy and Alvin had come up from Houston. That afternoon we'd watched a tape of *Lonesome Dove*. Texans do this.

They shouldn't'a took me, Gus.

I know, honey. But they did. They did.

Thus does fictional hero Augustus McCrae explain reality to Lorena, who has been brutally beaten and raped by outlaws. It shouldn't have happened. But it did.

What shouldn't have happened.

What did happen.

My mother shouldn't have given up on living after my father died, but she did, and every Christmas I got angry at her because I wasn't through needing a mother, even if until the last years of her life we fought most of the time. Holidays always put our differences into focus: I wasn't what she had in mind as a daughter. I hated pink and liked boys and, to her taste, was either too fond of them or too competitive with them. I wanted a career. Insisted on it. Mama had one. Once. She was the buyer for the children's section of a small Texas department store. My father told her to quit; people would think he couldn't support his wife. Mother refused. Later, at family holidays, somebody would always tell the story of how Daddy got Mama to stop working. Seems there was a big storm. When Daddy left his office for the day, he customarily picked up Mama at the store and drove her home. That day he didn't show. Mama walked home in the hard, cold rain. Daddy drove by her, waved, and kept going. It was a long walk. Saddened and sick, Mama quit her job the next day.

Everybody always laughed at that story.

After that, Mama turned herself into Daddy's corporate wife and my nagging mother. We were her only job. But I grew up and moved away, and my father died when he was sixty-four. Now Mama was really out of work. She stopped traveling. She stopped going out to dinner with friends. Soon she rarely left the house. Eventually she rarely left her chair. After the first stroke, she sat around, waiting for the second. Mama lived her last year in a nursing home, immobile, and deeply mad at God for taking from her all the things — the only things — by which she had been forced to define herself: her home, her husband, her child. My mother was an angry, moving, breathing human being who decided to stop moving and breathing.

It shouldn't have happened, but it did.

Usually at Christmas I enjoyed spending a little while alone with the tree, both of us twinkling in time. But that year in New York, thinking about Mama, wishing she were with me, knowing that at some level she had *chosen* not to be, only the tree twinkled. All is calm, all is dysfunctional.

"Tree," I said . . .

From the kitchen, a crash. Cousin Billy was making pies; earlier I'd heard him cussing the pots and pans. He must have dropped one. Upstairs my daughter was playing guitar; her song drifted, further interrupting a private conversation with a tree. The phone rang. It was my son. Had I bought the oranges to put in the toes of the Christmas stockings, or should he? The doorbell rang. *What now?* Only Cousin Alvin, who had locked himself out by mistake. He said he'd gone to buy a wreath to hang from the front door. Was this okay or would somebody come along and steal the wreath because it was New York City where everybody knew people would steal anything, even a few branches and a piece of ribbon and why Linda stayed here he really couldn't understand?

"Quiet time is impossible around this place," I harrumphed to the tree. I whined some more, and then got up to go do whatever needed doing, but by the time I got to the kitchen I discovered I was humming the song my daughter was playing. Billy smiled at me, and gently removed a piece of wreath stuck to Alvin's hair. Pretty soon they were humming too. Life had crept into the house and into me — loud, clumsy, and all at once. Life, served family-style. Mama, like Daddy, my grandparents and aunts and uncles and all the rest, would never again be here to celebrate it with us, but there *would* be a Christmas. The tree twinkled, and said nothing.

The best holiday is the Fourth of July.

Summer is the purest good time for the senses. I don't ordinarily find the odor of mothballs enticing, but in summer mothball smell brings back good memories of camp. Then there is the smell of chlorine, honeysuckle, geraniums, steaks on the grill, Coppertone, new-mown grass, and old roses. The air just before and right after a thunderstorm. The *sea*. There's more: certain sounds. I know it's summer if I hear the tinkle of bells on an ice cream truck. Mentally my feet start running and I'm hollering, "Mama — I need a nickel!" Baseball on the radio. Children's voices in a pool. Wind rustling through the highest leaves of a tree you're lying under. The squeak of a rotating table fan. My mother singing an old hymn.

Splash.

There is no better summer sound than that. And there is no better eating than this: homemade ice cream (only vanilla counts; all right, maybe peach, but don't invite me). Corn on the cob. Tomatoes. Melons. Mama's fresh summer-squash casserole. Green beans. Green anything. I love putting together a feast for Independence Day. I begin the morning by listening to the folks on NPR read aloud the Declaration of Independence. At the end, I shove my fist into the air and cheer — *Right on!* — and then go to the Farmer's Market to buy what looks most fresh. Next I go to Guido's, world-famous in the Berkshires, to buy meat, lemons, limes, whatever the farmers aren't selling. Once home, I blanch the green vegetables, laying them out next to a bowl of homemade mayonnaise. On another platter I alternate slices of dirt-warm tomatoes and cool mozzarella, showering them with olive oil and handfuls of basil. Rolfe grills chicken or steak or ribs. I grill corn, zucchini, red onions, and sweet peppers. The watermelon is cooling in a big tub of ice water. Once I had invited two friends for lunch. It was late August. There was homemade cream-of-tomato soup. I meant to serve it cold. Then we would have lump crabmeat salad made with baby arugula and capers I had smuggled back from Greece, plus a hunk of St. André and some peaches. All of which was well and would have been good, if the two friends had not brought two friends. I had enough crab, mayo, capers, and lettuce to stretch the salad. I had plenty of cheese and peaches. I did not have enough tomato soup.

Refrigerator staring is what you do when you can't think of anything else to do in a perplexing situation, of which a shortage of tomato soup is only one. Refrigerators, I'm convinced, hold the answers to all questions, possibly the secret of life itself. And so I stared. There must be something I could add to soup to make more soup.

Low-fat milk? Mostly water and sugar, and tastes gray.

More cream? It was tomato soup I was after, not gravy.

Soy milk? Never, unless pressed by a guest, had I allowed soy milk in my house. You have to draw the line somewhere.

Cranberry juice? Did we really want to pee all afternoon?

Beer? Always thought it must have tasted better going into the horse.

Maybe a bottle of red wine.

Maybe not.

Is that half a watermelon on the bottom shelf?

Well, it was red.

I chopped and seeded some chunks and threw them into the blender with the cold tomato soup, in batches. The result was a lovely pink-red, somewhere between a Cosmopolitan and blood. I topped each bowl of soup with a little stream of sour cream diluted with lime juice, and a few ribbons of fresh mint from the garden. Cold tomato-watermelon soup became a staple around our place and a symbol of how I felt about summer food; it had to be colorful, abundant, and most of all, fresh.

Which is why I was so shocked the year Rolfe and Josh said they didn't want any of that wonderful stuff for the Fourth of July. They wanted hot dogs. Ballpark or Hormel. The buns had to be the ones that look like split-open slices of bread. Mustard had to be French's. Ketchup had to be from a plastic squeeze bottle. No vegetables. Maybe some potato salad, but not that "funny" kind I made with weird green stuff (for these people I grew an herb garden?). In addition to dull potato salad, they wanted potato chips, Fritos, and bean dip in a pull-top can. They wanted grape Kool-Aid, the kind you put lots of sugar in. They wanted Oreo cookies.

Junk food? Processed food? Preservatives? Chemical flavors? Squeeze-bottle sauce?

Store-bought potato salad? What about *my* plans? Frankly, my dear, they didn't give a damn; they had their own. Thus began the family fight I have come to think of as the Battle of the White Man's Fourth of July.

"But Linda," Rolfe said, "why can't we have what *we* want?"

"Because it's dumb. And so are you. In summer, you eat *fresh* food."

"Mom, stop bullying us," my son said.

A tension convention in the making.

Sometimes you have to choose between being right and being happy. I passed the Farmer's Market and Guido's and headed for the chain-owned supermarket. At the deli counter there were large plastic tubs of different potato salads. One appeared to have nothing in it but potatoes and mayonnaise — so boring just looking at it made me yawn. When I bought some, the fellow behind the counter reacted as though I'd done something really intelligent.

"We sell a lot of this. Guys like it."

I couldn't help myself. On my way home, I stopped at the Farmer's Market and bought some perfect yellow squash, a red pepper, and an onion. I would make Mama's summer-squash casserole. *Real* summer goodness, just the way Mama made it. Maybe they wouldn't notice. The guys started the grill. The womenfolk set out jars, tubes, plastic bags, and tin cans, and made a pitcher of poisonously purple Kool-Aid. I started on Mama's squash casserole, sautéing minced onion in butter, adding chopped red pepper and mashed steamed squash. I stirred, seasoned, and tasted. Not right. I telephoned Cousin Shirley in Texas, the keeper of family recipes. What was I missing? What gave Mama's squash casserole that special fresh taste?

"Why, Linda Jane," Cousin Shirley said, "you forgot to add the Cheez Whiz."

I thought she was joking. She wasn't.

A high-speed dash back to the supermarket.

"Excuse me, where in this store might one find cheese with no cheese in it? You know — Cheez Whiz?"

I whispered in case he had taste buds.

"In the refrigerated cheese case. Where did you think?"

"But why?" I said, when we found it. "This stuff has the shelf life of a jar of cobalt. There's nothing in it that needs refrigeration — certainly not cheese. Look at the label. Made with *cheese food*. What the hell is that — something they feed the cheese?"

"Lady, you want it or not?"

Once I added the Cheez Whiz, it tasted just like Mama's fresh summer-squash casserole. It tasted right even if it was wrong. The hot dogs weren't bad either. Not even the Kool-Aid. And to think we nearly had a first-class family fight over a few weenies and a cup or two of chemicals. I forgave the men for wanting to eat trash. They forgave me for not understanding I wanted to eat trash too. Cousin Billy says that to love people, you must be prepared to forgive them a dozen times a day.

This year I'm planning a huge old-fashioned family Christmas in the Berkshires. Josh and Rebecca will drive up from New York. Vanessa and Blake will fly in from Oregon with Violet, my first grandchild. Cousins Shirley, Tom, Billy, and Alvin will fly up from Texas. My other, younger, cousins will fly in from Maine, where they emigrated and broke their parents' hearts. My cousins from Austin, with whom we haven't shared Christmas since we were children, will make their way here from Austin. Same for the cousins in Spokane. Who knows, maybe Mama and Daddy will drop in from wherever. We'll all be together one more time. Now we know how to do it without wanting to kill one another. Now we know how much we've missed one another, and how we need one another, and these special times together. It's been a long road home. We were lost, but now we're found.

Josh tells me he and Rebecca may go to England to spend Christmas with her family. Vanessa says she may not be able to get enough time off from work. My cousins say . . .

Their voices fade, and in the silence I am gifted with a moment of pure clarity — a laser beam of insight — in which I finally get it.

My plans aren't going to work. No plans are going to work. There are always going to be those who are missing. There is always going to be stress and strain among those who aren't. There is always going to be some Cheez Whiz in the fresh vegetables. And we are going to muddle our way through this holiday thing every year, through all the holidays of all the years, because families, despite all that is fine and precious about them, despite tradition, love, and hope, despite passing time and sweet memory, are — and always will be — *messy*. So what? I know what I know, and I know that every last one of them *will* be home for the holidays.

If only in my dreams.

Mama's Secret-Ingredient Summer-Squash Casserole

SERVES SIX

6 yellow summer squash, chunked
$1/2$ stick butter
1 onion, chopped
$1/2$ cup chopped red bell pepper (I add a
  little chopped jalapeño pepper too)
1 egg, beaten
$1/2$ large jar Cheez Whiz
$3/4$ to 1 cup crumbled saltines
Salt and pepper to taste
1 tablespoon melted butter

1. Cook, drain, and mash the squash. (I steam them, but you can boil them if you wish.) Put the mashed squash into a mixing bowl.
2. Preheat the oven to 350 degrees.
3. Sauté the onion and red pepper in the butter over a medium heat. Don't let

them brown. Add to the squash.

4. Stir in the beaten egg, the Cheez Whiz, and most of the crumbled crackers (save a little bit for topping the casserole) while everything is still warm. Add salt and pepper to taste. Stir again.

5. Put everything in a Pyrex dish (8 by 8 or 9 by 12 inches). Bake for 20 to 30 minutes.

6. Fifteen minutes before it's done, mix the reserved crushed crackers with the melted butter and scatter on top.

7. When people say how good this tastes and ask you what's in it, lie.

Superfresh Cold Cream-of-Tomato Watermelon Soup

MAKES TWO QUARTS, MORE OR LESS

Follow the recipe below or buy the tomato soup at a good takeaway market. For homemade soup, I use canned tomatoes. So shoot me. Everything else is fresh.

2 (28-ounce) cans whole tomatoes (preferably Italian) and their liquid
$1^1/_2$ tablespoons brown sugar
4 tablespoons butter
4 large shallots, chopped
1 tablespoon tomato paste
2 tablespoons flour
2 cups chicken stock or canned chicken broth (if using canned broth, don't salt until the very end; you may not need any)
1 cup heavy cream
Salt and cayenne to taste

1 quart chopped, seeded watermelon
1 tablespoon sour cream
1 lime
Fresh mint, chopped

1. Preheat the oven to 450 degrees. Spread the tomatoes on a nonstick cookie sheet, reserving their liquid. Sprinkle with the brown sugar. Bake 30 minutes. Peel off the tomatoes and set aside in a bowl.
2. Heat the butter in a saucepan on low. Add the shallots and tomato paste. Cover and cook, stirring occasionally, until the shallots are softened. Add the flour and whisk until everything is combined. Whisk in the chicken stock, the juice from the tomato cans, and the roasted tomatoes. Bring to a boil. Reduce heat and simmer for 10 minutes. Puree the mixture in a food processor or blender. Add salt and cayenne to taste.
3. Stir in the cream. Let it sit until it's room temperature and then put in the refrigerator to chill.
4. When the soup is chilled (overnight works best), put it in the blender, in batches, with the seeded watermelon chunks.

5. Serve the soup cold. Thin the sour cream with lime juice and water until it is the consistency of heavy cream and then drizzle it in ribbons over the top of the soup. Scatter chopped mint over the whole bowl.

THIRTEEN

The Woman Who Hated Cruising

(1986–2001)

Me on a big boat with plastic-clad people scratching around foreign ports for the best deal on T-shirts and gold chains? Cruising was what you did on a Friday night. Awright, a few Friday nights had passed since I'd done that kind of cruising, but was I ready for the bingo party? They were offering two first-class airfares to England, three days in London followed by a seven-day Atlantic crossing, the maiden voyage of a new ship. All I had to do was to give a speech, one little 45-minute talk. The cruise, they said, would be celebrity-laden. I asked which celebrities would be doing the ladening.

"Ann Blyth. Glenn Ford. Frankie Laine."

Aw shit. Those people were stars when I was a kid. Now they were, well, people on the beach.

"Helen Hayes," they said.

"*The* Helen Hayes? Why would Helen

Hayes want to . . . ?"

"Because it will be wonderful," they lied.

How had I arrived at this place so soon? I was only forty-four and until recently had been a small-to-medium-well-known network newswoman. I anchored. I scooped. I eavesdropped on other lives. Sometimes people gave me prizes for being snoopy. Once in a while young women sent letters asking how they could grow up to do what I did. I never knew what to tell them; I was never sure exactly what it was I did, but as they say in baseball, I had been to The Show, and as sometimes happens in baseball too, I had turned out to be a troublemaker whose salary at some point was not worth the cost of putting up with me. Ask Jim Bouton how it works.

When ABC canceled *Our World*, I told them I wanted out of my long-term contract. Roone Arledge, president of ABC News, said I was too valuable to lose, an interesting statement from the fellow who'd just stamped "invalid" on my best effort. I had to find a way to threaten Roone Arledge with something worse than my leaving.

"How," my agent said, "can *you* threaten *him?*"

"Tell Roone I said if he doesn't let me

out of my contract, I'll stay."

Roone thought it over and released me the next day.

Welcome to the beach.

I said yes to the cruise; I could become an old Glenn Ford at a much younger age. Rolfe and I flew to London, tooled around, took a bus provided by the cruise line to Southampton, and boarded the ship, which someone had worked hard to transform into a floating Las Vegas hotel. I met Helen Hayes. The boat ride went downhill from there. The seas were rough and the skies gray. Rolfe, an accomplished aerobatic pilot, took seasick the first day and spent the rest of the trip horizontal, doped up, and still moaning. The beds were hard and made funny noises when you rolled over. Some toilets flushed five minutes after you pushed the lever, or not at all. The food was indifferent, but there was plenty of it. The musicians played off-key and no one noticed. The pool had to be emptied because someone had shat in it, not that the weather encouraged anybody to want to use it for much else. On the next-to-last night at sea, Greek sailors, in an effort to breathe life into what I'd come to think of as the Voyage of the Dimmed, encouraged passengers to drink many small glasses of ouzo and dance around the deck with them, shouting *"Opa!"* Because of unanticipated rolling of the ship (something not quite right with the stabilizers, the purser said later), the Greek sailors managed to knock several passengers ass-over-teakettle, sending one old lady to the infirmary, where the ship's doctor, it turned out, was two decks up, shouting *"Opa!"* Those in charge of making people happy could be seen breaking down in tears before they got drunk too. When I got home, one thing was clear: I was the woman who hated cruising.

I am a slow learner. The next year the same line invited me on another cruise. The ship was going to stop at Leningrad, soon to be renamed St. Petersburg. I'd been in Berlin in 1989 when the wall came down. Being in Leningrad for the name change was an interesting idea, especially as I could, for once, watch something big happen without having to try to explain it thirty seconds later. I mentioned this to Rolfe, who said words I don't believe are worth recording here, the central theme being "Go alone." I did. On August 19, 1991, the day we were to dock in Leningrad, the act formerly known as the Soviet Union put on a coup. The ship turned.

The announcement came from the bridge.

"Due to circumstances beyond our control . . . not our fault . . . *force majeure* . . . and we're sure you will all enjoy the extra day in Stockholm."

Never again, I said. It helped that I was no longer on the beach. Lucky Duck Productions had turned out to be profitable. *Nick News* was a kid-TV phenom, and I'd morphed into an improbable, raggedy-feathered, journalistic Big Bird. Our shows on other networks were doing well. My dance card was filled. So why did I say yes when, in 1996, Crystal Cruises invited me to float around the Mediterranean for two weeks? Madness comes to mind. But there was more to it than that. Even on bad cruises, I had come to appreciate some of the advantages of messing about in big boats. Like takeoff. You don't have to sit down, strap yourself into a narrow, chemical-fibered, supposedly fire-retardant seat, or swallow a Valium to keep the boat from falling out of the sky. Departure by ship is gentle; one moment you're here and the next moment the ship moves — so slowly that at first you barely notice — taking you there. A plane gets you where you want to go faster, but most of us can't make our brains or bodies keep pace. We leave something behind that, like lost luggage, will take days to catch up, if it ever does. You can take a trip on an airplane, but you cannot really travel on one any more than you can travel by catapult. All airplanes do is expel you from here to there. You can't see the world by leaving it.

This ship, the *Crystal Symphony*? It was different. Everything worked. I lived in luxury. My stateroom had sliding glass doors and a private piece of deck. At night, with the doors open, I could hear (and smell) the sea rocking me to sleep. In addition to a bed, I had a sofa, two armchairs, a desk, a cabinet with a refrigerator and minibar, ample closet space, drawers for stowing my stuff, a satellite telephone and television, a VCR, and a tiled bathroom with a full-length tub and separate walk-in shower. Make a little speech and live like a duchess for two weeks? Justice is deeply nearsighted.

"Even so," people say to me, "don't you feel trapped on a ship?"

Some of these are people who belong to private country clubs, live in gated communities, and never meet anyone they don't already know. On a ship, I go to sleep in one place and wake up in another. Try that in Homeland Acres. Anyway, a cruise comes with choices. Be alone, or not. I go both ways. My time by myself is nearly as precious as time spent with people I might not meet rafting the Colorado River or hiking the Appalachian Trail or flying too fast down too steep a slope in Telluride. And if I hadn't met some of these people, the loss would have been mine.

I met Ruth and Bennie my first day aboard the *Symphony*. A woman of a certain age, with black-and-silver hair, red lips that seemed always to be smiling, and eyes that seemed always to be accepting, Ruth dressed in layers, usually black and/or white cotton, and never looked anything but chic. The night she showed up for dinner wearing a shocking-pink silk jacket, she was the most beautiful woman on the ship. Bennie was older than Ruth, a big man with a voice and generosity of spirit to match. He could not bear anyone in his presence to be unhappy, or see wishes go unfulfilled if there was something he could do about it. Bennie was the irresistible force. Ruth and Bennie were educated, curious, witty, happy people, and they took me into their hearts and made a home for me. When I first met them, I could not figure out why they were so kind to a stranger, a deeply flawed one at that.

And then I learned their stories.

Bennie, a German Jew, was the only member of his family to survive Auschwitz. A young Bennie had in fact escaped from Auschwitz. For all practical purposes, the war was over, but the camp had not been liberated. Bennie didn't want to wait to find out if, as a departing gesture, the Nazis would kill everyone they hadn't already killed. He ran. A German soldier spotted him and raised his rifle, aiming at Bennie's head. Bennie stopped running and stood still. It seemed like a long time, he said, before the German soldier, understanding the Thousand Year Reich had come to an end 988 years too soon, lowered his rifle and looked away. Bennie ran all the way to America. Ruth's father, seeing which way the wind blew, had taken his family out of Germany in the mid-thirties. His instincts were right, but he made a small compass error. He took them to Shanghai. Ruth spent the war in a Japanese prison camp, after which, at eighteen, she too made her way to America, to the University of Chicago, where she met Bennie. I like to think that having seen the worst men could do, the two of them were more tolerant of ordinary human failings. Certainly they were tolerant of mine. They forgave me

347

sins they didn't even know I'd committed. I fell in love with Ruth and Bennie. I know their children and grandchildren. When Daniel, their grandson, was only ten, they brought him on a cruise and turned him over to me to spend his evenings watching movies I thought he should see. The first was *To Kill a Mockingbird*. We both cried. When I go to Chicago, Ruth and Bennie are the first people I call. Daniel is the second.

And it all began on a big boat filled with strangers.

Apart from the gift of getting to know people like Ruth and Bennie, the best thing about cruising is that it is a tasting menu; it allows you to take small bites of places you might otherwise have missed. I leave certain countries or islands or cultures, knowing I have no need to go back, but others I leave, wanting more, and I have returned to those places on my own. Here are a few bites from my years with Crystal; some are tastier than others.

In Malta, I hook up with three new friends from the ship who share a desire not to see fortresses. We hire a car, leave Valletta, and head for St. Peter's Pool, a place of white rock as hot as the turquoise water is cold. We swim and dive and splash one another as children do when no grown-ups are near. *I see skies of blue and clouds of white*. In a nearby village, we stop at a small dockside restaurant. The man who greets us at the door speaks English.

"Are you the owner?" I ask.

He smiles. "The bank is the owner."

We're taken through the kitchen and out back to the harbor, where piles of still-living sea creatures lie in clumps on paving stones. He asks us to choose. We say we can't; there's too much. He says he will choose for us, but he doesn't. He gives us some of everything. After fried bay shrimp, grilled calamari, fresh anchovies (forget everything you ever hated about anchovies; you would love these), small clams in a spicy tomato sauce, sautéed giant crayfish, and a kick-ass plate of grilled scampi with an aioli that makes me want to lick the bowl, he's still worried. Are we sure we've had enough?

"Malta is not just a fortress," he says. "It's a good café."

When the *Crystal Symphony* leaves a port, it does so to Louis Armstrong's definitive version of "It's a Wonderful World" played over the ship's speakers. One evening I decide to throw a sail-away party, inviting eight people. We stand on my deck

349

and listen to Louis. Land recedes. The setting sun turns us from frogs into princes and princesses. *The colors of the rainbow, so pretty in the sky, are also on the faces of people going by.* I have put on a black leotard, opaque black tights, and high-heeled pumps. Over it I wear the long jacket of my best black pants suit. I tuck a white scarf under my lapels and add the black felt, snap-brim Sinatra hat bought for me at a flea market in Villefranche by Buddy, the six-foot-four, blond, blue-eyed Broadway singer with a showstopping baritone, who entertains passengers in the ship's big theater, a genuine leading man, especially if nice counts. (As you already know, Buddy has become a good friend and part of our "holiday" family.) I put on red lipstick, which I never wear, and cock the hat just so. A hat's not a hat till it's tilted. I'm Judy Garland in the "Get Happy" number from *Summer Stock*. Would I do this at home? Never. But I'm not at home. The sail-away party rocks. I add the slacks before we go to dinner.

Sailing out of Taormina, I stand on deck, flirting with the young Sicilian longshoreman nine stories below me on the dock. As he releases the last line and we move slowly into the harbor, he blows me a kiss. If the distance between us hadn't been so great, we would have ignored each other.

In Copenhagen, the statue of the Little Mermaid looks so sad on her rock, naked, violated by people who climb up to be photographed holding on to her legs where they puddle into fins around her feet. Her face is averted, eyes looking out to sea. I'm embarrassed for her. What this world won't do to a woman who's different.

Midnight on the Mediterranean. Thunder wakes me, scoring my world. Lightning clarifies my vision. I go out on the deck naked. Waves, the whiteness of their crests like icing spread over and over again on top of a black cake, slam the ship. I let the rain wash me. The storm sings. *The bright blessed day, the dark sacred night. And I think to myself* . . .

At a café in Lisbon, Kirk (a friend, and an executive at Crystal) and I chuckle over the English translation on our menu. Under the heading "cheese," it says:

1. Cheese from mountain.
2. Cheese not from mountain.

Under the heading "cakes and pies," it says:

1. Cake.
2. Pie.

We are both collectors of significantly silly signage. Kirk tells me about an announcement he saw on a menu in a Warsaw restaurant: "As for the tripe we serve, you will be singing its praises to your grandchildren on your deathbed." A notice in the lobby of a hotel in Ankara: "You are invited to visit our restaurant where you can eat Middle East food in a European ambulance." On the wine list at a Swiss restaurant: "Our wines leave you nothing to hope for." I tell him about the Holiday Inn in Seabrook, a small, run-down coastal town outside Houston until NASA got there. With the space age came a sophistication unfamiliar to Texas, certainly to Seabrook. The newly built Holiday Inn had a wine list. First I'd ever seen. Until recently it had been illegal to sell alcohol by the drink in Texas, but hey, astronauts will be astronauts, and with Lyndon Johnson leading the way, Texas was by God going to be modern. The wine list read:

1. Red
2. White

Beneath that it said, "Please order by number."

In Málaga, I go walking with Buddy. We

go to a tapas bar called Bar No Gueños, ordering many small plates. The bill comes to thirteen dollars. Elated by the quality of the meal and its paltry price, I convey to the waiter in my wretched Spanish that we would like a pound of the Serrano ham, sliced, and a pound of the smoked goat cheese, sliced — to go. Buddy says it will be his treat. We have only twenty minutes to get back to the harbor. The nice waiter says he understands. I make a run to the ladies' room; while I'm there, he brings Buddy the wrapped package of ham and cheese, and the bill. Buddy, whose arithmetic is worse than mine, gives the nice waiter his Visa card. We make it to the ship in time, barely. As we sail away from Málaga, I ask Buddy what the ham and cheese cost. He says he doesn't know; foreign money confuses him so, but lunch was so cheap it couldn't have been much. He shows me his Visa receipt. I convert it into dollars. The nice waiter has charged Buddy $500. The moral: If you're in Málaga, avoid Bar No Gueños, and if you don't, make sure not to let your mouth outdistance your math.

George and Lara, who work in the ship's computer room, and Lara's mom, Audrey; George's lover, Steve; Tim, a passenger from Seattle; and I decide to visit Cagaloglu Hamami, the oldest Turkish baths in Istanbul. At the front door, only the men are allowed to enter. Lara, Audrey, and I are sent to the women's entrance, a small door around back where the garbage is picked up. Inside, Alyla, the largest naked woman I've ever seen — not entirely naked if you count the red nylon panties — instructs us to disrobe, wrap ourselves in towels, and come into the baths. The "baths" are a gigantic damp room with arches and marble floors and slabs under a high, domed ceiling patterned with star-shaped holes to let in the sun, which, best I can tell, is the only light source. The place smells of mildew, almond oil, and something else — the girls' locker room at Lamar High School? There's no pool, no Jacuzzi, no sauna, no steam, just a faucet with dripping water. Alyla tells us to take off the towels and lie face down on marble slabs. She moves from one woman to the next, straddling us, kneading as though we were small lumps of dough, which, compared with Alyla's queen-sized loaf of a body, we are.

"Does this hurt?" Alyla says.

"No," I say, not wanting to appear a wuss.

"Then I do harder."

"Alyla? It hurts now."

"Good. I do more harder."

After she stops the pummeling, she lifts me into her arms, takes soap and a washcloth, and bathes me as though I were a baby. An odd sensation, being held close by a 300-pound woman in red nylon panties who's recently done her best to kill me with her bare hands. I close my eyes, relax, and realize it feels good to be a baby again, to be held by a big person. Alyla rinses me, rubs my body with almond oil, and moves on. I may be paralyzed for life, but I'm clean. I've never been so clean. When we recover enough to dress and meet our male friends outside, they tell us about the steam room, the sauna, the scrubbing with brushes, the heated soaking pools, the spiced tea, the fruit, the incense. They seem to have been to different baths, which of course they have — they've been to the *men's* baths.

But we had Alyla.

At sea in the Dardanelles I think about Winston Churchill's colossal blunders here during World War I — a man whose political career might have sunk without a trace, had it not been for an Austrian housepainter named Adolf.

"And off the starboard side," the captain says over the public address system, "is Gallipoli."

I stop thinking about Churchill and start thinking about Mel Gibson.

I like sea days, the days between ports, when I can lie on my deck and read for hours, or stroll the public decks, smiling at faces I recognize — joining someone for a hamburger outside or eating a Cobb salad alone at my window table in the dining room. I go to the ship's health club and work out until I feel so righteous I head straight for the make-your-own-sundae bar. The food on board Crystal ships is worth the calories. (The mushroom cappuccino they serve on the *Crystal Symphony* one night between Gibraltar and Barcelona is so delicious I ask the waiter to tell the chef how much I enjoyed it. The waiter returns; the chef says he would be pleased to make some for me every night. And I don't even know the man.) Usually I eat lightly when I'm on the ship — make believe I never said that about the make-your-own-sundae bar — saving my splurges for the days we're in port; however, once during every two-week cruise, the *Crystal Symphony* lays out an open-air lunch it calls an Asian Buffet. I think of it as the Pig Party.

There is an abundance of goodies, but for me there is only The Pig. I have a pigskin jones. Not my fault; I'm a Southerner — well, a Texan, but in matters of pig there is no difference. Pig is basic, necessary, transcendent. Call it hereditary swine fever. I suffer from the disease as often as I can. But I'm not a glutton; I add lettuce to the plate so people will know this. Eating roasted pigskin under the sun on top of a ten-story-tall ship in the middle of big water is one of life's little unexpected gifts.

In Stockholm, I take two women, fellow passengers, to Uriksdals Wardhüs, a restaurant in a park outside the city. They ask us where we're from, and when we tell them, they put a tiny American flag on our table. Raise it, they say, when you want service. I check: they have dozens of small flags. The smorgasbord offers thirty different kinds of herring. I try twenty-two, all of them better than herring I've eaten in America, and then finish off with a plate of crayfish boiled with dill. One of the women won't eat the crayfish; she says they look like things she steps on in the corners of her apartment in Palm Springs. After lunch I walk through the older part of Stockholm. Ingmar Bergman said Stockholm isn't a city, simply a rather large village in

the middle of some forests and some lakes. "You wonder what it thinks it is doing there, looking so important." Bergman may have been right in his description, but what's wrong with a rather large village surrounded by some forests and lakes? The man has seen too many Woody Allen movies.

Monte Carlo. Ruth and I are at an outdoor café in the square. To the left is the casino and across the square, the Hôtel de Paris. Both buildings are relics of La Belle Époque, wedding-cake structures from a time when a gentleman would no more think of showing up for dinner dressed in anything less than black tie than a lady would dream of leaving her diamonds upstairs. The square is lined with flowers, palm trees, and tourists. Ruth and I dish. The woman in the purple-and-green running suit — never ran anywhere but to her refrigerator, that one. The skinny broad in the four-inch platform sandals — ought to supply crutches with those shoes. I've made a reservation for dinner at Louis XV, the three-star Michelin restaurant in the hotel. I ask Ruth to join me for dinner. We decide to go confirm the reservation, but at the door we're stopped by a snooty French fellow in a morning coat who tells us only guests may enter. I see. This is how they keep the tourists from seeing the lobby, snapping pictures, and, heaven forbid, touching something.

"I'm here to confirm my reservation tonight at Louis XV."

He still doesn't look happy. We aren't wearing plastic and there are no cameras draped around our necks, but I'm wearing sneakers and there are, after all, standards to be upheld. Ruth speaks to him in rapid French. I don't know how many languages Ruth speaks. I'm not sure she does either. He turns red and opens the door for us.

"What did you say to him?"

"I told him I was watching the Grand Prix from my family's suite in this hotel before he was born in whatever backwater village his ignorant parents met and mated."

"Is that true?"

"Well, yes, but it doesn't matter, really."

I will never know all there is to know about Ruth.

Our reservation confirmed, we leave the hotel to roam the two or three shopping streets that surround the square, trolling our way through Gucci, Fendi, Armani, Tiffany, and Chanel, buying nothing. This makes me feel superior. Look at all the money I'm not spending. In the Yves Saint Laurent boutique, Ruth spots a black-silk-and-satin tuxedo cut for a woman.

"Now this," Ruth says, "is spectacular."

It is. Even feels good to touch. "You could wear it tonight at dinner, Ruth."

"Not me, darling. You."

"Me? And then what would I do with it?"

"Oh, come on. You're always speaking at some banquet or another."

"Not wearing Yves Saint Laurent."

"Nonsense. There is a time for splurging. Today may be one of those times, my darling."

She calls over the salesperson and the next thing you know, I'm wearing a black-silk-and-satin tuxedo over a black cashmere camisole with a thin, silver-buckled belt around my waist and high-heeled black patent sandals on my feet. Maybe Ruth is right. Maybe this is one of those times. While I'm still thinking about the price of splurges, Ruth tells the man to send in a fitter. She says the suit must be altered in time for me to wear it to dinner.

"Of course, madame."

"Ah . . . Ruth?"

"Linda, give the man your American Express card and let's go back to the ship. We need to rest after so much exercise."

She's right about that. Signing the bill totally exhausts me. It may take years to recover from the sticker shock. Just after sunset we return to the boutique, where I put on my newly fitted finery, hoping I can still make next month's mortgage payment. I look in the mirror.

Damn. I look as good as I've ever looked in my adult life.

"Ruth, walk slower. I'm not used to heels this high."

"It's only a block, my darling."

Ruth is wearing black too, with white at her neck and cuffs. Her hair shines and her skin glows as always, from within. Or perhaps it's only that how you feel is how you look.

This time the doorman cannot bow low enough.

The dining room is gilt and damask, with

chandeliers and cherubs on the ceiling, which is about a thousand feet high. I'm another person, in another life. We're shown to the best table in the room. Uniformed men rush over to cater to our whims. My whim is easily catered; a minion has rolled a silver bread trolley to our table. Ruth persuades me to stop after choosing only five different kinds. Soon we're presented with dishes of big fat white asparagus, plus little skinny green ones and several other varieties I've never tasted, sliced in clever ways. Fresh morels. *Moreilles.* "Mor-ay," Ruth says, correcting my terrible French. The mor-ay nestle among the asparagus, and everything rests in a puddle of lemon sabayon. I want to get up and perform Snoopy's little dance to spring.

The chef sends out some little goody before and after every course — a nugget of fresh foie gras inside a puff pastry, a perfectly poached shrimp topped with beluga, a dainty silver goblet of grapefruit and champagne sorbet. We don't order dessert, which means we have to settle for a plate of petits fours and a box of chocolate truffles. The box is made of chocolate too. Only my high heels keep me in my chair now.

Leaving the restaurant, we consider going across the street to the casino. I tell

Ruth I have this vision of sitting at the baccarat table and reaching for a cigarette only to have a lighter snap open in front of my face. I look up. Over the flame, Sean Connery looks back.

"Bond's the name," he will say. "James Bond."

And I will say . . .

But the casino, run by the Principality of Monaco, requires a passport to enter it, and Ruth has left hers on board. Just as well. I don't smoke and have no idea how to play baccarat, or what I would say to Sean Connery, who's probably somewhere in Scotland eating grouse — shaken, not stirred. We pass the hotel, the casino, and Gucci and are heading down the path to the yacht harbor and the ship's tender. Cinderella is going back to her room to take off her glass slippers and soak her feet. The streets down here are dark. A formally dressed man passes us going the other way, toward the casino. He nods. I nod back.

"Ruth."

"Yes, my darling?"

"That man we just passed was Roger Moore."

"Yes, my darling."

And I think to myself, what a wonderful world.

Grilled Scampi with Double-Garlic Aioli from a Café Called Malta

SERVES FOUR

There is confusion over what scampi is. The *Food Lover's Companion* says scampi is the Italian name for the tail portion of any of several varieties of a species that's actually part of the lobster family, the most well known being the Dublin Bay Prawn, which can be found in the Mediterranean. In the United States the term *scampi* is often used to describe large shrimp that are split, brushed with garlic oil or garlic butter, and broiled. Should you care to know, one scampi is called a scampo.

1 head of garlic, the cloves separated, peeled, and chopped
3 tablespoons chopped fresh thyme leaves
$1/_2$ cup olive oil (and a little extra for brushing on the shrimp while they grill)

Salt and freshly ground pepper to taste
2 pounds jumbo shrimp (Try to get them
with the heads still on, and if you do,
leave the heads on. In any case, leave
the shells on.)

1. Put the garlic, thyme, and oil in the jar of a blender and blend until smooth. Season with salt and pepper.
2. Put the shrimp in a large bowl, pour the marinade over them, and let them marinate at room temperature for half an hour.
3. Make sure your fire is hot. I mean really hot. Shrimp cook quickly and you want to make sure you get some of the fire taste (and markings) without having to grill the shrimp until they're dried out.
4. Grill the shrimp for $1^1/_2$ to 2 minutes per side (brush with some olive oil when you turn them). The time will depend on the size of the shrimp, but again, overcooking shrimp misses the point. All the sweetness goes south. Remember that they will keep cooking in their shells for a short time after you take them off the fire.
5. Serve warm or at room temperature with a bowl of Double-Garlic Aioli

(or Double-Quick Garlic Aioli) for dipping. Or spreading. Or drizzling. You'll know what to do.

6. Go to sleep knowing you're safe from vampires for the next 24 hours.

Brigit's Double-Garlic Aioli

MAKES 1 $1/_3$ CUPS

My pal Brigit is a pro. This is her recipe. Mine follows. You will notice certain differences.

20 medium garlic cloves
1 large egg
1 tablespoon red-wine vinegar
1 teaspoon Dijon-style mustard
$1/_2$ teaspoon salt
$1/_2$ cup extra-virgin olive oil
$1/_2$ cup canola oil
1 tablespoon boiling water
$1^1/_2$ tablespoons fresh lemon juice
$1/_4$ teaspoon ground white pepper

1. Place the garlic in a small saucepan and cover with cold water. Bring to a boil and simmer for 30 seconds. Drain in a sieve, return to the pan,

and repeat the process two more times. Let the garlic cool in the sieve for 5 minutes.

2. In a food processor, combine the egg, garlic, vinegar, mustard, and salt. Puree for 15 to 30 seconds, until completely smooth, scraping down the sides as necessary.

3. With the motor running, drizzle in the olive and canola oils very slowly at first, then a little faster after the first $1/2$ cup or so has emulsified. Add the boiling water, lemon juice, and pepper. Process again. If the aioli is too thick, add a teaspoon or two of water.

4. For a bigger punch, reserve 5 of the garlic cloves, then push them through a press or mince finely. Sir this in at the end and let the aioli stand in the refrigerator overnight to mellow.

Linda's Double-Quick Garlic Aioli

5 garlic cloves, smashed and then minced
2 cups Hellman's mayonnaise
Juice of $1/2$ lemon
Olive oil as needed

Put the garlic in the food processor. Add a big spoonful of mayo and hit the ON button for 10 seconds. Add the rest of the mayonnaise and the lemon juice. Hit the ON button again and with the machine still running, drizzle olive oil into the mixture until it reaches the right consistency (it should be thick enough to not slide off a scampo when you dunk one, or a green bean either).

Mushroom Cappuccino from Crystal Cruise Line

SERVES EIGHT AS A STARTER

I have adapted this recipe to make it simpler, quicker, and more accessible to somebody like me, who wants the flavor, the silkiness, and the conceit of a soup disguised as coffee but can't always reach out and grab seven varieties of fresh mushrooms. My apologies to the chef.

1 ounce dried morels or 2 ounces fresh morels

$2^1/_2$ ounces portobello mushrooms, minus the stems

$2^1/_2$ ounces white mushrooms

3 ounces fresh or frozen porcini mushrooms (if you can't find them, substitute more portobello)

3 tablespoons extra-virgin olive oil

3 medium shallots, finely chopped

2 garlic cloves, finely chopped
Salt and freshly ground white pepper to
    taste
1 cup dry white wine
4 cups chicken broth
1 cup heavy cream

1. Soak the morels for 10 to 15 minutes
    in warm water. Wash them several
    times to remove sand. Cut the stems
    off and cut the small morels in half
    and the large ones in three or four
    parts. Slice all the other mushrooms.
2. In a small pan, heat the olive oil over
    medium heat, add all the different
    kinds of sliced mushrooms, and sweat
    them for 3 to 4 minutes. Add the
    chopped shallots and garlic and con-
    tinue to sweat for about 2 more min-
    utes. Season with salt and pepper.
3. Add the wine and reduce by half. Add
    the chicken broth and bring to a boil.
4. Add half of the heavy cream and
    bring to a boil again. Reduce heat and
    simmer the soup for about 25 minutes.
    Blend the soup in a food processor
    until it is smooth. Strain through
    cheesecloth, pushing down.
5. Whip the remaining cream. Pour the
    soup into cappuccino cups and top

each with a half spoon of lightly whipped cream.

6. Drink as you would cappuccino, but don't dunk your doughnuts in this one.

FOURTEEN

Faces of Hope

(2002)

"What do you mean, I can't go on the streets alone?"

"You can't go on the streets alone."

"Sonofabitch."

"A mature response," says Josh, my son, the producer.

"Told you she wouldn't be happy about this," says Rolfe, my partner and, along with me, executive producer.

"There are," I say, "other women alone on the streets of Kabul. I've seen them."

"Maybe so," Josh says. "But *you* can't go on the streets alone."

"Why not?"

"Because we say you can't," Rolfe says.

Guys, let us review the situation. I am a big girl. I sleep without a nightlight. I have been places and done stuff with no one but me to take care of me. I ate stewed guinea pig at a market stall in an Andean village

372

and heated stones to warm my feet at night before one of you was born. I navigate quite well among people whose language I do not speak. You want to talk survival? I raised two kids in New York City. *This ain't my first rodeo.* But I don't say this. They mean well. They want to protect me because I'm a woman. So did the Taliban, which protected women by making it illegal for them to be educated, get proper health care, show their faces or bodies in public — or walk the streets unaccompanied by a man. The Taliban, whose butt we have spent several billion dollars kicking out of this country. Now my partner and son tell me I can't walk the streets unaccompanied by a man?

Here's where I must remember to stick to facts, which, as I recall, add a lot to a story. Fact: I haven't come to Afghanistan to assess the rights of women in these brand-new, post-Taliban days. Certainly I haven't come to help them in their struggle. We're here to produce a television show about the children of Afghanistan, but we're not here to help them either. If this makes me a hypocrite, I'm in good company. The United States hasn't come here to right wrongs against women or to ensure the future of children. Why would it? Who cares? Not the mainstream media. In America, what makes news is America. We are, all of us — military, diplomats, journalists, and aid workers — in Afghanistan for a much simpler reason. Storai says it when the two of us are in a car on our way to a village outside Kabul.

"Because you lost something, now you pay attention."

Tuesday, the eleventh day of September 2001, the day everything changed — not in Afghanistan, in *America*. New York City. Downtown. Where I live. I took it personally. I wasn't the only one.

We had an impossible task that week: put together a television program explaining the inexplicable to children. The thought of making television seemed trivial and was, but it's what we do for a living, and so we did it then. We told kids what we knew and *didn't* know (journalists regularly are accused of knowing more than we tell; I think the opposite is true). After our show aired, we were overwhelmed with letters and e-mails from American kids wanting to do something to help. At first, most were addressed to New York City firemen or their families, but soon after that many of the messages were meant for those who must have seemed as far away and perhaps no farther away than New York City: the children of Afghanistan.

In October, the United States began bombing Afghanistan to oust the Taliban, a government it had once supported (the Taliban, it was said, would help stabilize the area, and you can't say it didn't; the Taliban stabilized Afghanistan all the way back to the twelfth century). For my part, reality really went south when our government announced that because the Afghan people weren't our enemies, we'd bomb them with food too. Mental picture of Afghan children looking to the night sky and shouting to one another, "Run! Here come the Americans," or alternately, "Hold out your hands. Here come the Americans!" By November, the Taliban was reported to be gone. In December, we were still getting mail from American kids asking about the children of Afghanistan. We decided to take their questions and go get some answers. My son left for Afghanistan in January. In *The Lathe of Heaven*, Ursula K. Le Guin wrote of a young man, "He had grown up in a country run by politicians who sent the pilots to man the bombers to kill the babies to make the world safer for children to grow up in." I never wanted my son to be the fellow she was writing about. Instead, Josh ended up being a television producer, working for Lucky Duck Productions sometimes, for other organizations at other times. Now he was going to produce our Afghanistan show. Real irony is rare, but we live in rare times. Not only was my son going to a war zone, I was sending him. Oh yeah, he volunteered, but I can't recall which came first: my saying "Let's go" or his saying "Let me go."

On February 4, 2002, ten years to the day since I had been diagnosed with breast cancer, I found myself still on the right side of the grass and on an airplane to Central Asia. A family affair, this trip. I liked working with Josh, liked it that my son shared a passion for a craft, understood its possibilities and limits, spoke its particular language, the two of us finishing each other's thoughts and sentences, challenging each other, idea-building. Rolfe and I had years of experience at it. Josh and I were still working out how to work together; on the road, he was the show producer and I was the correspondent. My job was to do what he told me to do.

I spoke to Josh, who was already in Afghanistan, by satellite phone.

"First impression of Kabul?"

I said this with a raised voice — it's a long way from Greenwich Village to the Mustafa Hotel.

"Kitty litter," Josh said, quietly.

Rolfe and I flew to Pakistan and bought a ride on a United Nations plane to Afghanistan. The flight over the Himalayas was bumpy and then there it was — Kabul, a city in the middle of a 7,000-foot-high sand trap ringed by serious, snow-covered peaks. A brown city, except for buildings built during the Soviet occupation — they were gray. The plane touched down and taxied by the skeletons of Soviet military aircraft, dead metal reminders that this country was not easily captured or kept. The terminal was wrecked too. No glass in the doors or windows, no light, no heat. Pieces of ceiling hung down precariously. An Afghan wearing civilian clothes and carrying an AK-47 stamped our passports. He had nothing to wet the inkpad but his tongue. I couldn't figure out why his tongue didn't freeze to the pad; it was that cold. We shouldered our backpacks and walked out into the dust, noise, and sunshine of a "free" Afghanistan.

There are armed guards at the front door of the Mustafa Hotel and iron bars on the windows. Up concrete stairs, a series of small rooms serve as restaurant, general gathering area, and place to watch TV, when it's working; electricity is a sometime thing. Heat too. The Mustafa is filled with journalists. The first one I see is my son. He's grown a beard and looks tired. I want to put my arms around him but I don't. Apart from Josh, Rolfe, and me, our group is made up of our cameramen, Andy and Tom, and Chris — full name Christopher Stephen Geoffrey Cobb-Smith. When Chris retired from the Royal Marines, he pierced his ear, let his hair grow, and drove around Europe on a motorcycle. Now he makes himself available to news outfits that want to go places where people might be shooting at one another. His job is to protect us. As he is quite tall, mostly he does this by looming. Tarik is our interpreter. Zia is our Afghan guard. He can't speak English but is not hampered by rules that keep Chris from carrying weapons. If one of us splits off from the group, Zia follows. After a few days, Zia is an annoyance. When *will* I get some time alone on these streets? I understand that making TV is a group effort; still, traveling in packs is my least favorite way to see anywhere. But if safety is a problem, Zia is a solution. Before we left home, everybody said the same thing.

"Don't do anything dangerous."

What? You mean other than go to Afghanistan right now? We did not mention that we carried big backpacks loaded with everything we needed to survive unsupported in the mountains — should it be necessary to get the hell out of Dodge. If a friendly helicopter couldn't extract us in five days, we could eat dirt and die.

"At least you'll be in a city filled with American soldiers," they said.

Kabul is a city filled with men — some in uniform, some in blankets — carrying automatic weapons, but the only American troops are at the embassy and at Bagram Air Base outside of town. Officially, Kabul is patrolled by ISAF, the United Nations International Security Assistance Force, mostly British with a few Italian and Dutch troops thrown in.

"Those guys? They *like* killing," a journalist says.

Must be why they're called peacekeepers.

One afternoon Rolfe and I are checking out old postcards of palaces and parks — Afghanistan before it was target practice. Two ISAF soldiers are in the bookshop. I try to start a conversation. How long have they been in Afghanistan? What exactly do they do?

The oldest sneers.

"We're here to make Chicken Street safe for you tourists."

Gosh, and I was hoping he'd tell me how much he liked killing people. The younger soldier, out of earshot of his colleague, says, "I feel very strange shopping for books with a machine gun under my arm."

We spend most of our time meeting and talking with kids. I ask them questions American kids want us to ask.

How has your life changed since the Taliban left?

"We can go to movies." The boy smiles. "If there were movies."

"We can watch TV." The girl smiles. "If we had TV."

"We can learn about the Internet." The boy smiles. "As soon as we get computers."

"It's different because it's free." The boy does not smile. But his eyes shine. "Now it is not the kingdom of Taliban. Now is the kingdom of peaceful."

Computers, TV, movies — even going to school costs money. The national economy is based primarily on the illegal by-product of poppies. The interim government is shaky. This is still a dangerous place.

Bombs still fall. Al Qaeda is still around. The Taliban too. Warlords wait in the wings, ready to carve up the nation when the United States and its coalition, their geopolitical needs met, boogie out of here. The kingdom of peaceful may have a short run. But the kids are filled with energy, and something else. Dignity? Hope? How can that be? More than half the population is under fifteen and the country has been at war for twenty-three years. *No child in Afghanistan has ever known peace.* On what would they base an emotion like hope?

We visit a family — a mother, a father, and eight kids — who live in a house made of a timber frame supporting homemade bricks and covered by dried mud, looking much like adobe. There are four rooms; in winter they all sleep in the main room, the only one with a *sandali,* the traditional form of Afghan heating. A rug covers the floor. On the rug is a charcoal brazier, a *manqal.* The *manqal* sits under a low table covered by a duvet called a *liaf,* which is large enough to spread over your legs when you sit on the cushions surrounding the table. I sit. They serve me tea and a small dish of toffee candies. I wait for them to get theirs before I start the interviewing. But no one moves; it occurs to me that

Zarmina and her family

there's not enough to go around. To refuse
the hospitality of the house would be rude,
so I drink tea and eat candy, feeling piggy,
and say *tashe kur* a lot. It means "thank
you." My pronunciation is terrible. They
pretend it's not. Zarmina, the mother, a
middle-aged woman with a tired face and
anxious eyes, wears a maroon scarf with
navy blue flowers on it, an inexpensive
rayon thing, but it's pretty and I tell her so.
When she thanks me, I hear the uncer-
tainty in her voice. Will talking to American television make trouble for her family?
Am I friend or foe? I'm neither. I'm paid to
ask strangers questions. There are only two

basic questions in journalism. "What happened?" and "What is it like to be you?" I've come to ask the second question.

Zarmina says her husband works for the new government. She's vague about what he does, and he's still waiting for his first paycheck. Her oldest child is twenty, the youngest still a baby. I ask what she tells her children about the days of peace, before the Soviet invasion in '79. Before the mujahadin wars. Before the Taliban.

"I tell them we went to the parks arm in arm, me and my husband, and nobody asked us where we were going."

Lena, at eighteen, the oldest daughter, interrupts.

"In the past six years, I didn't go to the bazaar even once. I felt like a bird in a cage. Now I can go to school, to bazaar — and we're not so constantly afraid of bombs."

I do not ask whose bombs she has been afraid of lately.

Javid, Lena's eleven-year-old brother, has red hair, blue eyes, a freckled face, a giant chicken pox sore on his right cheek, a body language that speaks of spirit — and a sense of humor. He stands in the center of the room. Using English, Pashtun, and pantomime, Javid tells his story.

"During the time of the Taliban, I had to put this turban on my head when I went to school." He demonstrates, comically weaving a black piece of cloth around his head as fast as he can. "When my teachers would leave the room, I would take it off." He unweaves it even faster. "Sometimes I got caught." He grins. "They hit me, but when I would come home, I would throw it in a corner. Like this!" He wads up the cloth and tosses it as though it were something offensive. Grins again. Takes a bow. We laugh, as we are meant to do.

Would Zarmina show me her kitchen? At first she refuses. I persist. In the kitchen, a cold, windowless room, are two loaves of bread, one bag of rice, some bottles of water, a container of salt, and a few spices. A small charcoal brazier sits on the concrete floor. The fuel is grass. I think of my big Viking range, the butcher-block counters, good knives, cast-iron pans, a full pantry, a Sub-Zero refrigerator loaded with fresh food. Zarmina is embarrassed to show me her kitchen. I would be deeply ashamed to show her mine.

Zarmina's husband walks me along a wall bordering their house, giving a guided tour of bullet holes.

"These," he says, "are Soviet."

He moves down the wall.

"These are mujahadin. And those over there, Taliban."

The question hangs in the air between us.

"No, there are no American bullet holes in my wall," he says. He pauses. "But thirty yards down the street there is a large crater."

The morning passes and the family gets more comfortable around the cameras. They all talk at once, speaking of the future more easily than the past. The unknown is — so far — less frightening than the known.

"Zarmina, what are your hopes for your children?"

"My hope is that they all go to school and university, and that like all of you they may have good jobs and travel the world."

She wears the worried-mother smile, the one that strains your mouth.

"And *your* children?" she says. "Did they attend university? What do they do?"

I don't tell her that neither my children nor I graduated from college. I tell her I have a thirty-three-year-old daughter who organizes unions in American hospitals and a thirty-two-year-old son who produces television programs.

"Ah," she says, pointing to Josh, who's making notes and directing the cameramen. "Like that man?"

"Yes, rather like that man."

"Please," Zarmina, says, "will you stay for lunch?"

Ten of them and eight of us? If we eat their food today, what will they eat tomorrow? I make excuses. As we get ready to leave, Zarmina takes off her scarf, the one I've told her I admire.

"I want you to have this. To remember."

We go to one of the bigger outdoor markets; there are stalls with pyramids of spices for sale. I'm not surprised to see bags of rice or piles of onions and beans. I'm not even surprised to see meat, most of which I can't identify and about which I don't care to ask — a cameraman for another network suffered a nasty bite when he tried to pet a dog on the street, not understanding that most dogs in Kabul are either rabid or dinner. But stalls selling fresh oranges, apples, and pomegranates? Lettuces, hot and sweet red peppers, and curvy, deep purple eggplants? Clearly food is being trucked into Kabul from somewhere — probably from within Afghanistan itself. Parts of the country are subtropical. Afghan melons and grapes are highly prized. But who in Kabul has money to buy such things? Nobody we meet.

Josh wants me to "do a stand-up" in the market, an unnatural act and a part of television journalism I've always hated. You're in the middle of a crowd, talking to a television camera you're trying to pretend isn't there, sounding like an idiot and certainly looking like one. He wants me to buy oranges and walk through the market, describing what I see. I buy a bag of oranges. I walk and talk. Lord knows what twaddle comes out of my mouth. Within minutes I'm surrounded by a group of kids looking at my oranges. I am about to do something I probably should not. I begin to hand them out. Everything gets crazy fast. People rush at me from all directions, yelling and pushing, squeezing. They don't mean to hurt me. They want my oranges. Chris and Josh fight their way through to rescue me out of a mob of my own making. Once we are safely away, Josh grabs my shoulders. His hands are shaking and his grip is so tight it hurts.

"Don't you ever, ever do that again. Do you understand me? Never again! Promise me! Say it!"

He's right. When our guys pushed through the orange crush to protect me, it could have gone sour. You don't know who might be in a crowd like that or how they might feel about American men shoving Afghan women and children aside with no great gentleness. I've endangered my team and angered my producer. It's not what a good correspondent does. In the van, riding back to the hotel, I try to explain.

"I'm sorry. I'm just, ah, so accustomed to being in charge, making choices . . ."

"You're not in charge here," Josh says. "You're the talent."

The *talent*.

In our business, this is a term used (as a noun) to describe, often inaccurately, the person in front of the camera. I despise the term. I mention this. I'm a little huffy, and still shaken by what has happened in the market.

"Okay, you're the talent-droid," Josh says. "Is that better?"

Somehow it is, mainly because it makes us laugh and eases the tension. From now on, our crew will refer to me as the talent-droid. It becomes a running gag. I don't mind. As a parent, I've had years of experience being a running gag.

A bumpy country road outside Kabul: I'm in a car with Storai and her driver. Our van follows. Neither Chris nor Zia is happy about me being in a car where they aren't, but Storai, a young woman I've connected with through Mercy Corps, is taking us to a village where, during the Taliban years, women ran a secret school for girls. She has insisted I ride in the car with her. I get the feeling Storai is helping us because she wants something, but I don't know what, any more than I can figure out how she really feels about us. One day she tells me, "I thank Allah for Osama, because he brought the Americans back." Another day she says, "You didn't have to bomb us. You are like the Soviets." Storai no longer wears the burqa, but she wears a scarf that covers her hair, a tunic top with sleeves to her wrists and slacks down past her ankles. She goes nowhere without her male driver, but she will not shake hands with a man. Storai is modern and not-modern. She says she hates it that when the Taliban killed the father and brothers of her niece, the girl, who was twelve, was forced to marry in order to have a man to protect her. But Storai is getting married next year to a man she's never seen. Her father picked him. She says this is not Taliban; this is custom. There's a difference, she says.

The village has been lifted from my

childhood Sunday school reader. Square, whitewashed, flat-roofed houses join on different levels. Children play on the roofs. Women work in the houses. Men sit in the courtyards. A once-secret school for girls is now an open school for girls. We talk with the teacher and then meet her students.

Look at these kids. Kabul was the crossroads of the silk trade between Europe and Asia. Every nation and race that traveled through here left, along with its goods, some of its blood. You see brown skin, pink skin, black skin; blond hair and blue eyes, black hair and green eyes, redheads with freckles — children who might be Arabic, Chinese, Norwegian, Navajo, Irish, Indian, or all of the above; that is, they could be American. Norman Rockwell portraits. Calvin Klein models. Sitcom kids. Afghans may be the most varied, handsome folk on earth. This is diversity, more than a thousand years' worth. This is Central Asia.

One high-cheeked girl with Mongol blood sits tall, back straight, her head held high. A proud little person.

"My name is Shamila. I am thirteen years old. It has been five years that I have been studying here. We were very frightened Taliban would come, frightened they would catch us. People who came to us to teach would wear homely clothes. They brought us school material hidden under these clothes."

"We knew there would be a day when our country would be in need of educated people," the teacher says. "We had an obligation to prepare girls secretly."

"And if the Taliban should return to power?" I say.

"If Taliban should come back again, we will study in hiding once more. We will not give up."

The bravery of women and little girls shines over Afghanistan like a new moon.

Everywhere we go, we see children and teenagers (of both sexes) studying without light, heat, desks, chairs, blackboard, paper, or books, nothing but a desire to learn — sometimes a desire to teach: we visit an English class at one school in Kabul where the teacher is thirteen. He stands in the front of the room, reading, and the others, many of whom are older, answer him.

"Is that a chicken?"

"No, that is an airplane."

We ask kids what they want to do when they grow up.

"I want to be a doctor."

"A translator."

"An engineer."

"I want to work at the organization of United Nations."

There's another answer we hear but will not include in our television program, for obvious reasons.

"I want to be a pilot."

It has nothing to do with the terrorists. The kids have seen fighter planes and helicopters over their own heads; pilots have power. But it leads to another question children back home want us to ask. *What do you know about what happened in America on September 11?* The answer is complicated by perspective. Having no access to television, they've not seen the images, although they know passenger jets piloted by terrorists flew into buildings, killing thousands of people. They tell you it was very sad, but look at you as if to say, "And what's your point? Isn't death raining from the sky part of life?"

It is hard to remain a kid in Kabul. The city is filled with children begging, a risky job, but there is no security for these kids, only opportunity. There's this one little girl, maybe seven or eight years old. She wears a raveled-at-the-edges red blanket over her head and shoulders, and around a black jacket that bulges from layers of thinner clothes underneath. Little Red

Riding Hood. When I leave the hotel, she's by my side within seconds. When we pull out the cameras, she dissolves into the crowd, peeks out, teasing us, and then disappears again. She has a solemn face and almost never smiles, but when she does she takes my breath away and doesn't give it back.

One afternoon on Chicken Street (you can buy flowers on Chicken Street and chickens on Flower Street), Little Red Riding Hood and a group of her pals follow us, begging. No other kids are in sight. I reach into my pocket and give each child a 1,000-Afghani bill, worth about thirty cents. Little Red Riding Hood grabs my arm. Tries to tell me something. I keep walking. She keeps chattering. I stop and make hand signals. What? *What?* She indicates that I've skipped one of her gang. Uh-huh. I know how this will go down. If I pull out another bill, they'll all want another bill. Oh, so what, Ellerbee? I mean, really. I give the kid who allegedly was passed over his money. Little Red raises both her hands to the other children, palms facing them in a back-off gesture. She turns around and gives me a thumbs-up. The leader of the pack has spoken. Where did this peculiar sense of justice come from? Who does this child belong to? I begin to look for her everywhere, and when I don't see her, I miss her.

I miss food too. I don't mean I'm hungry. I'm a well-fed American. I would, however, like to eat something that tastes better than, say, wood. Most journalists eat dinner at the hotel. After several nights, I'm ready to brave the streets of Kabul — to hell with the curfew — for a chance to eat anything other than the fare at the Mustafa. Begin with the menu.

Rice and Lamb Meet.

And have been together so long it's hard to tell them apart.

Lamb Meet and Rice.

Their parents, I think.

And my favorite: Rice with Thin Shee of Carrots.

A thick shee would probably kill you.

Usually I go with Afghan Special Fried Chicken. What's special is that the pieces actually resemble fowl. No batter, no crust, just stringy old chicken parts, boiled and then fried in oil until reduced to half their size, plated, and covered with soggy french fries and sliced boiled eggs with green rings around the yolks. With this you get a choice of cauliflower, spinach, cabbage, or eggplant — all pureed and distinguishable only by slight differences in color: gray, dark green, pale green, or brown. Our first night, I notice an item on the menu called Afghani Traditional Food. I ask other reporters what it is. No one seems to know. The next night I ask the waiter. He says I wouldn't like it. I ask the owner of the Mustafa, Weis — an Afghan who spent most of his life in New Jersey, returning to Kabul to reopen the family's hotel when the journalists began to arrive — to explain the dish.

"God only knows," Weis says. "Don't try it."

I order the Afghani Traditional Food. What I get is a plate of frozen Chinese dumplings that appear to have been reheated in a microwave. On top of the frozen Chinese dumplings are canned Swedish meatballs. On top of canned Swedish meatballs is Italian spaghetti sauce out of a jar. On top of Italian spaghetti sauce out of a jar is less-than-fresh yogurt. I know this dish must have roots in real Afghan cuisine, but it's like ordering enchiladas at a Holiday Inn in Cleveland. Not unless you're starving.

On the streets, I see people with carts selling grilled meats, vegetable curries, eggplants with chiles — fried pastries filled with minced meat that remind me of Bolivian *salteñas*. No one in our group will let me try these foods. Unsafe, they say. Polluted air has fouled the outdoor food, they say. You can't trust the cleanliness of the vendors, they say. I say that after too many days and nights of refried chicken and baby-poop cabbage, bring it *on*. But I say it only to myself. I tell *them* my shopping genes are kicking in. I want to buy a burqa to show women in America what it feels like to wear a portable prison. I want to buy a beautiful wool blanket like the ones Afghan men wear as coats. I want to buy . . . jewelry. That there is no jewelry worth buying or that I'm not a woman who buys jewelry does not occur to them. To guys, a woman shopping for jewelry is a scary sight. None of them is going to want to accompany me.

I'm counting on it.

I can't go alone, they say, but I can go alone if I take Zia (and this sentence makes sense to you lads?). I point out Zia doesn't speak English. They say Zia doesn't need to speak English to watch my back. I agree to the terms, but once outside the hotel, I let Zia know with elaborate gestures that I'm happy to have him watch my back — from a distance.

In a small shop window, I stop to look at a blanket, but then my nose notices that up the block a street vendor is serving up great-smelling brown goop with a fried egg and chiles on top.

"Yoo-hoo, Zia . . ."

I wave my hands about, trying to make him understand that he should return to the blanket seller and buy the one in the window, the black one with the red stripe along its border. Zia shakes his head no. I wave my hands some more and make what I hope are boss noises. Zia looks uncertain, but heads back to the blanket store. The minute he's out of sight, I run up the block and buy a plate of what turns out to be mutton sautéed with ginger, onion, and garlic. The mutton is tender. The fried egg is fresh. The chiles make my eyes water. When I see Zia returning, I swallow the last bite and give the tin plate back to the vendor, who wipes it off for the next customer, with his sleeve. Zia is not carrying the blanket. I throw him my best question-mark look, and the guard who has no English says in perfect English, "I'm very sorry, but the price that man wanted was rather too much for such a poorly woven blanket. You can do better in the bazaar by the mosque. If you like, I shall be happy to escort you there."

Zia. My hero. *Who knew?*

Eventually we have our story, our show. We go to the new Foreign Ministry to get our exit visas. A man in a military uniform examines our passports.

"You are journalists?"

"We are journalists."

"You never registered as journalists with the Ministry of the Interior."

"There wasn't a Ministry of the Interior two weeks ago. Anyway, we're leaving."

"You can't leave."

"Why not?"

"Because you aren't here."

An interesting point.

He tells us to go to the new Ministry of the Interior and get a letter saying we are registered as journalists. The new Minister of the Interior is equally disappointed in us.

"How can I register you as journalists here when you're leaving the country tomorrow?"

Tarik, the interpreter, whose English is rotten compared with that of Zia, the man who speaks no English, finally proves his real worth. He takes the minister to another room. When they return, Tarik is carrying letters. Seems Tarik's uncle is head of the Eastern Alliance or, as a crass person might put it, one of the more powerful warlords. Tarik has explained to the minister that his uncle would take it as a favor if he could help the ignorant infidels. I'm assuming the "or else" was only implied.

Our last morning in Kabul, I have breakfast with Storai. I'm about to find out what she wants. She accepts a cup of green tea, nothing else. I have learned to sprinkle a bit of ground cardamom in green tea; gives it a kick, a heady little morning high, Muslim-style. Storai opens her purse and removes an envelope. A black-and-white photograph falls onto the table — a picture of a young man's face, strained and formal, as on a passport photo. I look from the photograph to Storai.

"My brother," she says, "was eighteen. He was bodyguard for the president of Afghanistan. They killed that president in 1992. Nobody knows what happened to my brother, but four years later someone said they saw him in Pakistan. I am certain he is alive. You work in television. . . ."

Storai believes I can take her brother's photograph and her page of carefully typed information and broadcast this on American television.

On Pakistani television too, she adds.

I think of the families in New York who have covered walls and the Web with pictures and information about loved ones

Little Red Riding Hood

"missing" in the World Trade Center. I tell her the truth. I can't do any of the things she thinks I can. I don't have the power. Also, does she understand her brother is gone, as those people in the twin towers are gone? She says I should take the photo and information anyway.

"The family," she says, "will not give up hope."

Having lightened our load by giving Zarmina's family our warm clothes, outdoor gear, freeze-dried food, paper, pens, everything we brought with us that we can do without, we're set to go. Outside the Mustafa, Little Red Riding Hood finds me, or I find her. I can't tell the difference anymore. Tarik asks if she will allow Rolfe to take a photograph of me with her. She agrees, but will not smile for the picture. Perhaps she knows better. Journalists are packing up and moving on. Businessmen are arriving faster than aid workers, and nothing they will do is likely to help Little Red Riding Hood either. She is not profitable. She isn't even good television.

I never find out her name.

At the airport, we're told we're to be searched. I'm taken into a pitch-black closet, the kind Patty Hearst would have interesting memories of. I can make out the shapes of three women. In my backpack is all the film and videotape we've shot in Afghanistan. I'm carrying the show on my back. They pat me down and begin to unzip the pack. Tapes spill out onto the floor of our dark little closet.

"Stop that. Please."

I say this with as much politeness as I can muster.

"Do you have money?" one of the women says.

"I beg your pardon?"

"Do you have money?"

Her voice is insistent. I know I'm being shaken down and I'm pissed. Especially because it's a woman doing the down-shaking. But there are certain advantages to being female in a patriarchal society.

"Of course *I* don't have money," I say. *"My husband carries the money."*

She sighs. "You can go."

Before the UN plane arrives, a 747, the first to land at the Kabul airport since the seventies, taxis by. It has been chartered by Mercy Corps and is filled with school supplies from Portland, Oregon. Some children in Kabul will have paper and pencils and books. A drop in the bucket, but do I hear the splash carry? It would take fifty years and billions of dollars to rebuild Afghanistan — money, time, and commitment I doubt the American government or its people have the will for. I have come to a hopeless situation, and yet everywhere I have seen hope. Every day I have asked myself how this is possible. Is hope something that can't be killed? Or is it that human beings, faced with overwhelming obstacles, will grasp at the absurd? Is hope absurd — merely a veil you drape over the naked truth? There are no victors here, only survivors who know that sometimes living takes more courage than fighting; and that the world is round — what seems like an ending might be a beginning. We're going back to the world of laptops, video games, and chat rooms, *girls'* soccer teams, hot showers, Big Macs, and snow days. Children here may not know about those things yet. They may not know about them for years, or ever. Nevertheless, children are the face of hope of Afghanistan.

The United Nations plane lands. Incoming passengers climb down stairs and walk across the tarmac, passing us. I want to say something to them, but what? A man with a manifest begins to call out our names. It would be so much easier if he spoke anything resembling English. People muddle about, uncertain whether their name has been called. A French (what else?) government employee is indignant.

"Who's in charge here?"

Everybody else in the departing group — aid workers, UN employees, and journalists — breaks into what might rightly be called hysterical laughter.

No one is in charge here.

I touch the maroon scarf tied around my

neck, the scarf Zarmina gave me, as she said, to remember.

As if I could forget.

Recipe

Buy a bag of oranges. Give them to children who don't have oranges.

FIFTEEN

Pass It On

(1971–2004)

I'm going to love being a grandmother. I plan to be available, understanding, and weird — as a mother I was mostly weird. Violet, daughter of my daughter, was born in December 2002. I intend to introduce her, and any other grandchildren I am fortunate enough to be granted, to my notions of adventure. I will go places and take them with me. Why not? It won't be the first time I set children on the road early. Vanessa wasn't two and Josh not even one when we packed up and along with Van, their father, and Magoo, the yellow dog, left the Texas-Mexico border and headed to Alaska. Two years later, all of us but their father returned to Texas on the wheels of a bruised dream and a tie-dyed VW camper Vanessa named *Callalee*. It took close to two months to drive from Seattle to Houston, but only because we stopped to smell a few flowers along the way, maybe all of them, if you include the ones Josh ate. That *Callalee* couldn't do more than 50 miles per hour helped. We slept and picnicked in parks: state, national, and undeclared. An undeclared park, I explained to the children, was a pretty piece of land with no fence around it.

We cooked our dinner in an iron skillet over an open fire. Rice mixed with whatever: Beans. Carrots. Broccoli. Hamburger. *Peanut butter.* We ate off tin plates and drank from matching tin cups: red for Josh, blue for Vanessa, yellow for me. It stopped so many arguments. Color Assignment was one of my parenting skills. As an only child and a self-taught divorced mother of two, I didn't have many, but the ones I used were rather brilliant, I thought. For instance, the Theory of Empirical Honesty is useful in many areas, but critical in teaching fair play and portion control. Let's say that for some reason or another you have two children but only one slice of pie. One child divides the slice of pie. The other child gets first choice. Simple and foolproof. The Theory of Empirical Honesty does introduce children to knives at an early age, but I think you'll agree it's a small price to pay for a little peace and quiet. Lying to Your Children — now there is a parenting skill you needed to practice early and often. I was a natural; I pretended our trip was motivated by something other than a lack of alternative. It was an adventure, I said, a word I also used whenever I didn't know where we were going. Or where we were.

"We are not lost. We are having an adventure."

Vanessa took to travel as if born to it, which I suspect she was. From her first step, she was always on her way someplace else. I admired the openness with which she met the world on its own terms, the adaptability and raw courage that enabled her to survive everything life threw at her, including me. Josh preferred no sudden moves. He placed his trust in staying put; ergo I was not trustworthy. But I knew travel was good for children. Everybody said so. While never abandoning the classics — *Are we there yet?* — they learn so many new ways to torture you.

"Mommy, Josh threw up on my head."

"I'll stop the car and we'll clean it off you."

"Magoo already ate it."

This was in Oregon.

"Mommy, who is God's daddy?"

"God doesn't have a daddy, Josh,"

Vanessa said. "His parents are divorced. Like ours."

"Actually, Vanessa . . . ah, never mind."

This was in Northern California.

"Mommy, there's a car with flashy red lights following us. Are we in a parade?"

Who knew they gave tickets in Arizona for driving too slow?

Are we there yet?

Along with explaining that wherever we were, we were *there,* and teaching my kids to relieve themselves by the side of the road, I used these early adventures to introduce them to the wonders of the world's foods. This occasionally required exercising the Theory of Enlightened Improvisation, which, although they are easily confused, is not the same as Lying to Your Kids.

"Mommy, why are we eating potato chip sandwiches?"

"Because they're world-famous in New Mexico. People come here from everywhere just to eat potato chip sandwiches."

Note to God: Help me remember to buy the baloney next time and I promise to explain to the children about your daddy.

Whenever we stopped at a grocery store, I would make a list with the kids, based on the Principle of Relative Reality.

"Let's see," I'd say. "We need a loaf of bread, a jar of mustard, a box of dreams, a carton of orange juice, a bottle of milk, a bag of rainbows, a sack of cookies, and a can of dead frogs. And baloney."

A pattern was established. We traveled. We got lost. We goofed off. We ate strange stuff, some of it imaginary. Magoo batted cleanup. This was so different from my own childhood that I was certain it must be the right way to raise kids. Like so many before me, I assumed that my parents had gotten it wrong, and that I would not. Too bad that being Mama, the most important job I would ever have, was the one for which I was the least trained, least equipped, and possibly the most ill suited; I hadn't known you had to stop being a child in order to raise one. We are supposed to give our children two things: a nest and wings.

I gave better wings.

If my parents, shaped by the Great Depression, were ants, I was, from birth and by choice, a grasshopper. I taught my children to wander down unmarked trails, take unpredictable turns, and appreciate the moment. I told them to enjoy today and laugh at tomorrow; they could learn other things (like how to spell) later, which helps explain why Vanessa and Josh could use chopsticks before they could properly add and subtract. If my mother thought any vegetable was better if it came in a box and was frozen, I would show my kids how to eat the flowers in the field. I would be surprising. Inventive. For instance, there was always plenty of raw cookie dough around our place because I taught my kids that going to the trouble to bake cookies was like stuffing a mushroom; life was too short. They came to agree with me on this. Once some Austrian friends of Vanessa's stayed with us in New York. When Vanessa visited them in Vienna, they served her raw cookie dough, carefully sliced and prettily presented on a cutting board, and were shocked to learn it was not a typical American delicacy.

Unlike my own mother, I was always happy to have my kids in the kitchen. The minute they would show interest in a dish, I would enthuse, rushing to explain how to make it. *In detail.* And then, as my voice would begin to take on the more charming characteristics of fluorescent hum, their eyes would glaze over. Josh, perhaps overinfluenced by one too many potato chip sandwiches and a bag of rainbows, found his answer in a blender. Over the

years he filled blenders with everything from ice cream and jelly to *chile con queso* and chips. Flipping the switch with an executioner's calm, he doomed otherwise normal foods to the degrading state of puree, often gray. Vanessa? Some people transform in kitchens; they become composers, conductors — virtuosos. Vanessa experienced a metamorphosis as well. She became Kaiser Wilhelm. With Prussian sensibilities she attacked food, smothering meat in garlic powder and onion flakes, drowning helpless vegetables in cheap, sugary stir-fry sauces, sinking salads in oceans of viscous Ranch Dressing, until eventually she would find herself staring down the trenches of her own Alsace-Lorraine. Another solution had to be found. In her first apartment, Vanessa stocked her refrigerator with chicken pot pies, bread, and cheese. When she found herself craving something not born in a toaster oven, she ate out.

In March 1999, when Vanessa turned thirty, the two of us celebrated her birthday (or as I sometimes referred to it, "our anniversary") on the Hawaiian island of Lanai. We went swimming, ate fresh fish, and wore flowers in our hair. I gave her gifts. For her gift to me, Vanessa said she loved me in spite of myself. I was giddy with joy. In April 2000, when Josh turned thirty, we went to the same island, swam in the same water, and ate the same fish. Josh balked at flowers in his hair. I gave him gifts. For his gift to me, Josh told me that come September he intended to marry an Englishwoman I'd never met. I was without words.

Was I ready for him to travel so far? So far from *me*, I meant. Oh I knew they would grow up, up, and away; I'd read the fine print. But still. I remembered my father standing in the doorway of our house and waving goodbye, tears running down his face, as I drove away with my new husband on a trip that was meant to last a lifetime but would never include him. I remembered thinking how silly I thought his tears were. I wished I could go back and apologize.

It rained the day before and it rained the day after, but when Josh wed Rebecca the sun was shining on the green hills of Wales, on the village of Llanidloes, on the bride and groom and on the rest of us who were gathered to witness the joining. The night before, I had thrown a party for out-of-town guests. As pretty much everybody at the wedding had come to Wales from either London or the United States, it was large. The Brits, who seemed never to have heard of a rehearsal dinner, thought an extra party was a swell, if odd, idea.

I very much wanted to do this correctly. My co-in-laws-to-be were English. English meant proper. I didn't have time to take lessons. I rented Garthmyl Hall, an old country house set on 14 acres of parkland and gardens in the rolling countryside of the Welsh Marches and filled it with the usual suspects: those of our family and friends who would cross an ocean to see

Josh wed, and would keep me from making a fool of myself. Nadine and David came from New York, Kit and Billy from New Orleans, Cousin Billy from Houston. Beth also came over from Houston, along with her son, James, who worked for Lucky Duck in New York. Josh and James were probably the only two living New Yorkers born in Eagle Pass, Texas. Then there was Vanessa, Rolfe, me, and — the night before the wedding — Josh. Although we had offered him a room, Van, my ex-husband and Josh and Vanessa's father, had chosen to stay somewhere else. Garthmyl Hall was exactly what I had in mind — elegant, beautifully proportioned, and simply furnished. Cousin Billy said with a couple of million dollars you could really do something with the place.

Most of us had brought too much luggage because we weren't sure what to wear to the wedding. What little Kit, Beth, Nadine, and I knew about English weddings we'd learned from novels or *Four Weddings and a Funeral*. We were thinking stone church, white gloves, big garden-party hats, and floaty chiffon. I had tried, as the mother of the groom is supposed to do, to take my cue from the mother of the bride, but whenever I spoke to Judy on the phone, she was maddeningly vague.

"Oh, just wear anything."

"What will you be wearing?"

"I haven't decided."

Determined to do right by Josh, I had three versions made of the same velvet dress, each with its matching cloche, silk stockings, and T-strap dancing shoes. The dress — had I been braver I might have called it a frock — was an adaptation of a 1924 Callot Soeurs couture design. It had a dropped waist and a handkerchief hem, a sensible choice, I thought, for a woman with good legs and no breasts. One version was black. "I'm from New York City; I'm sophisticated," it said (I hoped). Another version was a burgundy rich enough to play the West End but able to pass for maroon if Duchess Dowdy was the dress code of the day. The third dress was an entirely inappropriate blood red I'd chosen at the last moment. Nadine said I looked like Agatha Christie on crack.

My plan was to see what Judy wore to the party the night before, and then choose my costume for the wedding accordingly. Josh, already in Wales for several days, called to say he and Rebecca would be late; it had taken longer than they had anticipated to get the sheep out of the barn.

Barn? Sheep? He said I must greet the guests by myself. Okay, I could do that, if I had to. *Arrrghh.* When it was time, I stood on the steps of Garthmyl Hall, a cross between Melanie on the veranda of Twelve Oaks and Mrs. Danvers.

"Hello and welcome. I'm Linda, Josh's mother."

I shook their hands, a gracious, proper grown-up.

"Hello and welcome. I'm Linda, Josh's mother."

People kept coming. The light began to fade. It was nearly dark and I was too vain to put on my glasses, so I just stuck my hand in the general direction of the man standing before me. By now I had grown a slight British accent.

"Halloo and walcome. I am Lindah, Joshuah's mothah."

"And I'm Josh's father," Van said.

It would have been so much better if Rolfe and Kit hadn't been standing close enough to hear me introduce myself to my children's father. At least none of my co-in-laws-to-be had been there. Come to think of it, where were they?

I circulated, the hostess with the mostest, introducing myself to a young man with his wife and daughter, first

416

checking to make sure I'd never been married to him, and asked what their connection to the wedding party was. He said he was a former lover of the mother of the bride. Rebecca's father arrived. I knew he was a film director but hadn't expected this exuberant fellow with lots of curly, silver-striped hair and leopard-print shoes. He said Felicia, his wife but not Rebecca's mother, would be late. Rebecca's mother arrived with Chris, her longtime live-in lover, but not Rebecca's father. Judy's hair was even curlier and more silver than Richard's, only longer; it tumbled down her back and fell in tendrils around her lively, lovely, chiseled face. She was dressed, best I could tell, in a collection of unmatched silk saris, each more splendid than the next. Everybody hugged or shook hands with everybody else. Richard, Judy, and Chris began to explain why they were late: Seems that for the wedding reception, they had borrowed a barn on the top of a Welsh hill with a view of more Welsh hills trailing off into the distance, then talked the farmer into letting them remove one side of the barn to afford guests a view even while indoors. In return, they agreed to find temporary shelter for the animals, clean the barn, build a bandstand and dance floor, and then, when the party was over, tear down the bandstand and dance floor, rebuild the wall, and replace the animals. Richard said he had thought it would be easier. Judy said it *was* easy, once you got the hang of making sheep go where you wanted. I was hopeful. Not only was theirs, like ours, a blended family, but from what I could tell, they might not be normal.

Josh and Rebecca arrived, flushed and beautiful. The dining room where the buffet had been set up was tall, dark, and handsomely lit. There was a pair of silver candelabra on the mantel. The buffet was loaded with food of my own choosing. My general opinion of English cooking being that they were better at war, I had asked the caterer for plain foods, the kind that would be hard to screw up: cold beef and ham, salad, bread, and cheese. As I had eaten some fine Middle Eastern food in England over the years, I also ordered hummus, eggplant, chicken sate, veggie kebabs, and spinach-stuffed pastries. Too bad I neglected to order the Indian to prepare them. On the other hand, the Welsh Rarebit was nice if you liked melted cheese — and who does not? Dessert was tops; there were small miracles on the cookie platter. Meringues, but not like any meringue you ever met. This was an innocent bit of swirled cloud that exploded with flavor and then disappeared in your mouth. Kit and I felt certain that if you didn't have to chew, it didn't count as eating. We headed to the kitchen where, as any savvy guest knows, they keep the replacements. Overall, the meal wasn't fabulous, but it was, I thought, *normal*. Sort of.

People ate and partied. I watched my son talk to Rebecca's father. Josh was relaxed, perhaps more than Richard. Rebecca's parents hadn't known Josh any longer or better than we'd known Rebecca. Richard, Judy, Van, and I had taken on faith that our children had chosen well, but we were parents — what did we know? A few minutes later, we were given the opportunity to learn something about what they were made of when Rebecca's hair caught fire. She and Josh were standing near the mantel. He cupped a hand under her chin, tilted her face up, and kissed her, softly. Rebecca's hair was a dozen shades of brown and like her mother's, long and curly. Tonight she wore it up, with a silk flower tucked into it in just the right place.

Or just the wrong place, as it turned out.

The kiss was too long. The candelabra too close. The flower ignited. All of a sudden Rebecca's whole head seemed to be on fire. Josh didn't hesitate; he put his bare hands onto and into the flames until they were smothered. The smell of burned hair and hand settled around the room as most of us, frozen in place and face, waited to see how a bride would react to her hair going up in smoke the night before her wedding.

Rebecca held a fistful of singed hair in her hand. She looked at it, then at Josh, and then at the rest of us, and she smiled.

"Good thing I've got a lot."

My son had chosen a woman in full. I slept better than I had in weeks, got up the next morning, and without hesitation chose the red dress to wear to his wedding. And there could not have been a more co-ordinated pair of co-mothers-in-law-to-be if we had had Vera Wang do it for us. Judy was magnificent in a bright purple silk suit and red gloves to her elbows. She wore a hat of her own design, consisting of a base from which sprang, stalklike, a bunch of al-most invisible wires, each with a tiny red silk banner attached to the end. When she moved her head she looked like a field of poppies caught by a breeze. Richard wore a dark suit with his leopard shoes. Van wore an open-necked shirt and cowboy

Josh and Rebecca

boots. Our friend David wore a black tux, a green shirt, and red Converse sneakers, and for the wedding song, played his guitar and sang "It Had to Be You." The most traditionally dressed were the bride and groom and Cousin Billy. Josh wore a black Armani tux. Rebecca wore a strapless white wedding gown. Cousin Billy wore the air of one who knows he is always appropriately dressed, whatever he has on.

Although they publicly and legally declared themselves necessary to each other in the office of the town clerk, it became real for me later, when Josh swept Rebecca into his arms and carried her across the top of the hill next to the barn, the two of them lit, like the hill itself, with the magic light of that time in September we're supposed to try to remember. Beth and I watched them, held hands, and cried. We had become friends while pregnant with our sons. James was to be married the next year; they were moving on, our boys. Josh *had* moved on.

I sat at the head table with the bride and groom, the other parents, and our assortment of lovers and/or spouses, and the exes. A thoroughly modern wedding. When it was time for toasts, the father of the bride was eloquent while climbing a ladder and making sweeping gestures with his free hand. Having no props, when it was my turn I rose and said I had told a guest I had to make a speech and wasn't sure what to say. He said they wouldn't let him speak. I said I had asked why. "Because they knew I would ask how a bunch of silly British bastards let the wanker from New York steal the best woman in England," he said. I told the wedding guests that I had thought about this question.

"And so," I said, "how *was* a Yank able to take something valuable that belonged to your country?"

Nobody answered, so I did.

"Practice."

Only the Yanks laughed.

Rebecca had said there would be music and it would be called dancing. I wondered what we would call it. A group of Irish musicians climbed onto the bandstand, tuned up, and let loose with pipes, fiddles, and other stringed instruments, stomping their feet in time to the music while a man called out the steps to dancers arranged in patterns of four or more couples. Aha! *"Called"* dancing. Or as we who were from Texas had grown up calling it — square dancing. Well, *we* knew what to do next. *You folks step back now and watch us strut our stuff.* Most of the English guests were trying this sort of dancing for the first time and with varying results. Van was a popular teacher, possibly because nobody else was chewing tobacco and wearing cowboy boots. I haven't danced so hard or so happily or with such abandon since 1969, and that was different. After the wedding cake was cut, the father of the bride donned a red sequined jacket and played the spoons. And I was worried they'd think *me* weird. These Brits knew how to party.

Near dawn, Josh carried Rebecca down the valley to a glade next to a stream,

423

Vanessa and Blake

where their friends had set up an old Boy
Scout tent and furnished it with a soft rug,
and futons draped with sheets and throws
of many colors, and it was there a new husband and wife did spend the first night of
their journey together.

The Yanks returned to America, all but
Cousin Billy, who stayed over in London
an extra day so he could, in his words,
"move around without Linda Jane telling
me when and how." When he got run over
by a London cabbie "going too fast, and

on the wrong side of the street!" he called
to say he was resting comfortably in the
Princess Diana Hospital.

"I'm *fine*. They're so *nice* here, Linda
Jane. *Just like she would have wanted.*"

The drugs wore off the next day. It took
a full year for both broken arms to mend.
Just in time, as it turned out.

Vanessa phoned from Seattle.

"Hi, Mom. Guess what."

A risky proposition. With Vanessa,
"guess what" could mean a new vocation,
a political epiphany, a change of hair color,
or a severed limb.

"Ah . . . what?"

"I'm getting married."

I sat down. And Blake's last name was
. . . I thought hard.

"We've picked September 1, 2001,"
Vanessa said.

"Wright!" I said, as memory caught up
with reality.

"That's how I feel too!" my daughter
said.

"I'm really happy for you, Vanessa. But
so soon?"

Everybody knows daughter weddings are
different from son weddings. We're supposed to worry for months, stare at sample
wedding cakes, smell flowers, and argue

over menus, invitation lists, and lingerie.

"No reason to wait."

When Vanessa made up her mind to go somewhere, she went. Nothing had changed. I was surprised they weren't heading down to city hall the next day. Or maybe she only meant to say that her wedding would be a small, simple affair.

"Well, then, September it is. What size wedding were you thinking of?"

"Anyone who wants to come can."

"Gee," I said. "How welcoming."

I had a vision of Blake's family — his brother was a major in the army, his father a retired lieutenant colonel, his mother a retired civil service budget analyst, and they all voted Republican, I was sure — in the same room with Kit and Billy. Nadine and David. Rolfe and his cameras. Cousin Billy and his mouth. Van and his cowboy boots. Vanessa's union buddies. Vanessa's ex-boyfriends (seven showed up, referring to themselves as "The Loser's Club"). Vanessa's rock-and-roll pals.

Vanessa's mother.

What would they think of us? Would *they* think we were strange?

"Do you know what you'd like to wear?" I said.

"I have always known that if I ever married," my daughter said, "I would wear red."

2004. This afternoon in Portland, Oregon, I am babysitting Violet, my granddaughter, for the first time. Vanessa and Blake were nervous when they left.

"Don't drop her," Blake said.

"Don't warp her," Vanessa said.

Warp her. As if I would. As if I needed to. The child was doomed from birth. Funny, isn't it, how we go out of our way to warp *our* children *our* way and then are surprised when they turn out to be as weird as we are, only *their* way. Because of me, both my children knew how to be good strangers in a strange land. They knew how to get along in uncertain situations and changing circumstances. Josh, who once resisted crossing the street on grounds he didn't know what was on the other side, was a documentary producer who roamed the world in search of the unfamiliar, but he always kept his apartment in New York, his nest. Vanessa regularly had moved her nest. Vienna. Istanbul. New York. La Jolla. Juneau. Seattle. Portland.

Doing it their way.

As for food, Josh had gotten past the blender phase, even before he married

Rebecca. I would like to say that Vanessa now creates culinary masterpieces in her nest, only this would not be completely true. Although she has learned to cook at the most basic level, a forgiving palate remains her greatest asset. She still doesn't bake the cookie dough unless she has company, but now and then, when nobody is looking, she does make a great Caesar salad, with a raw egg yolk and anchovies, as God intended. And she is a terrific mother, much better than I was. Vanessa and Josh had survived my deficiencies to become interesting, interested people who married people who also were those things.

Fantasticks, all of them.

Both my children had chosen to marry in September; Josh because of a play, a story — a song — that he had loved since I first took him to see and hear it when he was a boy. The night before his wedding, I gave him a letter.

"Dear Josh," it began.

I'm not qualified to advise anyone about marriage. But I do at last know one or two important things worth passing on. It's been said that the only joy in the world is to begin. This is wrong. What happens next is what counts. Life is lived with dailiness, not drama. This is why a wedding is easier than a marriage — why giving birth to children is easier than raising them. Try to remember to cherish the dailiness, and accept this basic truth: No marriage, no great love, or love lost, no divorce, no change of profession or country or code of belief has any significance compared to having a child, the one thing in life you can't change, get over, or beyond — the only absolutely final commitment you may ever make. I have loved being your mother. I shall always love being your mother. Meanwhile, it is September, before a rainfall. A perfect time to be in love.

I'm not really weird, no matter what anybody says. In the rocking chair, Violet is a sweet, heavy weight in my arms. She stirs, wakes, opens her eyes, and smiles her baby girl smile at me. I think I'll take her to China next year. It's really the easiest way to learn to use chopsticks.

Proper British Meringues*

4 large egg whites
8 ounces superfine (or S&W bakers') sugar
1 cup whipping cream

1. Preheat the oven to 350 degrees for 20 minutes.
2. Whisk the egg whites until stiff. Keep whisking as you slowly add the sugar.
3. When the mixture is stiff and glossy, put it in a piping bag with a star nozzle. Squeeze out little rosettes (about $1^1/_2$ to 2 inches in diameter) onto a cookie sheet lined with baking parchment.
4. Put the meringues in the oven and turn it off. By the time the oven has cooled, the meringues should be cooked and crisp.
5. Whip the cream until stiff. It's going

to be your glue. When the meringues are cool, take one in your hand and spread whipped cream on the flat side. Paste it to the flat side of another meringue (think Oreo cookies). Continue until all the little rosettes are little meringue Oreos. Serve immediately.

*NOTE: This recipe comes from Mary Bunner, who made the meringues for the party.

Box of Dreams Cake

SERVES EIGHT OR FOUR
(DEPENDING ON WHO'S EATING IT)

This is a pudding cake. A friend of my mother's gave me the recipe years ago. My kids started making this cake when they were ten. Grown-ups can make it too, but it's harder for them.

$3/4$ cup granulated white sugar
2 tablespoons unsweetened cocoa plus $1/4$ cup
1 cup flour

$1^1/_2$ teaspoons baking powder
$1/_4$ teaspoon salt
$1/_2$ cup low-fat milk
2 tablespoons vegetable oil
$1^1/_2$ teaspoons vanilla extract
1 cup brown sugar, packed
$1^3/_4$ cups boiling water
1 box of dreams (they are stored in the pantry of your imagination)

1. Preheat the oven to 350 degrees.
2. Put the white sugar, 2 tablespoons of the cocoa, flour, baking powder, and salt in a 9-inch square baking pan and stir.
3. Add the milk, oil, and vanilla. Stir again.
4. Mix the $1/_4$ cup cocoa with the brown sugar and sprinkle over the top of the batter. Pour the boiling water over the batter. DO NOT STIR.
5. Shut your eyes and wish a box full of your own dreams onto the top of the cake.
6. Bake for 40 minutes. When you touch the top it should spring back. Serve warm.

Vanessa's Caesar Salad

CROUTONS
12 (1-inch) cubes of crusty white bread
3 tablespoons extra-virgin olive oil
2 teaspoons minced garlic
Salt

SALAD
3 garlic cloves, minced
2 large egg yolks
1 tablespoon Dijon mustard
4 to 5 anchovies, chopped
1 tablespoon fresh lemon juice
Coarse salt and freshly ground pepper to taste
6 tablespoons extra-virgin olive oil
4 heads romaine lettuce torn into 2-inch pieces (Use only the inner parts of the romaine; that is, lose the big outer leaves.)
Parmesan shavings

CROUTONS

Preheat the oven to 350 degrees. In a bowl, toss the bread cubes with the oil, garlic, and salt. Put them on a baking sheet and toast for 10 to 15 minutes, until golden.

SALAD

1. In a large wooden bowl, whisk the garlic with the egg yolks, mustard, anchovies, lemon juice, salt, and pepper. Add the olive oil slowly, whisking, until the dressing is emulsified.
2. Add the lettuce and toss until the leaves are coated. Add the shaved Parmesan. Sprinkle the croutons over the salad. Toss again (gently) and serve.

NOTE: The American Egg Board states: "There have been warnings against consuming raw or lightly cooked eggs on the grounds that the egg may be contaminated with salmonella, a bacteria responsible for a type of food-borne illness. Healthy people need to remember that there is a very small risk and treat eggs and other raw animal foods accordingly. Use only properly refrigerated, clean, sound-shelled, fresh, grade AA or A eggs. Avoid mixing raw yolks and whites."

Vanessa states: You're more likely to die in a traffic accident. Enjoy a Caesar made the right way.

SIXTEEN

Nadia's Room

(2002)

Once upon a time there was a woman who tried to write a book in her spare time. Trouble was, like most people, she didn't have any, and so she decided to run away from home, to escape life in order to write about it. She would go live, not visit, but *live* for a month in another country, on an island perhaps — one far, far away. Elsewhere was always a good idea. Taking a month off from her day job would be a challenge, but with careful planning she thought she could find a way. She had the will; disengaging from the busyness of everyday life was such an appealing notion on so many levels. This is the story of what happened next.

A woman on an edge, I chose a place on an edge — the village of Oia, on a cliff 800 feet above the Aegean Sea at the far northwestern tip of the Greek island of Santorini. Five hundred people lived in

Oia full time. Thousands came in the summer. I would go in the spring. I had never been there. I knew no one there. No one there knew me. We didn't speak the same language. Writer heaven. Few of my family and friends took the idea seriously. No one but writers thinks writing is work.

"Yeah, sure. Have a good vacation."

The word "boondoggle" was mentioned.

On April 29, 2002, I arrived in Athens hardly believing I'd done it, or was about to. New York already seemed part of the past, not merely last night, something more distant. I had no luggage but a carry-on bag and my laptop. In the Athens airport, I found a coffee shop and settled in to wait for my flight to Santorini. Two airline pilots were at the next table, drinking ouzo with their coffee. I hoped they weren't my pilots. They were. We made it to the island anyway. On the half-hour taxi ride from the airport to Oia, we passed fields peppered with red poppies and the occasional donkey. Everywhere you would expect to see grass you saw daisies. The last part of the drive was equally stunning. We were on a narrow, twisting road cut into the side of a mountain. The road had no shoulders. To my left, the mountain went up. To my right, the drop went down.

The driver found my fear encouraging.

"Many die on this road," he said, turning to wink at me before passing a bus on a blind curve. I searched once more for my seat belt. There wasn't one. He wasn't wearing one either. Greek fatalism? In a shop at the Athens airport, I had seen a T-shirt with lines written on it in Greek. The clerk translated for me.

"I hope for nothing. I fear nothing. I am free."

I hoped to arrive in Oia alive. I feared I might not. I was not Greek.

Until I saw Oia.

Someone had upended a box of slightly melted sugar cubes along the top of a cliff and partway down its ruddy, rocky face. The light was crystal; it ruled, altering everything, shocking awake senses I didn't know I had. *Zowie!* That's a sense, isn't it? The seventh. I think. I wanted to stop to wallow in light, but I was anxious to see the place where, for a month, I would live this other life. All I knew was what I had learned online and from a string of e-mails exchanged over the past year: Perivolas, "a complex of private houses" on the outskirts of Oia, was owned by the Psychas family, who had restored a group of 300-year-old caves (carved into and out of the volcanic rock cliff) that once had been the wineries, stables, and homes of fishermen and farmers. They said it was a simple place. They said it was quiet. They said it was beautiful. As it was too late to turn back, I hoped they hadn't lied.

I got out of the car, feeling fortunate to have lived to do so, and followed a path along the top of the cliff until I came to a low, black-painted wooden gate on which the words "Perivolas Traditional Houses" were hand-lettered in white. The area below formed an amphitheater. Wide stone steps outlined in white paint curved down to a central terrace. Whitewashed caves — *houses?* — were next to, on top of, and below one another, wedged together in a seemingly random but appealing pattern. I could see stands of bamboo, wild fig trees, olive trees, and orange flowering cactus. Terra-cotta pots of scarlet geraniums lined steps and terraces. Grapevines and fuchsia bougainvillea trailed over low walls of dark stone and up white plaster. I walked down the steps. A yellow puppy was tethered by a two-foot rope to the leg of a table on the terrace in front of reception. I bent down and patted one end. The other end wagged.

"What's your name?" I said. But the

puppy spoke no English.

My "house" was at the top of the complex. The only way to get to it was by climbing a stone staircase that wound up the outside of the building below — and went nowhere else. Privacy. Great. I went inside.

I would be tempted to call my "house" a room. Studio might be a better definition. After I saw it, labels didn't matter. Everything was curves and light. Edges of walls were rounded. Ceilings were vaulted. Walls, ceiling, and floor were white. The center part was about twelve feet wide and twenty long. There was a faded lavender nubby cotton rug, the kind that feels good to bare feet. A built-in sofa with a mattress covered in coarse-weave white cotton spanned the far end of the room. Pillows formed its back. The pillow covers were striped in shades of plum, strawberry, and raspberry — handwoven fruit for leaning on. In front of the sofa was a low, round, primitive wooden table about four feet across. There were purple flowers in a glass bottle. There was an alcove containing my kitchen — a teak countertop with a two-burner hot plate and a sink set over a small refrigerator and a white-painted wooden cabinet containing the

440

necessaries. The bathroom was large and spare and had a big hole near the ceiling so that light, too, could bathe you under the open shower. The most outstanding part of my "house" was at the front of the cave and on the left. A bed on a white-plastered stone platform fit perfectly into a high, curved niche. A lilac cotton bedspread was tucked in around the mattress. Where the foot of the bed met the front wall, there was a window. I opened the white wooden shutters and gasped. To lie in this bed was to see, just beyond your toes, nothing but sky and the essential beauty of the Aegean, sliced in the distance by the edge of another island. A white-and-violet womb with a view — who could ask for anything more? I walked out the shuttered double doors onto my small terrace, pulled a canvas deck chair up to a little round table, sat down, took a deep breath, let it out, smiled at the sea, and said to myself, This is where I shall begin work on the book.

But not yet.

It was late Wednesday afternoon. I had given myself permission to do no work until Thursday morning. I also planned to take off Sunday to see how Greeks celebrated Easter. (If you've read this far, it will come as no surprise to you that what they ate was of more interest to me than how they worshiped.) But now I wanted to explore Oia before dark. The village was a ten-minute stroll from my cave along a cobbled footpath that traced the cliff, passing a dead windmill or two. The sea was on my left, a long way down. A quick geological note: This area of the Aegean was a volcano that blew its top three thousand years ago, give or take a thousand years. The sea filled in the crater, called the caldera. The surviving parts of the volcano — a few pieces of land now separated by water — formed a broken circle around the caldera. One of these pieces is the scimitar-shaped island of Santorini.

The buildings of Oia were old, small, short, and made of plastered and white-washed stone, but for the wooden doors and window frames, many of which were painted the same blue as the domes of the churches, and the sky. Streets were too narrow for cars. I would see donkeys carrying suitcases, baskets of vegetables, and cartons of T-shirts, toothpaste, and Tampax to shops, hotels, and tavernas. The Mamara, the ancient main street that ran the length of the village, was lined with shops and paved with marble, the slabs worn smooth and rounded by centuries of

footsteps. I stopped at an ATM to get some drachmas, and would have, if not for the sign taped to the screen.

"Sorry. This machine not yet works."

Me either.

I came to a taverna. Across from it was a large terrace with no tables. In summer there would be tables and they would be filled with tourists. But it was April and I was no tourist. Feeling like Shirley Valentine, I asked the taverna owner if he might move one of his tables out to the far edge of the terrace where it overlooked the sea. He did. I ordered a plate of Atherina, tiny fish — whitebait, I think — that are fried and eaten whole, by hand, like french fries. If french fries had heads and tails and eyes. I settled back with my little fish to enjoy the theatrical extravaganza they call sunset in Oia. The village was on fire. When the sun sank below the horizon, the show got gaudier; the bottoms of clouds looked bruised. It was dark when I asked for the check. The waiter put it on the table, weighted down with a small beige ball. I love marzipan. Didn't know it was Greek. I popped it into my mouth. The waiter motioned for me to return what I had only just discovered was not marzipan but a rock. I gave it back and told him that where I came from it was good luck to lick a rock after eating. Back in my cave, I slept like a different person. Must have been the bed. The room. The quiet. The sea. The sunset. The island. The marzipan. Maybe for breakfast I would eat a brick.

Thursday morning I woke up rested and ready to write. There was a piece of framed embroidery hung on the wall by my front door that I had not noticed the day before. Pink and purple wildflowers surrounded a word, which — even though it was in the Greek alphabet — I recognized as *Kalimera*. Good morning. I said good morning back at it and decided to put off opening up my laptop for another day.

The yellow puppy was still tied to the table downstairs. There was a bowl of food, but three large cats had managed to push it out of the puppy's reach and were eating as fast as they could. I had seen a small market on the path to town. This morning I would go buy a few things I needed for my kitchen: eggs, cheese, olives, tomatoes, lettuce, dog food.

At the store I introduced myself to Koni and Christos, who ran Market Oia, and told them I would be here for a month. They said not many people came on holiday for so long a time. I informed them I wasn't on holiday; I was *living* here. They said in that case would I join them and their children at the house of a friend on Easter Sunday. There would be many people, they said. We would eat a lot of food, drink a lot of wine, and dance until we fell down. I had come to work and to be alone — making friends was not in the plan. No time for it. But who could refuse such a kind offer?

Thursday I explored Oia some more.

Friday and Saturday too. There would be time for work later. Sunday morning, when church bells rang out Jesus' wake-up call, I hopped out of bed and threw on wide, floppy cotton pants, a loose-fitting cotton shirt, and a pair of sandals, my uniform for a different life.

The yellow puppy had managed to twist her two-foot rope around three table legs and her neck. I sat down on the ground and untangled her.

"Who does this dog belong to?" I said to the woman who had been enjoying her coffee at a table while beneath it a puppy slowly strangled.

"She is stray. Perivolas owner's girlfriend found her on road. But owner's girlfriend is tour guide. She is not here much."

"Why is the puppy tied up?"

"Owner doesn't want dogs here."

I decided not to point out the dog was already here. Instead, I turned her over and tickled her puppy belly.

"Does she have a name?"

The woman laughed at me.

"Who knows? I told you. She is stray."

The stray yellow puppy had a white streak down the middle of her face that spread out around her nose to make room for a patch of yellow freckles. She had two big brown eyes in the center of all that yellow and white.

"Daisy," I said, remembering the fields.

I patted Daisy some more. When I stopped, she gave me the patented disappointed puppy look, the one that says, "I thought it would go on forever."

It never does, Daisy. Not for puppies. Not for big girls either. And then, before I could figure out what I meant by this, I was overcome by a smell. It came from houses and tavernas, from alleys and courtyards, from the plains west of the caldera and from the higher mountains to the south. It came from the entire island of Santorini. It came across the sea from other islands, from the mainland. From every corner of Greece, it came.

The scent of rosemary and roasting lamb.

I raced down the path to the market.

"Is it time to eat?"

Koni stopped stacking jars of what we call Vienna sausage and German tourists call food long enough to laugh at me.

"Not for hours."

She said we would go to the house of their friend at two o'clock. But wouldn't the lamb be overcooked by then? I was a concerned citizen. She laughed again. The waiter, the woman at Daisy's table, now

Koni — a lot of people seemed to enjoy laughing at me no matter which life I was living.

"Lamb takes a long time," Koni said. "Meanwhile, don't eat anything."

Oh man, I hate those words. I went back to Perivolas and sat down at Daisy's table with a murder mystery, reading parts of it aloud to the puppy. Maybe she knew who did it. Daisy said probably it was the cats. Her English was improving. I kept checking my watch. Okay, I was living on a Greek island; I could wait a few hours. Hadn't Penelope waited twenty years for Odysseus? I asked Daisy if she knew how to weave. She said no. I went to my cave and brought back a sock. We took turns unraveling it.

Finally it was time. Koni and Christos were waiting with their two children. Vassily was five. Alexandra was three. Koni was thirty-nine. Christos was forty. I was hungry. At the house of their friend, several long tables had been pushed together on a shaded terrace. Fifteen or twenty people greeted Koni and Christos. Deciding I already knew enough people, I followed my nose to a patch of ground next to the house. Five men were gathered around a bed of glowing coals, taking turns hand-cranking two spits, drinking wine and heatedly discussing the endeavor. I knew this song; it was only the Greek version of men and their grills. Rolfe would have felt right at home.

A baby lamb rotated on one spit. I looked at Christos, who had followed me. Or his own nose.

"Can't they turn it faster?" I was only going to be here a month.

"You turn fast at first, and then slow, slow," Christos said. "You brush on olive oil and rosemary, or oregano, or both, over and over. Takes hours."

"What's that thing on the other spit?"

It resembled a sausage about two feet long and three inches in diameter, with something stringy-looking wrapped around it.

"*Kokoretsi tis souvlas,*" he said.

I didn't know any more than I did before I asked, and must have looked it.

"Liver. Heart. Kidneys. Lungs," a fire tender said.

"Lamb guts," Christos said.

Another man spoke up. "We marinate the meats overnight. Maybe in some wine and olive oil. Today we wrap the intestines round and round to hold the meats together. Then we slide the *kokoretsi* onto the *souvla*. This word means 'spit.' You know *souvlaki?* Just means meat on spit."

Slow-roasted lamb guts. Yeah, we always had that for Easter back home. Right after the baked ham and deviled eggs. I decided to go see if I could help out in the kitchen, but when I got to the terrace the table was already cocked and loaded. There were plates and bowls of Crayola-colored food from one end to the other, a very long distance indeed. There were gallon jugs of wine. Koni said it was homemade. Women were shuffling dishes around, trying to make table space for still more food. Easter is the most important Greek holiday. I barely had gotten a good drool started when the men came up to the terrace triumphantly bearing enormous platters of *kokoretsi* and lamb. The *kokoretsi* was sliced crossways, like salami — well, sort of like salami. Thicker. And funkier. The lamb was in chunks.

Roast lamb perfume is a powerful incentive. There was a rush for chairs. I might have been trampled if I hadn't had so many years' practice in chair rushing, and if Koni hadn't saved me a place between her and Christos. What nice people they were. What nice people they all were. I was the only non-Greek at the party, a stranger, but they made me feel welcome. Now they

450

fought over who would explain the food to me. I hoped it wouldn't take too long.

A woman handed me a loaf of bread. She said to pull off a piece. This, she said, symbolized Jesus breaking bread with his disciples. Small bowls of creamy white yogurt dip reeking of garlic were passed. Another woman said this was *tzatziki* and I should spread it on the bread. The garlic would protect me from Satan. A man with a gray beard that needed trimming and black eyes that couldn't be avoided put chunks of lamb meat on my plate.

"Baby lamb," he said, "the most traditional Easter food of all."

"Must it be *baby* lamb?"

"Baby lamb is God giving up his only son to be crucified — or in this case, eaten — in his honor," he said. "Also, babies are the most tender."

I was almost sorry I asked.

The man put a piece of *kokoretsi* on my plate. I doubt everybody looked to see what I would do, but it felt that way. I did what I usually do when faced with a new food. I ate it. And guess what? Slow-roasted lamb guts were delicious, the flavor as complicated as the texture. New York needed a *kokoretsi* café.

Christos added eight or ten oven-roasted

small potatoes, crisp outside, soft inside. Somebody else put on my plate a heap of finely shredded romaine tossed with sliced green onions and fennel, fresh dill, lemon, and olive oil.

"This symbolizes the beginning of spring, the rebirth of life," he said.

A young woman with full lips, hollow cheeks, and an attitude gave me a bowl of sliced tomatoes, green peppers, cucumbers, red onions, black olives, capers, and chunks of feta cheese.

"We call this *choriatikisalata*," she said.

"We call it Greek salad," I said.

"But Linda," Christos said, "in Greece all the salad is Greek."

I had a feeling somebody was laughing at me again. Maybe everybody. Let them laugh. I ate lamb and lamb guts and potatoes and salads and bread and dip until I finally could see part of my plate. If the early Greeks had eaten as much as I ate that day, they could never have fit inside that horse.

Koni reached for a bowl of hard-cooked eggs that had been dyed deep red. She took two and handed one to me.

"Hold up your egg," Koni said.

"Why?"

"Just do it."

I held up my egg.

"Now," she said, "when I say *'Kristos anesti,'* you say *'Alithos anesti,'* and tap your egg against mine."

"Huh?"

"We'll try it in English," Koni said. "When I say 'Christ is risen,' you say 'Risen indeed' and then we tap eggs until one of them cracks."

"Why?"

"You ask too many questions," Koni said.

A really old woman leaned across the table.

"The egg cracking open means Christ is breaking out of his tomb. The red color is his blood."

Too much information.

"The one whose egg cracks last," Koni said, "has good luck the rest of the year."

"But Koni," I said, "why wouldn't the one who breaks Jesus out of his shell first get the good luck?"

"Shut up and bang eggs with me."

I asked too many questions.

We tapped our eggs. Koni would have good luck for a year. Okay by me. I would settle for good luck for the month. Several men pulled out stringed instruments, the names of which I do not begin to know, and started to play. People around the table sang. The dancing began. Old men, middle-aged women, three-year-old children, and everybody in between got up to join in. I declined. When it came to dancing, I didn't have to drink wine to fall down. After a while, the dancers took to smashing plates on the terrace. Breaking dishes? This I could do and did, but tentatively, until Koni told me they were cheap plates sold for this purpose. Well, hell, I broke some more. It was getting dark and the party was only beginning to find its second wind when I made my goodbyes and left to walk home. On the path I hummed a Greek tune I'd heard the men play, tried a dance step I'd seen a four-year-old do, and fell down.

Back at Perivolas, on the terrace where Daisy had been, there was nothing but one foot of rope tied to a table. I went up to my cave. On my bed was the other foot of rope. Attached to it and sound asleep was a yellow puppy. I climbed in next to Daisy and whispered.

"*Kalo Pascha*, Daisy *mou*." Happy Easter, my Daisy.

I was so glad I had moved to Greece.

The next morning I opened my laptop and went to work. By the end of a week I had found my rhythm. I got up early and wrote sitting cross-legged on the floor at the low wooden table. If I looked up, I could see the sea and sky beyond the double doors. Never once during that month did I shut those doors. Around four in the afternoon, I would close my laptop and go for a long walk. Some afternoons I made my way to the backside of the island, where I could scramble down a mini-cliff to a small rocky beach, take off my clothes, jump into the water, and swim; the birds and fish, having seen naked ladies before, were not impressed. I would put my clothes back on, hike back up to Oia, get something to eat, follow the path to my cave, and watch the sunset from my terrace. When it got dark, I went to bed. And then got up and did it all over again. But I made sure not to get bogged down by routine. Some days I ate first and then went for a walk. For one month I did not produce TV shows. I did not watch TV. I did not listen to the radio or read a newspaper. I did not miss my children. I did not miss Rolfe. Not only had I never lived alone — as the only child of two parents and the single parent of two children — I had been outnumbered all my life.

Yeah, sure. Alone for a month. Could you do it for a year? For a *life?*

I didn't know and didn't know if I would

ever want to try. But for now I was living alone and loving it.

Except I wasn't really alone.

Daisy had more or less moved in with me. When we were finished writing for the day — she would let me know by placing her front paws on the keyboard, which made for some lively paragraphs — I would close the laptop and say, *"Ela."* Come. And she would. She liked our walks. She liked going to the tavernas with me. Tavernas, you understand, are not taverns, exactly; they are cafés that serve a certain kind of food: taverna food. This included *mezedes* — the small plates one eats with a glass of ouzo or as the first part of a meal — traditional home-based dishes, and grilled meats and fish. Daisy loved pork chop bones, so I ate a lot of pork chops. I didn't mind. Having never fallen for the New White Meat scam, Greece had never bred the fat and, therefore, the flavor, out of their pigs. The only thing Daisy didn't like was going in the water. While I swam, she worked on her tan. At night we slept side by side, arguing over whose pillow was whose. This made Kostis, who (along with Maria Irini, his sister) owned Perivolas, unhappy.

"No dogs in the houses!"

Daisy would be tied back up. Then she would chew through the rope and come find me. As cats apparently were acceptable at Perivolas, I took the attitude that if my studio was a "house," Daisy was a cat. I felt bad about breaking the rules, but if Daisy kept chewing her way free and didn't come to me, she might wander off, get run over on the highway (as strays regularly did), or get herself poisoned. Some Greeks, many of the same ones who didn't believe in neutering dogs — *It's not natural!* — put poisoned food on the street as a means of controlling the puppy population on an island that had no animal shelter. The only time I willingly relinquished Daisy was when Kalli (Kostis's girlfriend), the pretty, kindhearted woman who had rescued the puppy from the streets in the first place, was back from one of her tours. Kalli had first dibs. It was only fair.

Besides, if I wanted more than Daisy's company, Koni and Christos's store was just down the path and across the road from Anemomilos, a taverna where I took many of my meals. There were four generations at Taverna Anemomilos, often at the same time. Spiros, the grandfather, a white-haired man with big mustaches and a wise smile, was usually at his table drinking coffee in the sunshine. Iorgos, the father, a native of Oia who had traveled the world, cooking on boats, before he came back to open this taverna, was usually behind the grill. Spiros, the son, ran the place and spoke the best English. Iorgos, the grandson, spoke no language yet, but was happy to sit in his stroller and accept compliments. Spiros, Iorgos, Spiros, Iorgos. I began to get the naming process here — and why so many people had the same names.

I ate outside on the shady part of the terrace. When Koni or Christos would see me there, one or the other would leave the store to come sit with me, which is how I got to know two extraordinary people who led equally extraordinary lives. Koni, a slender woman with long brown hair and brown eyes, had been born in Italy and was the youngest of twelve children. Her real name was Concetta. When she was seven, her family migrated to Canada, where Concetta became Connie. Concetta-Connie (now Koni) and I would sit at a table at Anemomilos and talk about everybody we saw. There was an old woman who hung around Market Oia. Her face was more wrinkled than God's grandmother's. She wore black. Her clothes were dirty. She smelled. I felt sorry for her. I asked Koni if the old woman would be offended if I offered her money enough for a decent meal.

"Yeah, Linda. You go do that," Koni said. "That old woman owns the building our store is in, the building next to it, the windmill, and the land below it all the way down to the sea. Go give her some money. Tell her to buy a bar of soap with it."

Koni had no patience with fools (present company excepted) or what she considered foolish notions.

"Here I can't have men friends. This is not how I was brought up, but it's the Greek way," Koni said. "So once in a while I tell Christos, 'You are a Greek man. Go out with your men friends tonight.' He goes out, stays one hour, and comes home. 'Koni,' he says, 'you're my best friend. Why do I want to go out?'"

Koni took a small sip of Anemomilos's homemade honey-colored wine. "Sometimes I'm not sure Christos is really Greek."

He was. Christos was born in northern Greece and raised in Athens. As a teenager, he moved to Germany to study graphic design and then returned to Athens, where, for the next twelve years, he applied his talents working for a newspaper. In 1988, he met a man who, on learning that Christos was a smart fellow who also happened to speak five languages, offered him a job running tours on Santorini. Christos moved to Santorini. Two years later, Connie, now an assistant bank manager in Toronto, came to the island on holiday. She met Christos. They fell in love and began one very long-distance romance. After five years, enough apparently was enough.

"We can't keep this up," Christos said to Connie. "You must come to Greece and marry me. I am going to find something for the both of us to do. Something where we will always be together."

And so it came to pass that a Greek graphics designer and an Italian-Canadian assistant bank manager invented a life for themselves that was as rewarding as it was strange. For six months of the year, they leased Market Oia, stocked it, and ran it, working seven days a week from 8 a.m., when the store opened, until 11 p.m., when it closed, living with their two children behind the store, in one room. The other six months of the year they lived in their house in Preveza, a city of 30,000 people on the other side of Greece, next to the Ionian Sea, where they did nothing but enjoy their kids and each other.

"A typical day in Preveza? In the morning when the children are in school Christos and I play tennis, go walking, or ride our bikes. After school we — the family — eat the main meal of the day. Christos helps the kids with their homework. Then we all go for a walk. We stop at one of the waterfront cafés for coffee or ice cream. When the children go to bed, Christos and I open a bottle of wine and sit in front of the fireplace. We hold hands."

"If I work twelve months, I am going to lose my life," Christos said. "This way I buy my freedom for half a year."

Work life was in Oia. Real life was in Preveza.

One life paid for the other.

My work life was in New York, but what if my *real* life was here (except that eleven months in New York paid for only one month in Oia), where I had found something for which I had been searching a very long time? Everybody talks about the importance of balance. Koni and Christos had found theirs, and I had found mine, maybe for the first time. Because I had to concentrate on only one thing — writing a book — twenty-four hours was long enough to encompass everything. There was time to write, walk, swim, eat, and visit with friends, and still get a good night's sleep. If elsewhere was the answer, simplicity was the key.

I ate simple too.

Along with Anemomilos, I discovered Oia's Café inside the village, run by Tony and Panagiotis, who served food a step up from a taverna and defied local custom by putting out napkins made of cloth instead of the little paper cocktail napkins everybody else used, the ones that blew off your lap unless you tucked them under your butt, in which case they were useless. I also ate at Santorini Mou, a taverna in the nearby village of Finikia, where Mikhailis, the owner, played the bouzouki and sang his own songs, wearing a gray beard, a Greek fisherman's cap, and the smile of a guiltless child. Dimitri, a Greek, and Joy, his American wife, owned and operated a fish taverna down at the tiny harbor of Amoudi, where you could sit at a table three feet from a clear green bay, watch the sun set, and eat fish you picked out by pointing (the photo on the cover of this book was taken there). But Anemomilos was my regular hangout. Maroussa (wife of

Iorgos the Father), a woman my age who worked harder but looked younger, would greet me.

"*Ti kanis?*" How are you?

"*Kala. Esi?*" I would answer. Fine. And you? (I had been learning a little Greek.)

"*Poli kala,*" she would say. Very good.

"*Ti ine to fagito tis horas?*" I would say. What's the food of the hour?

At this point, having established my intention, I ran out of Greek and Maroussa ran out of English. We would go to the kitchen so she could show me what had been made that morning. Often I would ask Maroussa or Spiros, her son, to choose for me. In this way I learned to eat what Greek people ate and not what tourists ate, which was almost always the same thing. One day an English couple was sitting at the table next to Koni and me, staring at the menu and looking puzzled. I decided to enlighten them.

"Try the *giouvetsi,*" I said. "It's a lamb stew cooked in a clay pot. Or maybe the *stifado* — that's veal cooked with wine, onions, and tomatoes. If you're vegetarian, see if they made the green peppers stuffed with rice and . . . ah, stuff."

They listened with the greatest of interest to everything I had to say and then

463

asked Spiros for one Greek salad split for two and an order of souvlaki. Meat on a stick.

Koni and I smiled at each other. Tourists. Spiros smiled along with us and told me to try the rabbit braised in wine with garlic, onions, and tomatoes. The rabbit was very tender, very flavorful, he said.

It was. I told him so.

"I am glad you liked it," Spiros said. "I took one bite, remembered the look in the bunny's eyes before it was dead, and, well, I was lucky, I made it home before I threw up."

I was a continual source of amusement to Spiros. By now I had a favorite corner table on the patio at Anemomilos. One day it wobbled.

"Ah," Spiros said, "your table dances. Better than you, I think."

Who told?

"You write anything good today?" Spiros said another day.

"I'm not sure. I never am."

"To write, first you must know yourself."

"Some of us write in search of ourselves," I said.

"That is very silly."

"You think so too?"

One night a full moon centered itself in

the window beyond my bed. I went out on my terrace and sang to it. My huckleberry friend. The next day, I happened to mention this to Kostis, Perivolas's owner.

"You sing at the moon. You let a dog in your bed. What is the matter with you?"

"Do you really care so much what I do in my room, Kostis?"

"It is Nadia's room."

For once we agreed it was a room, not a house.

"Who is Nadia?" I said.

"She was my mother," he said. "She and my father made this place. My father died in 1984. The details here — all Nadia's. She believed in harmony. You know what I mean? She wouldn't let you sit with a plastic bottle on the table. Even in dying she put things in order. I still find notes from her."

Kostis made a sweeping motion with his arm, indicating everything around us.

"Perivolas was her dream. She would have liked more time to enjoy it. But she died in 1999. The cancer . . ."

Kostis was a tall, good-looking guy with straight blond hair that brushed his shoulders, a soft voice, blue eyes, and a brooding air. There was Russian blood there; I already knew this. He could be amiable, even charming, but he wasn't a big talker. Suited me. I was afraid he'd bring up the matter of Daisy. Again. Later I asked Maria Irini, his sister, to tell me more about their mother.

"Nadia was an artist," Maria Irini said. "She made the world nice in simple ways. She gave life to things that have no life."

"What does that mean?"

"Nadia took classes in weaving. She wove bedspreads and all the exquisite pillow covers you see around Perivolas. Her weaving, it lives."

Maria Irini pushed her streaky brown-gold hair back from her face. She spoke without looking at me.

"Her loom was in your room," she said.

"You mean her room."

I was never able to learn to live on Greek time. I could not get up at six in the morning, go to work at eight, eat lunch at three or four in the afternoon, eat dinner between ten and midnight, and go to bed at three the next morning. Seemed to me the entire country had to be sleep-deprived. But near the end of the month I tried. I would rearrange my day, taking a nap instead of going to lunch or taking a walk, in order to stay up to meet Koni and Christos at Anemomilos after they closed the store. It was only then that both could relax at the same time. The fun we had on those nights! I'd fallen in love with Koni's husband. She understood. Many people fell in love with Christos, who had a high forehead, a sharp nose, curly black hair, and green eyes that missed nothing. He used his wiry, animated body to punctuate his funny, often wise words, and like all philosophers, Christos let no one do his thinking for him. They had gone to Canada to visit Koni's family. They were in a car on a road near Toronto and Christos was driving. A police officer stopped him for speeding.

"Speeding?" Christos said. "How can I be speeding if there are cars still in front of me?"

The cop thought this over and then gave Christos a speeding ticket anyway. Christos refused to pay. He insisted on going before a judge; he said it was his right as the citizen of a democracy far older than Canada's. Koni mentioned something about Canada not being, technically speaking, a democracy. The word "dominion" entered the conversation. Christos said this didn't matter. Greece was a democracy. He was Greek. He wanted his day in court.

Christos told his story to the judge.

"So you see," he said, "it is unfair. There were *always* more cars in front of me."

The judge, apparently more impressed by this logic than the cop had been, offered to reduce the fine. Christos refused.

"*Partarchidia!*" Christos said to the judge. Take my balls!

"What did you say?"

"Put me in jail now. Otherwise, in a week I'll be back in Greece. You are going to come to Greece to make me pay? Take my balls!"

Christos never paid the ticket. The judge didn't put Christos in jail. Canada never sent cops to Greece to hunt him down. Christos continued to make friends with tourists who came to Greece, even Canadians.

"It is easy to make friends here, Linda, is it not?" Christos said.

"Many Greeks don't," I said. "At least not with tourists."

"Ah," he said. "Not to do so is to lose. There is much to learn. Everybody has a story."

"You like tourists. You invite strangers to family feasts. You prefer staying home with your wife to going out with other men, and you care more about family than fortune.

You say this is very Greek, but I don't see other Greek men arranging their lives in order to be with their wives and children all the time. What is it with you?"

"There are two kinds of Greeks, Linda."

"Which kind are you?"

"The other kind."

A month by yourself when you're grown is much like summer when you're a kid — or maybe like a puppy when it's being patted — you think it will go on forever. But it never does. I guess this is what I was trying to tell Daisy my first day in Oia. Beginnings bring promises that time can't keep. My month was nearly over. I had written a chunk of book, enjoyed myself, learned I liked eggplant — couldn't get enough of it — and breathed deeply the odor of a different life. Christos was right. It was easy to make friends here. When I walked through the village, I was no longer a stranger.

"*Yassou*, Linda," said Violetta or Alekos or Nikos or Mikhailis or Phenix or Tony or Panagiotis. Or Vassily, from his little bike.

"*Yassou, Leenda!*"

My last night, Daisy and I lay in bed listening to the sea and looking out our window. Goodnight moon. Goodbye Oia. I used to wonder what in the world would become of me if something happened to Rolfe. What if I were alone, and moved to a strange place? Could I survive? Would I be lonely? I had come in search of total solitude and found I was so incapable of sustaining such an unnatural (to me) existence for any length of time that I took a stray puppy as a roommate and made new friends who would, in time, become old friends. Bloody Mary was right: most people do long for their own special island, but not necessarily the Robinson Crusoe kind. I had found mine. It wasn't the island of Santorini, a poster-perfect place (so *over*, some will tell you) where German tourists flock like fat white birds, lying near naked in precise rows, working at tanning their pale bodies even on days when there is no sun. The English come because they think it exotic, although many limit their desire for exoticism to what they can see from a bus. Greeks from Athens come because to them Santorini is quaint. Americans come to get married on a cliff overlooking the sea — or because they are on a cruise ship and this is where the ship has docked for the day.

My own special island was Nadia's room.

In that clean, white, uncluttered space,

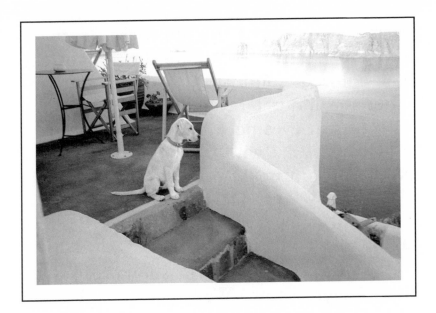

sitting on the floor, writing, sleeping in a bed that had the sea for a footboard, I had found the center point of my balance. I like to imagine that Nadia helped, that she was there with me, lending some of what she knew. Nadia gave life to things that had no life, her daughter had said. Please know that anything in this book that is good, if anything is, was born in Nadia's room.

A photograph of Nadia's room hangs over the fireplace in our bedroom in New England. It is the last thing I see before I fall asleep and the first thing I see when I wake. Our bed comforter is the same color as the bedspread in the photograph. Two reminders of my time there — and a hint to try to replicate in my life here some of what I loved about my life there. In this I have help. I roll over, lift the top of the lilac-colored comforter, and peek at another reminder I brought home with me. Two brown eyes peek back.

"Daisy *mou,* who do you think is in Nadia's room now?"

"Nadia is?" my Daisy says.

I suspect she's right. She always was a smart girl.

"Get up, Daisy *mou.* It's snowing. You've never seen snow. We'll go outside and play."

"Take my balls!"

Daisy's English is just about perfect now. She's a real Greek-American, even carries her own bottle of Windex. But when it's winter, she gets cold. We snuggle back under the comforter, fighting to see who can get closer to Rolfe, who is always warm, and go back to sleep, maybe dreaming of Nadia's room.

An island far, far away.

Greek Spring Salad

This tastes like summer all year round. Most tourists don't run into it because on taverna menus it's usually translated simply as "lettuce salad." Boring. But it isn't!

$1/2$ head romaine lettuce, shredded
Olive oil
Lemon juice
1 fresh fennel bulb, thinly sliced and then, if it's big, chopped as well
1 bunch fresh dill, stems removed and fronds chopped
1 bunch green onions, chopped
Salt and pepper to taste

1. Put the shredded lettuce in a big bowl. Toss with only enough olive oil to coat lightly.
2. Add a little lemon juice and taste. If it needs more, add more.

3. Add the fennel, dill, and green onion. Toss again. Let people salt and pepper their salads to their taste. This salad wants a lot of pepper and not much salt.

Phenix's Tzatziki

MAKES ABOUT TWO CUPS

Phenix, who was not born Greek but has lived in Oia eight years, makes great *tzatziki*.

1 quart yogurt (do not use low-fat)
1 cucumber, peeled, seeded, and grated (or minced)
2 to 3 garlic cloves, minced or pushed through a garlic press
2 tablespoons olive oil, the greener the better
Salt and pepper to taste
French bread, for serving

1. Wrap the yogurt in a big square of cheesecloth. Put it in a strainer inside a large bowl in the refrigerator overnight.
2. Pour out the water in the bottom of

the bowl. Strain the grated cucumber and garlic with your hands. Use a towel if you don't like to touch food, but if this is the case, you are reading the wrong book and I'm sorry it took you so long to notice.

3. Stir in the olive oil and salt and pepper to taste.

4. Serve with French bread for dipping.

SEVENTEEN

The River of No Return

(2004)

The secret of life is enjoying the passage of time.

— JAMES TAYLOR

I turned a corner and saw it. Them. Spaced evenly across nearly half a mile of river, silver in the gray light and not a little ugly, they looked like the periscopes of gigantic alien submarines, instead of what they were: the sole visible parts of the world's largest movable flood barrier (built to protect London from tide surges), otherwise known as the Thames Barrier. For my purposes, they should have called it the finish line. This was the end of my big sixtieth-birthday hike. I touched the trail marker to prove I'd really made it, but instead of being elated, I was bummed, on edge and off balance. Worse, it was Friday the thirteenth. I'm not superstitious; what mattered was that it was August

13, and my birthday wasn't until August 15. I'd finished two days early. My fault. I'd rushed the walk, gulped the meal without tasting it, even known I was doing so at the time, known it when I passed up an extra swim here, a nap there, another conversation with an interesting stranger (or swan), another side trail that led to — elsewhere? And for what? Why had I treated what was meant to be a slow and serene and significant solo stroll across England as a race? Exactly what or with whom was I competing? A clock? Or some part of me that just had to keep moving.

Maybe I wasn't handling this sixty thing so well after all.

Six months earlier, I'd decided to celebrate my birthday by hiking the River Thames from its source in the Cotswolds to the Thames Barrier, here, where the estuary widens to meet the sea. Unlike my wilderness birthday hikes, this one would be easy. The path followed a river, which meant the path was flat, or downhill. I planned to lollygag, to take twenty days to walk roughly 200 miles. Rolfe said he'd be waiting in London with caviar and congratulations.

From the beginning, nothing much went as I envisioned.

In late July, I flew to England to start where I would ultimately end, at the Connaught Hotel, only to discover they'd played with her. The bar had been redecorated; the beautiful crystal water pitchers were gone. Thank goodness I still had mine. The Grill Room had been altered too. A much-heralded new chef had replaced the silver trolleys and big joints of meat (and the little old men who carved) with a menu featuring Mediterranean cuisine. *Mais oui!* London is so close to the Mediterranean; you've only to follow the English Channel past England, France, Portugal, and Spain, and then hang a louie at the Rock of Gibraltar. The new Connaught restaurant? It wasn't that what was here was bad. It was that what was no longer here was sad. The next morning I caught a train to the Cotswolds, got off at the tiny station at Kemble, hoisted my pack onto my back, and walked a few miles until, in a meadow, under a tree, I came to what looked like a gravestone but for the words carved into it.

"This stone was placed here to mark the source of the River Thames."

I touched the stone, turned around, and began to walk east. There was no water in sight, nothing but folds of fields, black-

and-white cows, a church spire, and the rest of England. No worries. In time there would be puddles that turned into a stream that turned into a river, but this trip was about more than following a piece of water. I was on a quest. I meant to try, as the Navajo say, to walk in beauty, to be at one with my soul, mindful of the life around me and my connection to it; to stay in the moment while, at the same time, I would rummage about in the mental attic, dusting off memories and holding them up to the light. Wasn't looking back on one's life to live twice?

Brilliant idea. Bad execution. I struggled under a backpack that weighed too much on a body that did too. After only a few days, my poor feet, patched with Band-Aids, moleskin, and gaffer's tape, were a sore sight for eyes, worse when you removed the patches. I sweated in the heat, crouched on my pack during electrical storms, slipped in the mud when the rain ended, hauled myself up and over a million stiles — and pushed on, uneasy and unsteady. Once I fell down and thought about staying where I was. Several times I got lost — following a river. What was *wrong* with me?

There ain't nothing to it . . . any fool can do it . . .

So maybe I wasn't just any fool. This cheered me up. I stuck a poppy behind my ear, winked at a squirrel, put my face into some honeysuckle that grew by the path, and inhaled my childhood. *Linda, come inside to dinner . . . Linda Jane, I mean right now!* But sometimes at night I cried into my pillow. The walk, the world — more to the point, my time in it — was passing too swiftly. When I put my watch to my ear I could hear my life ticking away. *Too fast, too fast, too fast,* it ticked. Despite James Taylor's advice in what was one of my favorite songs, at the moment I wasn't especially enjoying the passage of time. As for being mindful of the beauty around me, it's hard to stay in the moment when you've got a bad case of monkey brain. The chattering inside my head would not quit. I would sit down to rest under a willow tree hanging over the river and find my mind occupied with business or family issues, how many miles were left to walk that day, whether I would like the inn I'd chosen on the Internet, if I should take time to walk extra miles to see this castle or that museum, why I couldn't seem to think straight — or if thinking were something I had forgotten how to do, like playing the guitar. This hike was a bad idea. Should have thrown a party instead. Nobody thinks at parties.

When anyone from home called me on my cell phone, I lied.

"The hike? Perfect!"

Why burst their illusions?

I hated that I had to spend part of every afternoon making work calls on my cell phone, trying to walk, talk, and think at the same time. Thank God there were no french fries to trip over. Speaking of food, if I hadn't known where I was, I wouldn't have known where I was. I love it that because I live in New York, most of the cuisines of the world are readily available to me, but when I travel to foreign countries, I don't want to eat "foreign" food; I want to go native. I'm aware this is selfish. Why shouldn't the cuisines of the world be readily available to the English too? No reason at all, but I bet I'm not the only traveler who, when in Greece, wants home-made *moussaka,* not transplanted *mole.* At the pub where I had dinner the first night on the Thames Path, the featured item on the menu was that old Cotswoldian dish, *gravlax* with dill. At the Trout Inn, I waited while the woman next to me ordered the day's special: chili con carne with tortilla chips. At an Oxfordshire pub, dinner was a salad of Parma ham, mozzarella, and arugula, as Italian as the waiter who brought it. On the menu at the Talbot Inn in Enysham, it said, "Charles and Arthur welcome you." Whoever was in the kitchen probably was not named Charles or Arthur; more than half the dishes were Thai. In Marlow-on-Thames, I was offered *chile con queso* made with four cheeses, one of them Parmesan. At a pub in Henley, the menu listed *phô*. Those plucky Vietnamese, they got around. Like everybody else, apparently. Once upon a time the English flag flew over more than half the world. Now more than half the world seemed to have returned the favor. A woman in a yellow sari checked me in at the 250-year-old New Inn in the ancient English market town of Lechade-on-Thames. The Chicken Tikka was better than passable, as were many other "foreign" dishes I ate — they just weren't part of my *plan*, my carefully constructed vision of walking and eating my way across Mr. Shakespeare's blessed plot, this earth, this realm, this England.

Breakfast had always been my favorite meal when I was in England. At the Cove House B&B in Ashton Keynes, Roger, wearing an apron that had "His Lordship" printed on it, cooked up a dandy Traditional English Breakfast, blood pudding included, for another couple and me, but I'd barely gotten my teacup to my mouth when my tablemates attacked. They wanted me to defend the U.S. invasion of Iraq so they could tell me how wrong we were. I said many Americans were against the war.

"But one must stand responsible for one's government, mustn't one?"

I remembered why I hate B&Bs and got out of there before the toast was properly cold.

On the path, when waterfowl rose up from bushes at my approach, making fowl noises, I flinched, rattled by their flapping flurries. Sometimes white butterflies circled my head the way they do when a cartoon character's been knocked out. Did butterflies know something I didn't? Flowers I couldn't name bloomed next to bushes I couldn't name under trees I couldn't name. This pissed me off. Why was I forced to study algebra but not the world around me? If I could do it over . . .

If I could do it over.

I could not look back without looking ahead and I wasn't ready to look ahead. What if I didn't like the view? Hell, I knew I didn't like the view. I sat down on the riverbank and put my naked feet into the cold water to numb the pain. The bank was wide and green and flat. I lay back in clover and slept, fitfully, dreaming anxious, labyrinthine dreams. A rhythmic sound woke me up. Step. Clunk. Step. Clunk. I sat up and looked around. An old man using a walker was coming up the grassy path, going someplace on his own two feet, plus four metal ones. He smiled as he passed me. It took a long time. He held the smile.

Nobody knows how we got to the top of the hill. But since we're on our way down, we might as well enjoy the ride. . . .

The old man made me think of Montana. Five years after getting cancer, I had leaned out of a raft, dangling my fingers in the clear waters of the upper Missouri River on what would have been a perfect afternoon, except for a herniated disk and a sore throat. Was my body meant to disintegrate a piece at a time? I saw a bighorn sheep with a baby that looked to be a day or two old. Its eyes took up half its face. Was I ever that young? I stopped to climb a small hill. I thought about rolling down it. Nah. Would hurt too much. Suddenly, from nowhere, I was a *furious* fifty-two-year-old woman. My rage exploded over the hill, the river, the state of Montana, and the known universe. I began to holler.

"I didn't want to fall off a cart in Rome and rupture a disk in my neck! I didn't want a sore throat! I didn't want cancer! I want my breasts back! I want to be well again! I want to be young again! And I want it all to last forever!"

And I wanted the Tooth Fairy to put Johnny Depp under my pillow.

That day in Montana I had come to a fairly hard truth. A hard truth is one you wish were a lie. For the rest of my life, there would be times when, if I were to seize the day, I might have to do so through what doctors like to call discomfort and we know as pain — or nausea, dizziness, diarrhea, sore feet, sore throat, or a cold. Or cancer. What were my choices? Stay home, sitting on the pity-pot, moaning? Drug myself to the point where I wouldn't feel bad but wouldn't remember what happened? Or just give up on life and wait to die, the way my mother had?

If this was what was on the menu, I wasn't hungry.

But I wasn't ready to leave the table.

I recalled Earl Shaffer, writing about his landmark thru-hike of the 2,000-mile Appalachian Trail, saying that it was life's difficulties that gave him the wherewithal to carry on. I won't say that remembering

Earl Shaffer or Montana, or watching the old man with his walker, put me in a state of grace, but it gave me the will to get up and keep moving, and despite the noise inside my head, the walk got better.

Try not to try too hard. It's just a lovely ride. . . .

Eventually I found, if not my inner peace, my stride, and when I did, I began to see the green, living river as my sidekick. There were dawns so clear that spiderwebs in the weeds along the path looked like Edwardian diamond necklaces, afternoons when hayfields were painted Constable pink by the setting sun, nights when stars were distant polished pieces of Georgian silver. Early every morning, when the mists still lay on the path, snails were out in force. As a show of solidarity — my feet go where the escargot — I tried to avoid stepping on them. It was high summer, but except for snails and other critters, and the humans who walked their dogs near towns and villages, I had the Thames Path to myself. Most people I met had no idea that all the towpaths and footpaths had been connected (since 1996) to create a trail that followed the entire length of the river they lived next to.

Along the upper and most remote part

of the Thames, water traffic consisted of skiffs and "narrow boats." Once, these skinny barges had been loaded with produce for London. Now they were pleasure vessels enameled in pretty colors, with pots of blooming flowers on their roofs, and names like *Dream Weaver*, *Happy Days*, and *Toad Hall*. I heard what I thought was a narrow boat coming around a bend. They moved almost as slowly as I did, and they were quiet; as a consequence, while answering the call of nature, I had accidentally mooned a few as they passed by. But this wasn't a boat. More than two dozen swans came down the Thames in a triangle formation: The Swanish Armada. You didn't see *that* from the deck of a cruise ship. In Oxford, to mark finishing half the trail, I booked myself into a day spa called Heavenly Bodies for the "Steam *Rasul*," which turned out to be a modified version of the Turkish baths I had been to in Istanbul. The ceiling even had the same kind of small star-shaped holes to let in light, but there was no Alyla to pummel me into blissful infancy.

The food seemed to improve as I went along. The Chilterns, what passes for mountains in this part of England, lined my horizon on both sides, but for a short distance the path had been diverted away from the river to a lane (America needs more lanes), and then back down to the water at Moulsford-on-Thames — and The Beetle and Wedge. It was midmorning. I stopped anyway; the day and the place were too pretty, the tables by the river too inviting. Vines. Flowers. Old brick. White tablecloths. Lunch, which, as we know, is the sexiest meal of all, began with a half-dozen oysters flown in from Cornwall. Raw oysters are either a whole meal, in which case it takes at least a couple of dozen, or simply something to get the juices (all kinds of juices) going, in which case they don't count and you can eat a great deal more food after them without regret. Which explains the grilled fresh sardines I finished off after the oysters. Richard Smith, proprietor and chef, said the two biggest mistakes people make when they grill are a fire that's not hot enough and meat that's not dry enough, and then showed me how lamb kidneys cooked over an open fire were meant to taste. The salad and cheese were exceptional, too. A very sexy lunch, it was, all things considered.

In Wallingford, at the George Hotel, a sixteenth-century inn on the High Street, a young chef named Chris Hope introduced me to Stilton-and-smoked-bacon cheese-cake, a starter served with grape chutney and an herb salad. A savory cheesecake? Remarkable notion — English, but with a twist.

I'd never been much of a fan of what Brits insist on calling chips. Everybody knew Belgians made the best french fries. Everybody was wrong. The best french fries in the whole world are the Triple Fried Chips at the Riverside Brasserie at Bray-on-Thames. This is not open to discussion. Pasting those potatoes directly on my hips would have been a sin against nature.

One Sunday afternoon I passed through a campground packed with hundreds of people, mostly Indian or Pakistani, now residents of Great Britain out for a picnic by the river. I smelled lamb and eggplant roasting over charcoal. Chiles too. And then I came upon a family eating what looked like meatballs on what looked like Chinese dumplings topped with what looked like yogurt. I stopped for a closer look, and struck up a conversation with the family. Badria said she and Fakoor, her husband, and their children, Fowzia, Roxanna, and Nadir, had gotten out of Afghanistan when the Taliban came in. Now both her daughters were at English universities. When they finished, they planned to return to Afghanistan, where the daughters planned to teach young girls. I had been to Kabul? How amazing. Would I join them for lunch? She said what they were having was called potato *boulanee* with kofta and *chakah* sauce, and that it was Afghani Traditional Food. *Aha!* After tasting it, I hoped that when they went home to remake their country, they might find time to drop the recipe off at the Mustafa Hotel.

Rural Thames. Victorian Thames. Royal Thames — it still didn't take me long to look at a palace, whether I was in La Paz at nineteen or at Hampton Court at fifty-nine.

London sneaks up on you. And then you're there.

What followed was some of the hardest walking I did. The path, being mainly sidewalks and streets, was smoother, but filled with people who didn't look you in the eye or offer up their dog for an ear scratch and a compliment; Daisy would have hated London. Besides, I'd already seen most of what I was about to walk by during the next and final few days. Dutifully, I gave mental applause to monuments as I passed them, but it was from habit. Nothing touched me. When I stopped at a London pub to eat a tiny steak and grilled tomatoes, all I could think about was how much I wished it were a Monster Steak and that Rolfe were here to eat it with me. Elizabeth, Rolfe's mom, who would be ninety-two in November and had enjoyed a life of near-perfect health, had been in and out of the hospital in the last few weeks. Elizabeth was depressed about being sick. Didn't blame her one bit. Nor did I blame Rolfe for deciding he would stick closer to home for now, for his mom. Past London, in Greenwich, I came to where *Cutty Sark*, one of the last great clipper ships, was permanently moored. She was completely surrounded by a concrete pier, her masts and spars empty of sail, her prow forever facing the estuary that could take her out to sea, to all the seas, racing with the wind to China or Australia or India. If she could have sailed through concrete. She made me sad. Like Rolfe's mom, *Cutty Sark*'s only flaw was that she was no longer new.

Another hour of walking and I was at the Thames Barrier, two days too soon and without having attained the internal harmony I'd come seeking — and been so certain I would find — somewhere in 200 miles of being alone with myself and a river. I wanted a do-over. This being unrealistic, I considered what to do next. More nights at the Connaught would break the bank. I could call friends in London and stay with them. I could take a train back to someplace along the trail where I wished I'd spent more time, but that was almost every place. I could catch a plane to New York. Surprise! I'm home! Is it too late for a party? Too agitated to think sensibly, I called my office in New York. Holly Camilleri, my assistant — and a much saner person than I — said she had some bad news. Why was I not surprised?

"Okay, hit me with it."

"Julia Child died today."

The next words out of my mouth were a measure of my self-absorption.

"Nonsense. We share the same birthday. We always exchange cards. Julia is going to be ninety-two on Sunday. How can she be dead?"

Julia Child had been one of my teachers. Yeah, she'd taught me, along with a nation of home cooks, to look at food differently, taught me to stretch, get enthusiastic, make mistakes, laugh at them, and keep on cooking. Then she taught me more. We met because Julia was a breast cancer survivor too. I spent an afternoon at her house in Cambridge, where we talked, not about food but about life. And death. Julia's attitude about cancer was much like her attitude concerning dropping the chicken on the floor while you were preparing to cook it, which she claimed was an apocryphal event that had never happened on her show, but, she said, in that unique, often imitated but never matched voice, if it *had* happened, there was only one thing to do — what any person with gumption would do about a chicken, or cancer.

"Pick the chicken (or yourself) up off the floor and soldier on. Don't look back. Don't waste time thinking about it. And don't *whine*."

And hadn't I just finished whining my way across England, measuring what was lost, not what was left? I was ashamed of myself. Julia would have set her big feet and tall, strapping body to that path, energetically squeezing every minute of joy from the experience. She would have greeted every day, every piece of that river, every step of that walk with gusto, savoring a moment here, a meal there, a new, unexpected turn in the trail anywhere. Which is why Julia had endured. For ninety-one years and 363 days, Julia Child had endured, a testament to the benefits of staying keen on life. I thought about what a woman named Alice Warden had said to me in a letter ten years earlier, when I'd turned fifty.

"Oh, Linda, what a baby you are."

Back at the hotel, I looked in the mirror, something I'd purposely avoided during this journey, and saw a woman who wore no makeup but the sun, hadn't used any comb but her fingers since she left London eighteen days ago, and smelled right gamy — and she looked radiant in her shorts, T-shirt, and yes, her aging face. That woman wasn't a baby anymore, but she wasn't old either; she was still in the middle of growing up and into herself. Good to know. I only wished it hadn't taken Julia Child's death to remind me how alive I was. So what would Julia do now? Wasn't there some appropriate way I could celebrate my birthday *and* Julia's? The woman in the mirror and I smiled at each other.

Since we're only here for a while, might as well show some style. . . .

Saturday morning I took a plane to Naples, hired a car, and headed up the mountains to the village of Sant'Agata sui Due Golfi. At Don Alfonso 1890, Livia and Don Alfonso were waiting with hugs and kisses; they had a room over the restaurant where I could stay, and seemed to think it was only natural I had come to spend my birthday with them.

Give us a smile . . .

Sunday. August 15, 2004. Sunrise. I'm floating on my back in the Mediterranean Sea, possibly the only awake person in Positano. I was born at dawn. May be why it's my favorite time of day. Waves float onto my face and into my mouth.

Water.

The finest food of all.

I float some more. Hum a little more of that James Taylor song that's been in my head this whole trip. But now, at last, the chatter in my head has ceased, and I can really *hear* the words of the song. Better than that, I can hear myself think. James knew. Julia knew. Alice Warden knew. Now I know. I am as young as I ever will be. I am *never* going to be any younger than I am this minute. This second. Oops. There goes another second. And there's no way to stop that. I can go on whining. Or I can enjoy the passage of time. As always, a lack of alternatives clears the mind wonderfully.

Now the thing about time is that time isn't really real. It's just your point of view . . . how does it feel for you?

Right now it feels like this: Getting older doesn't mean you forfeit all the other ages you've been. If I were to die today, it would be wrong to say I lost my life, for I have lived one.

Happy birthday, Linda Jane.

I dry off and head for the café that has finally opened, standing in line for my double espresso, which I carry to a table by the sea and sit down where I can see the town, the beach, the people, Italy, the world wake up one more time. Good morning, life. A young hunk of a waiter comes over and tells me I can't sit here. The tables, he says, are for "waiter service," which doesn't begin until 8:30. I tell him this is silly; I bought my coffee at this café. If he'd been around, I would have let him take my order, but he wasn't. Not my fault. I had my coffee and I meant to drink it sitting down.

"You can't," he says, unmoved.

What is he — French? He waits for me to obey. I don't do obey well, and I'm not going to start on this particular day. I can sit if I want.

"It is my birthday," I say to him. "Today I am sixty years old."

"I am so sorry," he says.

I crack up. He's young enough to blush. And does.

"*Signora*, you misunderstand. I mean I am sorry for saying you cannot sit down at your age."

Now I totally lose it, trapped in the best laugh of all, the one you have on yourself.

"Kid, you are flat breaking my heart."

"*Prego*," the hunk says. "I do not say this right. I want to say that I am sorry for saying you could not sit down on this, your *compleanno*. Your birthday! Today you are *sedici!*"

"Not sixteen, you fool. Sixty! *Sessanta!*"

"*Sedici!*" says the grinning waiter, who turns out to be Italian after all.

I take a taxi up the mountain, dress in white cotton slacks I bought two years ago in Oia and a red silk shirt I bought nineteen years ago in Da Nang. I brush, even blow-dry my hair, and put on a little lip gloss, nothing else — the thing about makeup is that the more you need it, the less it can do for you — and hang antique rose-cut diamond drops from earlobes so long they would have done Lyndon Johnson proud. The earrings were a gift from Rolfe, the odd fellow who turned out to be the great love of my life. Having been a fool for love more than once, how lucky I am that Rolfe didn't enter the picture until I was old enough to appreciate that Sam

Keen was right: we come to love not by finding a perfect person, but by learning to see an imperfect person perfectly. What I know about Rolfe is what I love.

The secret of love is in opening up your heart. . . .

The extra-long earlobes were a gift from Daddy, the uneducated life-insurance salesman from East Texas who first set my foot, and heart, on the road to adventure. He was with me today, as he had been on all my other trips. I was sure of it. Every time I talked to a stranger, I was sure of it. Daddy was the first to teach me that when you talk to strangers, they stop being strange.

It's okay to feel afraid . . . but don't let that stand in your way. . . .

Mama? Her anger lit a fire under me, pushing me to do whatever she didn't want me to do. She didn't want me to drop out of school; she wanted me to get the education she'd never been offered. So naturally I dropped out of school to do exactly what Mama had done: be a wife, which, it turned out, took more courage than I could muster. Well, Mama, as a journalist and traveler, I got myself an education, of sorts, and two weeks ago, I walked to Oxford, a Roads Scholar. I spray myself with a big cloud of Shalimar, the perfume of grown-up ladies — the perfume of my mother, bless her Braveheart.

Fluffed and buffed, I am ready for my big birthday meal.

Mario, one of Don Alfonso and Livia's two sons, shows me to my table. I say I would like to buy a bottle of champagne and invite Don Alfonso, Livia, Costanzo, the maître d' who never stops smiling, and, of course, Mario to toast my becoming sixty. Let the revels begin. Mario says he's so sorry, but Don Alfonso left early for a long-planned hunting trip. Livia is working in the office, and it's Costanzo's day off. Do I still want the bottle of champagne? I say no, thank you. *I've come here to be with them and they're all gone?* Ah, well, and so it goes.

I ask Mario to choose my meal for me. *Might as well enjoy the ride. . . .*

There are delicious starters. And then they bring out the Vesuvius. *Il Vesuvio.* The volcano has been recreated in a show-stopping dish — Southern Italy on a plate. Cooked pieces of rigatoni stand upright, propped against one another in a circle about four inches across the base, forming the sides of the mountain. When you stick your fork in, the volcano erupts, each rigatoni spewing red sauce, white cheese sauce, basil sauce, and "rocks" of home-made sausage. Deep inside, the core of the "mountain" is melted mozzarella filed with tiny, fresh, bright-green peas, symbolizing the inevitability of spring — the rebirth of life that comes after a mountain has blown its top. I feel a kinship with my food. I blew my top and now I'm a sixty-year-*fresh* little green pea!

Clearly this dish is a masterpiece created by a master chef. But the master chef is off shooting birds, so who . . . ?

"*Leenda!*"

Livia kisses me on both cheeks, apologizes for being late, and sits down. Do I like *Il Vesuvio?* Do I wish to meet the man who made it? I follow her to the kitchen.

"*Leenda,* meet Ernesto. Our other son." She smiles that mother-smile. "The one who cooks."

Ah, yes. Family. The first, final, essential masterpiece.

Ernesto kisses me on both cheeks.

At the end of the meal there's a birthday cake, which seems to be composed of flowers, sugar, whipped cream, a box of dreams, and a candle. I'm about to blow it out when Costanzo shows up.

"*Buon compleanno, Leenda!*"

"But, Costanzo, Mario said it was your day off."

"I would not miss your birthday, *Leenda*," he says. "You are so . . . *Latina!*"

He kisses me too.

Well fed and kissed and in the finest of moods, I go for a long walk on feet that seem even lighter than my birthday cake, take a nap, and waddle to the town square in time for the fireworks. If your birthday is August 15, try to celebrate it in a Catholic country. It is the Feast of the Assumption. There are parades and fireworks and bands that play all day and most of the night — and all for *you* (that's my story and I'm sticking to it). At midnight, about to be sixty years and one day old, I sit at a small café on the square, drinking espresso, nibbling on biscotti, and listening to a string quartet that segues straight from Verdi into the theme from *The Godfather*, which somehow seems right, as it seems right that I am here to enjoy this mix of cultures, which is more *meld* than mix — just as it was in English pubs, cafés, inns, restaurants — and picnic grounds. We are all of us travelers, tasters. It's possible I travel so as not to take beauty for granted, or because I really can't stop moving, which, considering the fate of *Cutty Sark* and my mother, may be a wise idea. Or maybe it's something else. On one of our anniversary trips Rolfe and I went to Nantucket, where I met Jane Lamb, who was seventy-three and had lived all her life in the house where she'd been born. What, I had wondered, must it be like to stay in one place while the world revolved around *you,* year after year? Here comes spring again. Again. Again. There's that rosebush blooming again. Again. Again. You stay, maybe turning round and round with the seasons as they come and go, but not leaving. Part of me envied her, and then I was reminded of the time I decided I wanted to be a boatman on the Colorado River: a good life, but not mine. Having only one life is a hell of an inconvenience. In the end, it's not the going or coming, or being young or being old, or living and dying. It's the impossibility of being in two places at once.

But we can be seen trying.

Einstein said he could never understand it all. . . .

Einstein was right. Mathematics is well and good, except nature keeps dragging us around by the nose, singing its own song, choosing its own path.

'Cause anyone knows that love is the only road. . . .

This is what I hoped to pass on to Vanessa and Josh, and to Violet, my grand-daughter, who will be two years old in a few months.

Tomorrow morning I leave for that scariest of all destinations.

Planets spinning through space . . .

Home.

The smile upon your face . . .

Rolfe.

Welcome to the human race. . . .

And the rest of my life.

I'm not done with adventure. As has been pointed out, ships are safe at harbor. But that is not what ships are for. The best place? The one I haven't seen. The best bite? The one I haven't tasted. So often we applaud the past and condemn the present as, well, insufficient, but I have walked through England (and am now proud as punch to have done so) and considered its past and my own. I have flown off to a mountain in Italy for no other reason than it was where I wanted to eat my sixtieth-birthday meal — I like to think Julia would have approved. And I'm very clear about one thing: every new beginning comes from some other beginning's end.

The future?

An acquaintance of the nineteenth-century French composer Daniel-François-Esprit Auber once stopped him as they were coming down the grand staircase at the opera.

"My friend, we're all getting older, aren't we?"

Sliding down . . . gliding down . . .

Auber sighed.

"Well, there's no help for it. Aging seems to be the only available way to live a long time."

Isn't it a lovely ride.

Stilton-Bacon Cheesecake

This is my adaptation of Chris Hope's Stilton-bacon cheesecake. As for the ring molds, you can go to a cook store and buy them, or order them from various sources, or you can do as I did and go to the hardware store or plumbing supply store and, for much less money, ask them nicely to cut you 6 pieces of PVC pipe, 2 inches across and $1\frac{1}{2}$ inches high. I add a handful of chopped walnuts to the cheesecake, but it's dealer's choice on the walnuts. Serve this savory cheesecake as a starter or, with a bigger green salad on the side, some chutney and good bread, as lunch.

Softened butter, for preparing the ring molds
5 or 6 digestive biscuits (Carr's makes good ones) or graham crackers

505

3 tablespoons unsalted butter, melted

4 to 6 slices smoked (or regular, or even Canadian) bacon, diced

1 (8-ounce) package cream cheese, at room temperature

4 ounces imported Stilton, at room temperature

A handful of chopped walnuts (optional)

A few leaves of baby lettuce, for serving

Your favorite chutney, for serving (optional)

1. Generously butter the inside of the ring molds and place them on a large baking sheet.

2. Crumble the biscuits (or crackers) in a food processor. In a bowl, combine the crumbled biscuits with the melted butter and mix together thoroughly. Divide the mixture among the molds and press down firmly with your fingertips to completely compact. Refrigerate for 1 hour, to firm.

3. In a pan, sauté the bacon until golden brown. Drain on paper towels.

4. In a bowl, thoroughly mix the cream cheese and Stilton together with a fork and fold in the bacon. With a spoon, pack the cheese mixture over the crust in each mold and smooth the top with a knife you've heated by

dipping it in hot water. Refrigerate for at least 3 hours and up to overnight. Let stand at room temperature for 10 minutes before unmolding.

5.   To serve, transfer each mold to a plate (use a metal spatula), and run a small knife around the inside to release the cheesecake. Ease out onto a plate. Smooth any nicks and dents from the cheese and wipe the edges of the plate. Place a pinch of baby leaves on the edge of the plate. Chutney on the side is optional.

The Vesuvius

I am tempted to say, "Kids, don't try this at home." The trouble began when Don Alfonso faxed me the recipe in Italian. Colman Andrews at *Saveur* magazine was kind enough to translate, adding this note: "This is (as is common with chefs) a pretty wacky recipe, requiring a fair amount of second guessing." Turned out to be the understatement of the year. I e-mailed the recipe (in English) to Brigit Binns — (still) my friend and a cookbook writer — who read it and said something that sounded like "omigod." I then asked Bob

Palmer, friend and neighbor in the Berkshires, and a first-rate cook, if he would like to spend a day in the kitchen with me, figuring out this recipe. Foolishly, he said yes.

It was a long day.

Brigit sat by her phone in Los Angeles in case we needed emergency conferences. We needed twelve. Bob put his brain to work while I acted as his sous-chef and dishwasher. Without Brigit and Colman, and especially Bob, I would have flung my hands into the air and denied I'd ever been to Italy, which is what Don Alfonso may do when he reads our adaptation.

The thing is, this dish is all about presentation, timing, and being able to duplicate ingredients we were unable to duplicate. It helps if you are a three-star professional chef who knows certain things instinctively (like proportions and measures), makes his own pasta and cheese and olive oil, grows his own peas and basil, probably raises his own pigs, and has a kitchen full of minions to play backup.

Our first obstacle was the pasta. Don Alfonso says to use rigatoni, but we couldn't find any long enough to stand up high enough to form a volcano. Bob suggested substituting ziti rigati. That worked. Next we ran into the mozzarella wall. Don

Alfonso says to use fresh mozzarella. We bought some locally made, extremely fresh mozzarella, but it wouldn't properly melt in the sauce, or inside the volcano. No matter how hard we tried, our mozzarella stayed stringy. Finally we substituted goat cheese, which melted perfectly and tasted good but wasn't Italian.

The little meatballs that become the "rocks" that pour out of the volcano when it "erupts." Bob and I spent close to half an hour trying to roll meatballs the size of marbles and peas and tiny beads, until Bob pointed out that at this rate, we'd still be rolling come Tuesday. He put the rest of the pork in a pan in which he'd heated some olive oil and, as the pork mixture began to brown, took a spatula and broke it into pieces of varying sizes. Perfect little "rocks."

Now we turned to the problem of the molds that form the volcanoes. Don Alfonso's instructions said to use "an aluminum foil container about 3¹/₂ inches lined with wax paper." *What?* The volcano I'd eaten was conical, and about 3¹/₂ at the base, but I couldn't figure out how to make a "container" out of foil that would hold steady. Bob, an imaginative fellow, solved the problem. He brought four little terra-cotta flowerpots, 4 inches across the top rim. Brilliant! He also brought a small scale for weighing ingredients — the only one I have is huge; I use it to weigh what I put in my backpack, along with turkeys, hams, small pigs and, okay, my granddaughter, one time when my daughter wasn't looking.

We began. We experimented. We adjusted. Scratched our heads a lot. Turned up the volume on the oldies station. Stared blankly at the walls and each other. Did and redid the math until smoke could be seen rising from the tops of our heads. Laughed until tears came. And kept on cooking.

Although we'd assembled and used the right amount of ingredients to make four volcanoes, at the last minute we decided to make only three, which resulted in some leftover pasta, peas, and sauces. While our three volcanoes baked in the oven, we threw the leftovers in a bowl, tossed them, and ate them. They weren't as visually stunning (or funny-looking, depending on your view) as the volcanoes, but dammit, they tasted the same, and it would have taken about twenty minutes to make that dish, start to finish.

But that wasn't the point of the exercise, was it?

In the end, we triumphed, more or less. We had three volcanoes stuffed with little meatballs, peas, and melted cheese, topped with three sauces, one red, one white, and one green — the colors of the Italian flag. We called Brigit, hugged each other, and promised never to try this again. Never. Let me say it again. Never.

But if you wish to be so bold, here, with apologies to Don Alfonso, is our adaptation of *Il Vesuvio*.

The Vesuvius

SERVES FOUR AS A MAIN COURSE — THAT IS, ONE VOLCANO PER PERSON

4 new (or at least clean) terra-cotta flower-pots, 4 inches across the top rim
Nonstick spray
Baking parchment
1 ounce fresh bread crumbs
6 tablespoons milk (2 for the meatballs and 4 for the cheese sauce)
1 garlic clove, chopped
1/3 to 1/2 pound ground pork
1 egg, lightly beaten (you will not need all of it; I hope you have a puppy)

Salt and pepper to taste

Extra-virgin olive oil as needed (about 2 tablespoons)

$1/2$ cup cooked baby green peas (thawed frozen peas work fine)

1 hard-cooked egg, chopped

$1^1/2$ cups warmed tomato sauce (bottled, canned, or homemade)

50 fresh basil leaves plus 12 basil leaves for decorating plates

3 ounces soft goat cheese

$1/2$ pound dried ziti rigati, preferably imported

1 pound fresh mozzarella, finely chopped

1. Coat the inside of each flowerpot with nonstick spray. Line the insides and base with baking parchment. Put them on a cookie sheet and set aside.

2. Put the bread crumbs in a small bowl, then pour 2 tablespoons of the milk over them and let them soak. Combine soaked bread crumbs, garlic, and pork with just enough beaten egg to bind the mixture. Add salt and pepper to taste. Heat 2 tablespoons olive oil over medium heat. Add the pork mixture and sauté, using a fork to break it apart into different-sized little balls as it browns. These are the

"rocks" that will "erupt" from the volcano. Do not overcook; remember, all this is going into an oven later.

3.   In a bowl, mix the meat, thawed peas, chopped hard-cooked egg, and 2 tablespoons red sauce.

4.   Make a simple basil sauce by blanching 50 basil leaves in boiling water until tender and bright green (about 30 seconds), then drain them, squeeze them, dry, and puree them in a blender with a little bit of olive oil.

5.   Warm the remaining milk gently over extremely low heat. Remove from the heat, and then stir in 3 ounces of goat cheese to make a white cheese sauce.

6.   Cook the ziti in boiling water for 6 to 8 minutes. Drain and toss with 2 tablespoons tomato sauce.

7.   Preheat the oven to 325 degrees.

8.   Stand the ziti upright around the bottom inside circumference of the flowerpots. This takes about 13 ziti per pot. Don't worry that they don't reach the tops of the pots. They're not supposed to.

9.   Pack the bottom inside of the pot with a layer of chopped mozzarella to seal what will eventually become the top of the volcano. Fill the cavity with

the mixture of meat, peas, and chopped egg. Pack the remaining chopped mozzarella on top of the mixture to make a seal on what will eventually become the bottom of the volcano.

10. Bake the flowerpots (right side up) for 15 minutes (or until the mozzarella melts). Remove the pots from the oven.

11. Take a large round dinner plate. Place it over the top of a flowerpot, invert both, and then gently lift off the pot. The volcano should slide out, centered on the plate. Peel off the baking parchment. Repeat with the others.

12. Drizzle the three sauces — red sauce, green basil sauce, and white goat cheese sauce — on the top and down the sides of each volcano. Try to keep them separate so the colors remain distinct.

13. Decorate each volcano with a few basil leaves and a drizzle of olive oil. Serve immediately. Then check into a spa.

I WISH TO THANK

(or blame, as the case may be)

Neil Nyren, my editor since 1985 (when he refused to take back an advance and made me go write a book instead). *And So It Goes* was our first trip together. *Move On* was our second. This is our third. Without his initial and constant encouragement, inspiration, help, and generosity — we don't need to speak about his nagging, do we? — I would never have had the nerve to write about a subject that, as a television journalist, is really none of my business. Neil is more than my editor. He is, I believe, my friend.

Holly Camilleri, my assistant and mentor, who tirelessly read, researched, corrected, and enthused; then booked, canceled, and rebooked flights, hotel rooms, and restaurant reservations while keeping my schedule — and my television work — running smoothly as I scribbled away at a book that interfered with that work.

Lori Seidner, my longtime manager of speaking engagements, panels, and roundtables, who generously arranged those to accommodate my predilection to go spend time on unprofitable journeys to places where nobody gave a damn about what I had to say.

Brigit Binns, personal friend, professional chef, and world-class cookbook author, who graciously edited all the recipes and helped me test some of them. If there are mistakes, they're mine, not hers. Brigit never makes mistakes.

Kit Wohl, dear friend and coconspirator on this and too many other capers to list here, for reading, remarking, testing — and even eating food from this book — and never, ever giving up on me.

Bob Palmer, my neighbor and friend in the Berkshires, who, after saving Vesuvius from extinction, made seventy *salteñas*, plus twenty jars of Daddy's steak sauce for the sales staff at Putnam, who, I hope, were so impressed they will try to sell the hell out of this book.

Lloyd Dobyns, longtime curmudgeon and friend, who read every word at least twice and tried to remind me what commas, semicolons, colons, dashes, parentheses, and ellipses are, and are not, for. Verbs too.

Sometimes I even paid attention.

James Taylor, poet laureate of my generation.

Willie Pearl Ellison, who first introduced me to great home cooking and even pretended that one day I might be as good at it as she is. That day hasn't come. I still love her to pieces anyway.

Vanessa and Joshua, my children, who helped me to accept that I wasn't ever going to be Paul Theroux or Mother Teresa — especially Mother Teresa — and that it didn't matter.

And Rolfe. There's no place like home. He is mine.

ABOUT THE AUTHOR

A veteran of award-winning shows on NBC, CBS, and ABC, including the pioneering late-night program *NBC News Overnight* and the prime-time series *Our World*, LINDA ELLERBEE now runs Lucky Duck Productions. For eighteen years, she has produced a wide variety of programs across the television spectrum, and is especially known for her highly praised *Nick News* series and topical children's specials for Nickelodeon. Among the awards Lucky Duck has received are four Emmys, three Peabodys, and an Alfred I. duPont–Columbia University Award.

Besides her two bestselling memoirs, *"And So It Goes"* (which introduced the word "twinkie" into our journalistic vocabulary) and *Move On*, she is the author of a series of middle-school paperbacks entitled *Get Real*. She gives speeches nationwide on surviving breast cancer, and appeared as herself in an episode of

Murphy Brown (for which some say she was the inspiration).

She lives in New York City and Massachusetts with Rolfe Tessem, her partner in work and in life.